DOOMED BY CARTOON

"WHAT ARE YOU LAUGHING AT? TO THE VICTOR BELONG THE SPOILS."

How Cartoonist Thomas Nast and *The New-York Times*

Brought down Boss Tweed and His Ring of Thieves

JOHN ADLER

with Draper Hill

New York

DOOMED BY CARTOON

© 2008 John Adler. All rights reserved.

Paperback ISBN: 978-1-60037-443-2
Library of Congress Control Number: 2008929769

Published by:
Morgan James Publishing, LLC
1225 Franklin Ave. Ste 325
Garden City, NY 11530-1693
Toll Free 800-485-4943
www.MorganJamesPublishing.com

Cover & Interior Design by:
Greg Weber
HarpWeek.com
gweber@harpweek.com

Richard Samuel West

In 2002, on the occasion of the 100th anniversary of his death, I observed that no other political cartoonist throughout our history has dominated American consciousness as much as Thomas Nast. He is remembered as a heroic loner who toppled the powerful with the most unassuming of weapons: a pen.

In my opinion, these were Nast's strengths:

- He got results! No other cartoonist has influenced—or can hope to influence—American politics to the extent that he did.

- He was a wickedly good caricaturist, and knew how to use a person's features, shape and dress against him.

- He had a fine sense of humor and enjoyed puns.

- He understood the power of repetitive images. When he set out on a path, he stalked his game relentlessly. Some judged his method tiresome, but it almost always worked.

- He never lacked for moral outrage. Even when he was on the wrong side of an issue, he was ready to go to the mat for what he believed to be true.

Recent scholarship has chipped away at some of the details of the Nast-Tweed face-off. But the core of the battle and its images remain intact. Moreover, if Nast bull-dozed his contemporaries and then historians into accepting a version of Tweed that was not entirely accurate, isn't that just one more testament to his extraordinary power?

In this book, John Adler has done a great service—bringing together into one volume all of Nast's Tweed Ring cartoons and the serial story behind them. Here for the first time we can observe the awesome breadth and impact of Nast's campaign, and appreciate anew why Nast is and always will be America's greatest political cartoonist.

Richard Samuel West has written extensively on American political cartooning and is the author of *Satire on Stone: The Political Cartoons of Joseph Keppler*. (Keppler became one of Nast's principal rivals after 1872.)

Author's Note: How This Book Came About

iv

Draper Hill

This book could not have been written without the input and knowledge of Draper Hill. Ever since he graduated from Harvard fifty years ago, Draper has been engrossed by the life and cartoons of Thomas Nast. He has visited more than twenty libraries and museums that owned parts of Nast's collection, which was widely dispersed after Nast's death in 1902. His private collection includes unique Nast prints and publications, as well as contemporary publications related to the topics which Nast caricatured. Literally, Draper probably has forgotten more about Thomas Nast than anyone else in the world knows.

Unfortunately, Draper's professional career as a political cartoonist for the *Quincy (MA) Patriot Ledger*, the *Worcester Telegram*, the *Memphis Commercial Appeal* and the *Detroit News* kept him too busy to write the books on Nast that were in his plans. However, Draper has published numerous scholarly writings, including a biography of English cartoonist James Gillray. In 1990, he was awarded the Thomas Nast Prize by the city of Landau, Germany—Nast's birthplace

It would have been a significant loss to historians for Draper's deep knowledge and insights about Thomas Nast to escape publication. Consequently, beginning in 1995 and continuing periodically through 2001, I commissioned Draper to prepare several different projects on Nast.

We started by taking the approximately 2,250 cartoons and illustrations that Nast drew for *Harper's Weekly*—almost all between 1862 and 1886—and trying to identify the 450 different characters that Nast drew in his cartoons. I also had the assistance of the late Roger Fischer, a history professor at the University of Minnesota, Duluth, in this identification project. We ended up identifying 440 of the 450 characters.

Then Draper undertook three specific projects for me over seven years, including: Nast's 100 best cartoons (in Draper's judgment); his campaign against Boss Tweed; and his 1872 campaign against Horace Greeley.

Draper's completed projects contained many wonderful insights and details probably unknown to anyone else. However, to put them into a fast-moving, reasonably complete, logically sequenced book—in the way I thought the story should be told—required significant editing, almost total reorganization, quite a bit more research, and the selection of many additional cartoons and cartoon extracts.

Caricature by George Fisher

John Adler

I am an accidental amateur historian, who never took a history course during my time at Dartmouth, from which I graduated sixty years ago. My business career was primarily as a management consultant and entrepreneur.

Forty years ago, I started a marketing business which broke new ground in measuring the effectiveness of television advertising and testing new products. By 1972, I had conducted several hundred meaningful advertising tests, and became interested in the history of American advertising. One day, I answered a *New York Times* ad for the sale of some duplicate annual volumes of *Harper's Weekly*—America's de facto "newspaper of record" from 1857 to 1912—and soon found myself the owner of a complete set of 56 volumes.

Twenty years later, as a retirement hobby, I decided to have all 2,912 issues of *Harper's Weekly* manually indexed. That included 173,000 ads, but it was the 10,000 cartoons and 65,000 illustrations by artists like Winslow Homer and Frederic Remington, that really captured my interest.

Thomas Nast's 2,250 cartoons and illustrations stood out in particular. In addition to retaining Draper Hill to flesh out the stories behind the cartoons, I commissioned original articles from more than a dozen college professors, who had expertise in some important areas relating to Nast—eg., political scandals; nineteenth century journalism; Shakespeare; and even the connections between Nast and Vincent Van Gogh and, separately, Edgar Degas.

My company, HarpWeek LLC, manually indexed, scanned and retyped all 73,000 pages of *Harper's Weekly* and created a proprietary digital database, which was licensed to academic institutions and public libraries. For this, and another database called *Lincoln and the Civil War.com*, I was awarded the 2003 E-Lincoln prize.

As a public service, we created and mounted 30 historical, literary and educational websites, many of which are available free at www.harpweek.com. Several hundred Nast cartoons are included on them. One website: "Cartoonist Thomas Nast vs. Candidate Horace Greeley: The Election of 1872" is predicated on Draper Hill's commissioned project. It was edited and prepared by HarpWeek historian Robert C. Kennedy under my direction. Another site is "Nast and Shakespeare", which Rob also created.

For this book, about 60% of the interpretive content, as well as the narrative, came from Draper Hill's commissioned writings. Rob Kennedy helped sequence that material and also added some meaningful interpretation and commentary of his own.

Using Draper's content as a core, along with Rob Kennedy's contributions, I have written the book I envisioned thirteen years ago when I first retained Draper and hired Rob. I have made heavy use of my own library, which contains several dozen books and articles about Tweed, Nast and their era; studied hundreds of Nast's cartoons; and read biographies of many of the important characters in them. Where appropriate, references to specific sources have been incorporated into the text, rather than being footnoted at the end of the book.

Other authors have written good books about Tweed, beginning with Denis Lynch in 1927 and going through Kenneth Ackerman in 2005. (See Bibliography.) In 1977, Leo Hershkowitz took a well documented "Another Look" at "Tweed's New York," and stressed a more positive side of Boss Tweed's regime—championing the immigrants, developing Central Park, establishing hospitals and schools, widening Broadway, etc.—while blaming greedy contractors as much or more than Tweed and his Ring for the rampant graft.

Where "Doomed by Cartoon" differs from previous books is its focus on looking at circumstances and events as Nast visualized them in his cartoons, almost like a serialized but intermittent comic book covering 1866 through 1878. It has been organized to tell the Nast vs. Tweed story so that ordinary readers with an interest in politics, history and/or cartoons—or just in a uniquely caricatured political adventure story—will enjoy it. I hope that includes you.

*   *   *

In addition to Draper Hill and HarpWeek historian Robert C. Kennedy, two other people have been extremely helpful in the preparation of this book.

- Bonnie Currie typed my many drafts and helped with non-routine page layout, providing lots of hours with customary good cheer.

- Greg Weber, HarpWeek's Vice President for Technology and Operations, scanned more than 200 cartoons at high resolution and customized the digital sizing and layout for each of them. In addition, he created the relevant Nast websites under my direction.

This book is dedicated to my beloved wife Vi, who kept a smiling face in spite of all the time and effort required to write it as part of my "retirement."

This book contains more than 160 different cartoons and cartoon extracts drawn by Thomas Nast. Its primary objective is to provide you with the same background understanding and vision that contemporary readers of *Harper's Weekly* had for the fifteen years from 1863 until 1878 when they saw Thomas Nast and Boss Tweed in action.

Early on, you will be introduced to 20 of Nast's Cast of Caricatures—17 Bad Guys and 3 Good Guys, including Nast himself. One of the so-called Good Guys—Samuel J. Tilden—later was portrayed by Nast as a Bad Guy, so his Cast is predominantly villains as befits a cartoonist.

The early chapters are intended to familiarize today's readers with explanations and relevant cartoons (or parts of cartoons) dealing with the political, ethnic, religious and journalistic topics and environment of the time. The cartoons illustrating these topics have been selected without regard to their chronology in *Harper's Weekly*.

Beginning with 1866 and the early days of the Tweed ring, and continuing through its downfall in 1871, Nast's cartoon are shown in serial sequence as they reveal his lonesome campaign before the *New-York Times* joined the battle in September 1870. After that, the tempo picks up through the decisive election in November 1871.

After the Ring's collapse, the book follows what happened to each of the 17 Bad Guys—with Tilden now a Bad Guy, it's really 18—and Nast himself. The chronology follows each of the principal characters individually—over as many years as necessary to conclude their caricatured careers.

On occasion, Nast's cartoons have been used more than once to illustrate a particular topic or person, as well as the serial portrayals of individual Bad Guys after the Ring began to fall apart in September 1871. When textual references are made to earlier or later cartoons or topics, relevant page referrals have been incorporated into the text.

With a bow to the page-numbering modification that *Business Week* adopted in 2007, the page numbers in this book have been enlarged and put on the upper sides of each page. That should enable readers to refer to previous or later references more easily than with standard page references.

After the Table of Contents (which follows this page) is a list of cartoons in chronological order, along with page references for the entire cartoon or for extracts of specific cartoons. Many of the extracts are blown up, so the subtleties of Nast's peripheral vignettes can be appreciated. Numbers in bold text denote pages which include explanations of the cartoons or extracts on those or adjacent pages.

The key to understanding the context of Nast's cartoons and the story of the Tweed Ring relates to the cartoonist's serial approach to portraying events. While this book's approach may seem unusual, we believe it is the best way for today's readers to appreciate Nast's unique talents in what he, with the help of the *New-York Times*, ultimately accomplished.

Table Of Contents

All cartoons are listed in chronological order. Numbers in bold text denote pages which include explanations of the cartoons or extracts on those or adjacent pages.

List of Illustrations

I • Introduction

After the Civil War, William Magear Tweed became the unquestioned political boss of New York City through a combination of bribery, threats, patronage, graft and illegal voting. His hand-picked governor, John T. Hoffman, ran New York State, and Tweed effectively controlled the state legislature. His next potential target was to "rule the general government" by having Hoffman win the presidency in 1872.

John Hoffman is in the shadow as George Washington weeps in the background.

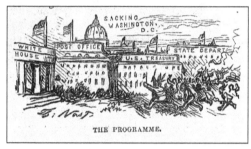

Along with Boss Tweed, New York's mayor, chief financial officer, head auditor, top police officials and most of its judges were active participants in his frauds. In addition, Tweed controlled or bought off almost all of the New York newspapers, so there appeared to be no effective way to combat him and his Tammany Hall Ring of thieves. They stole from $30 million to $200 million—possibly as much as $4 billion in today's dollars.

"WHO IS INGERSOLL'S CO?" N.Y. TRIBUNE.   MR. INGERSOLL. "ALLOW ME TO INTRODUCE YOU TO MY CO?"

TWO GREAT QUESTIONS.

"STONE WALLS DO NOT A PRISON MAKE."—*Old Song.*
"No Prison is big enough to hold the Boss." In on one side, and out at the other.

Into the breach stepped Thomas Nast and his editor, George William Curtis, of *Harper's Weekly*. Nast, whose combination of creativity and execution as an American cartoonist has never been equaled, challenged the Ring as early as 1867. Finally, with significant help from the *New-York Times* after August 1870, Tweed and his Ring were soundly beaten in the November 1871 election. Six and a half years later, after escaping once from prison, Tweed died in jail.

Both Tweed's and Nast's lives peaked in this 1870-71 period and its immediate aftermath. Nast put **"What are you going to do about it?"** into Tweed's caricatured mouth, and then with the help of the *New-York Times*, did something about it. As Tweed allegedly himself said: **"Let's stop them damned pictures. I don't care so much what the papers write about me—my constituents can't read; but damn it, they can see pictures."**

The *New-York Times* made the same point with the proof of the pudding in hand. (March 20, 1872).

"His (Nast's) drawings are stuck upon the walls of the poorest dwellings and stored away in the portfolios of the wealthiest connoisseurs . . . Many people cannot read leading articles, others do not choose to read them, others do not understand them when they have read them. But you cannot help seeing Mr. Nast's pictures, and when you have seen them you cannot fail to understand them . . . An artist of this stamp . . . does more to affect public opinion than a score of writers."

November 8, 1873

Boss Tweed was a huge man—just under six feet tall and almost 300 pounds. Thomas Nast was a head shorter and probably weighed about half as much in 1871. Figuratively, indeed, David slew Goliath.

Primarily through Nast's cartoons, this book tells the story of how that happened. At their peak, they were seen by more than a million people, week after week after week. They enraged the voters sufficiently to "do something about it" against great odds. Enjoy the story, just as the audience of *Harper's Weekly* did 130-140 years ago.

WILLIAM M. TWEED
The high-living Boss, who led the Tammany Hall Ring in stealing millions of dollars from the public.

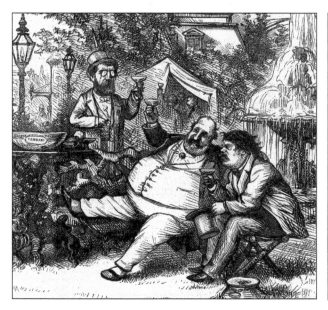

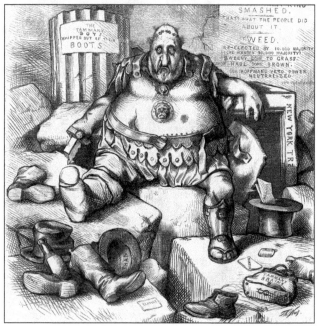

PETER B. SWEENY
The "Brains" behind the organized theft, who originally was considered to be the ringleader.

A. OAKEY HALL

Tweed's elegant, hand-picked mayor, and front man, who authorized the Ring's fraudulent payments.

RICHARD B. CONNOLLY

"Slippery Dick," the comptroller and chief financial officer of the Tweed Ring, who devised and manipulated its crooked multiple-entry accounting schemes.

THE CLOWN IN THE JUDICIAL RING

To what Base Usage the Bench is put.

"The court-room of Judge Barnard has been a place of amusement, where lawyers and others go to hear something 'good,' especially if a case is on the calendar in which the Judge is supposed to be strongly interested. Every day his indecent sarcasms and vulgar jests keep his court-room crowded with laughing spectators. Many of these 'funny things' have been reported in evidence before the Judiciary Committee now in session, by men whose presence in court has afforded opportunities of hearing them."—*N. Y. Tribune*, March 25th, 1872.

GEORGE G. BARNARD
A corrupt, hard-drinking, poker-playing chum of Boss Tweed, whose biased judicial decisions enabled otherwise illegal Tweed and Erie Ring activities.

THOMAS A. LEDWITH
A former Tammany Hall opponent who ran unsuccessfully against Mayor Hall in 1870, only to jump aboard the sinking Tweed Ring ship in 1871.

"A DOG RETURNETH TO HIS VOMIT."

(Prov., xxvi., 11; 2 Pet., ii., 22.)

As Solomon and the Apostle Peter compare Sinners who continually relapse into their sins.

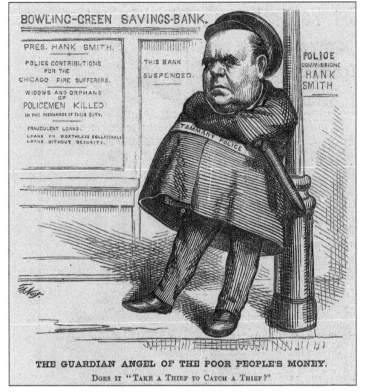

THE GUARDIAN ANGEL OF THE POOR PEOPLE'S MONEY.

Does it "Take a Thief to Catch a Thief?"

HENRY "HANK" SMITH

President of the Police Commission, who used his influence to protect Tweed Ring, operations, and also served as president of one of the Ring's crooked banks.

JAMES J. KELSO

The police superintendent who helped foil a coup against Tweed, met regularly with the Boss, and allowed police corruption to flourish.

MATTHEW T. BRENNAN

The sheriff, who treated Tweed and other defendants with extraordinary leniency, and ultimately spent time in jail for doing so.

ANDREW J. GARVEY
The "Prince of Plasterers," who took huge kickbacks for inflated construction, repairs and rent, and also served as front man for other illegal payments.

JAMES H. INGERSOLL
A furniture manufacturer, known derisively as "Chairs," who provided furnishings for Ring boondoggles at fraudulently inflated prices, and also was a front man for other illegal payments.

ELBERT A. WOODWARD
Tweed's shadowy, personal financial assistant, and former clerk of the Board of Supervisors, who became wealthy by processing, depositing and sharing in many of the fraudulent payments, but operated so far behind the scene that his picture was never published in Harper's Weekly nor caricatured by Nast.

JAMES (JIM) FISK JR.

Jay Gould's partner and Boss Tweed's high-living business associate and close personal friend, who was gunned down by his former mistress's new lover two months after the Tweed Ring fell.

JAY GOULD

The extremely wealthy financier, who bought the political support of Boss Tweed for his Erie Railroad manipulations.

HONOR AMONG ——.

JAY GOULD. "For the Sake of Peace!"

"WHAT A FALL WAS THERE, MY COUNTRYMEN!"

In the fall of 1869, Fisk and Gould tried to manipulate and "corner" the gold market with the help of President Ulysses S. Grant's brother-in-law but were unsuccessful. As Nast's cartoon shows, Wall Street was shaken.

JOHN T. HOFFMAN

The gentlemanly mayor of New York City, and later governor of New York State, who provided the Ring with valuable cover.

A RESPECTABLE SCREEN COVERS A MULTITUDE OF THIEVES.

THOMAS C. FIELDS

"Torpedo Tom," the thoroughly corrupt city official, who played a more prominent role in Nast's cartoons than he may have warranted in real life.

A FIELDS OF ACTION.

"He that runs away will live to *steal* another day."

NATHANIEL SANDS

The former anti-Tammany educator and reformer, who became a secret double agent for a price.

HEEP — OF SANDS.

DAVID DUDLEY FIELD

The renowned and talented lawyer, who had considerable success in defending Boss Tweed and Erie Ring culprits Jim Fisk and Jay Gould.

Harper's Weekly

Thomas Nast, Cartoonist

The *New-York Times*

George Jones, Publisher

This Nast cartoon, dated November 6, 1869, was published two years prior to the Tweed Ring's downfall. George Jones is at the far left, running behind Horace Greeley, publisher of the *Tribune*, who, in turn, trails the diminutive Nast. (The point of the cartoon is to enlist the German vote, symbolized by Civil War General and German immigrant, Franz Siegel, against the Tammany Ring.)

SAMUEL J. TILDEN

The Chairman of the New York State Democratic Party whose late intervention—always questionable to Thomas Nast—was important in toppling the Tweed Ring, and who used his success to build a political career as a state legislator, governor, and presidential nominee.

A BOX STEW; OR, AN ENVIABLE POSITION.

USUFRUCTUARY TILDEN. "WILLIAM, we *would* miss you—until I am in the White House." (Hard on TWEED.)

William Magear Tweed came into this world on April 3, 1823 at 1 Cherry Street in New York City, now in the shadow of the Brooklyn Bridge. George Washington lived at Number 3 in 1789-1790, when New York was the nation's capital, and John Hancock lived at number 5 while president of the Continental Congress. In 1823, Tweed's father, Richard, ran a chair-making business in numbers 3 and 5. Richard Tweed was the third generation of Tweeds in America; his Protestant ancestors emigrated from Kelso, Scotland—a town on the river Tweed—in the mid-1700's.

Bill Tweed was 21 in November 1844, when he observed outright vote-buying on the street, along with bully-boy tactics, in the first election in which he was eligible to vote. He probably didn't see the actual ballot-box stuffing which led to 10,000 more ballots counted for presidential candidates James K. Polk and Henry Clay than there were eligible voters. Tweed married Mary Jane Skadden, 17—his neighbor, childhood sweetheart, and daughter of his father's business partner—that same year.

January 22, 1870

Although his father gave him a first-hand business education, and he operated a small brush-making and then a chair-making business for several years, Tweed ultimately turned to politics. He began with Volunteer Fire Company No. 6, which had about 75 men in it.

His service as a volunteer fireman lasted eleven years (1839-1850), culminating in his election as leader of the Americus "Big Six" Fire Company for a few weeks in the late summer of 1850. He then embarked full time on a political career, beginning with his election in late 1851 to the New York Board of Aldermen, part of the Common Council notoriously known as the "Forty Thieves." The following year, he was elected to his only term in Congress—which he found very dull—and began serving while still acting as a New York City alderman. Tweed spent the turbulent 1850s as a minor Tammany Hall figure, assembling alliances and waiting out the flamboyant career of Fernando Wood, who was twice elected mayor on the Tammany Hall ticket (1854 and 1856) before winning with his own rival organization, Mozart Hall (1859).

Tweed learned many of the tricks of his political trade from Wood. Not the least of these was the state legislature's passage in 1849 of a charter amendment which removed the last vestiges of a property qualification for city voters, effectively ending politics in New York City as a "gentleman's game." Thereafter, the widespread use of votes from newly naturalized immigrants (see below) helped entrench "machine" politics, for the benefit of Tammany Hall.

April 16, 1870

Tammany Hall—named after Tamarend, a Delaware Indian chief—started as a patriotic social club prior to 1800, but soon became a political organization whose support often decided New York elections. As the number of Irish and German immigrants rapidly increased in the 1840s and 1850s, Tammany mobilized them for support, and they ultimately became the basis of its control of New York City.

One of Tammany's rare defeats came in April 1844 when James Harper, the founder of Harper & Brothers (Nast's later employer), was elected Mayor on an American Republican Party (anti-immigrant) platform. He started the first organized and uniformed police force in the city, but banned the sale of alcohol on July 4th and closed saloons on Sunday. The latter actions helped lead to his defeat for re-election

The sketches below are taken from Nast's 24-drawing panel of July 22, 1871. The initial capital letter "F" of "Friends" is fashioned into a gallows on which a ballot box hangs, symbolizing the death of voting rights from vote fraud. (See pages 108-109).

THE DAY WE CELEBRATE.

RIENDS AND BRETHREN,—In accordance with time-honored custom, the Tammany Society have assembled here to-day for

THE ELECTORS.

MIGHT MAKES RIGHT. MIKE TO PAT: "WHERE'S THE SINSE OF COUNTING THESE? WE KNOW HOW MANY THERE MUST BE."

Tammany Hall continued as *the* power in Democratic politics up to the middle of the twentieth century. After the Tweed Ring's downfall, muscleman John Morrissey (see pages 41 and 62-63) struggled for control of Tammany with the urbane "Honest John" Kelly. Both of them sided with Tilden against Tweed, and Kelly took unchallenged control after Morrissey's death in May 1878, (three weeks after Boss Tweed died in jail). Kelly died in 1886, and was succeeded by the notorious Richard Croker, who ruled until 1901.

"The Tammany Phoenix" on the left, from the November 29, 1873 issue of *Harper's Weekly*, shows Morrissey with a crown on his head as a fighting cock, appropriate for an ex-boxer. The Tammany "Ring" has been replaced with a champion's belt around Morrissey's waist, while his feet stand on a fallen Tweed (with a $ sign on his forehead).

Four years later, Kelly had practical control of Tammany Hall, but Morrissey was still battling him, as portrayed in the cartoon on the right from the *Harper's Weekly* issue of November 24, 1877.

THE TAMMANY PHŒNIX IS A FIGHTING-COCK.

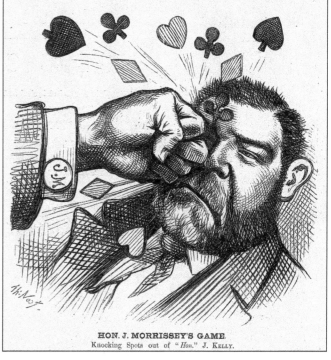

HON. J. MORRISSEY'S GAME.
Knocking Spots out of "*Hon.*" J. KELLY.

By 1855, the majority of New York City's population of about 630,000 was foreign-born—28% from Ireland, 15% from Germany and 9% from other countries. By 1870, with American-born children of the immigrants in the mix, the foreign-born population was down to 44%—21% from Ireland, 16% from Germany and 7% from other countries—of a total population of 942,000.

The Irish immigrants, in particular, were trapped in poverty by a lack of skills, a glutted labor market, language, illiteracy, their Catholic religion, and the desire to cling together. An important factor was their love of whiskey from both saloons and grog shops, which Tammany supported and which the prohibition and temperance policies of first the Whig and then the succeeding Republican party opposed.

April 16, 1870

January 22, 1870

THE USUAL IRISH WAY OF DOING THINGS.

September 2, 1871

"M'CUNN manufactures Citizens at the rate of 8 a Minute, or 480 an Hour."—*N. Y. Tribune.*

A Harper's Weekly cover cartoon just prior to the 1868 election (which is not by Thomas Nast) shows Judge John McCunn's naturalization mill manufacturing "Citizens at the rate of 480 an Hour" for the benefit of Democratic presidential candidate Horatio Seymour (at lower left). It was in the issue of October 24, just prior to the 1868 election which Seymour lost to General Ulysses S. Grant.

An incident in the 1866 election is related as typical by John L. Davenport who, at that time, was Chief Supervisor of Elections for the New York area, a federal post. (In his 1894 book, *New York Election Frauds and Their Prevention*).

An Irishman tried to vote "when the following conversation ensued:

"What name?" asked the inspector.

"Michael Murray, sir," replied the would-be voter.

"Michael Murray? No such name on the list, called the inspector, adding "There's a Michael Murphy!"

"Hould on, gintlemen," exclaimed the excited Irishman, as he pulled a piece of paper from his pocket and proceeded to read, "Sure and it is Michael Murphy instid of Michael Murray!"

According to Davenport, the man who had forgotten his instructions did not vote—at least not in that polling place.

Young Thomas Nast

Thomas Nast was born on September 27, 1840—seventeen years after Tweed—in the military barracks of Landau in the Alsace region of Bavaria, Germany, where his father, Joseph Thomas Nast, played trumpet in a military band. Joseph's liberal political views motivated him to send Tom and his mother to New York City in 1846 when Tom was five, and to join them there in 1850 when his enlistment on an American ship expired. Coincidentally, both Tweed and Nast attended the same primary school in New York City, although many years apart.

Tom's father became a member of the Philharmonic Society and played in the band at Burton's Theatre on Chambers Street. His son often accompanied him and was exposed to Shakespeare's plays, among others, as well as to the leading actors of the time. Young Tom's early theatrical exposure provided useful knowledge as references and models for many of his later caricatures. In fact, he used Shakespearean references in more than 100 cartoons.

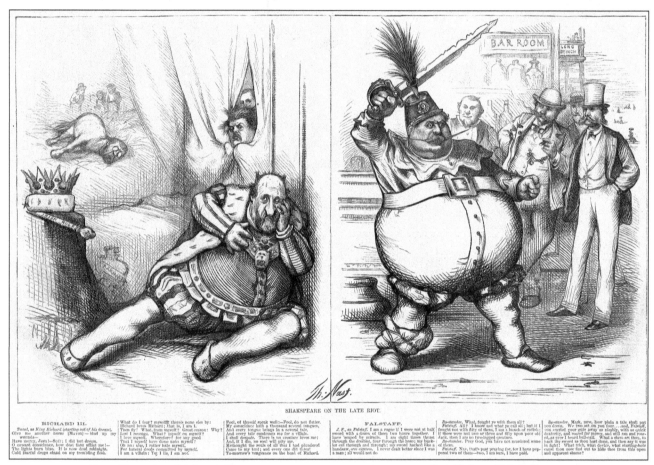

Boss Tweed as Richard III   Jim Fisk as Falstaff

The future cartoonist was probably aged nine to eleven when he first encountered the future political boss, who was then a local celebrity of sorts in his late 20s, renowned as the leader of the much admired Volunteer Fire Company No. 6. In his 1904 biography of Nast, Albert Bigelow Paine makes it clear that the cartoonist had been partial to fires and firefighting:

"He found a great joy in running to fires. In Landau he had never seen a fire . . . Now [in New York City], there were fires almost daily. The little boy was at first terrified, and then fascinated. He made a fire engine of his own and became chief of the crew. Less than a dozen blocks away, the Big Six—the fire company of which big Bill Tweed was chief—had its headquarters. On the engine of the Big Six was painted a tiger's head—a front view with fierce distended jaws . . . The boy Nast used to regard this tiger's head . . . with admiration and awe. Little could he guess then what use he would make of that sinister emblem in later days. For it was the Big Six tiger that was to go with Tweed into Tammany Hall, and it was Thomas Nast, the man and cartoonist, who was first to emblazon it as the symbol of rapacious plunder and civic shame.

"But in that long ago time, the Big Six boys with their polished engine and glaring tiger meant only excitement and joy. He pursued them when fires broke out—running and shouting with a crowd of other boys that mingled with a tangle of frightened teams and a score of yelping curs."

January 22, 1870

Thomas Nast always wanted to be an artist, and studied on his own and at the Academy of Design under skilled tutors. In an 1885 interview with the *Indianapolis Times*, he reminisced: "I was never fit for anything but picture-making, and I suppose I never shall be . . . . The teachers rather pitied me. They thought I was an idiot in other respects, and finally concluded it would be better to let me spend my time in drawing than in doing nothing. My parents had no sympathy with my desire to become an artist. I had to help myself unaided . . . "

From his early teens, he aspired for achievement and recognition as a serious painter in a grander manner than that of illustrator. He was enthralled by the urban world about him and anxious for success in its many spheres. His first job was as a journalist-draftsman for *Frank Leslie's Illustrated Newspaper* in August 1856 (a month before he turned 16), at a salary of $4-6 per week.

Nast gained useful experience in the areas of sanitation reform, political mischief, municipal corruption, and even a bit of personal caricature during Frank Leslie's energetic exposé of a "swill milk" scandal, affecting New York and Brooklyn, waged in the pages of his Illustrated Weekly from May to August 1858. This carefully documented and promoted crusade of pictures and words involved an attempt to halt the sale of "Pure Country Milk" from diseased cows, which were fed distillery refuse and then literally milked to death. Frank Leslie was in total control of this project with little or no credit going specifically to his "special artists," none of whose drawings were signed. The 17-year-old Nast appears to have performed the lion's share of the draftsmanship, ostensibly working under the supervision of Leslie's senior artist, Albert Berghaus. The illustrated series commenced in the May 8, 1858 issue with a large Nast page-one drawing of four young "milkmaids" (as the distillery henchmen were derisively labeled) hauling a dead cow out the door of a distillery.

Leslie's successful campaign of awareness and outrage continued throughout the summer—surely a calculated maneuver to offset the competition it faced since the birth in January 1857 of a rival periodical, *Harper's Weekly*.

The cartoonist's debut in *Harper's Weekly* occurred in the issue dated March 19, 1859, "The New York Metropolitan Police. A Pictorial Analysis of the Report to the Legislature." Two years before, in April 1857, the Republican-controlled state legislature had created the New York Metropolitan Police, headed by a state-appointed board, in order to undermine the political power of the city's Democratic mayor, Fernando Wood. Complaints about the allegedly poor administration and performance of the Metropolitan Police culminated in a scathing report prepared under the direction of Senator Francis B. Spinola, Democrat of Brooklyn, and presented to the state senate on March 4, 1859. Three days later, the *New-York Times* reacted harshly against the police.

The editors of *Harper's Weekly* shared that sentiment, and Nast's assignment to draw a satirical cartoon of the police placed him under a tight deadline. Since the postdated March 19 issue would be published on March 10, the artist only had hours to finish the illustration before it was sent to the engravers and typesetters. His sketches reinforced highlights from the legislative report criticizing the police force by depicting its alleged thievery, moral laxity, violence, bribery, and extortion. However, the accuracy of the Democratic legislative report was soon challenged, and the state police board remained in authority until abolished under the influence of Tammany Hall in November 1869.

THE NEW YORK METROPOLITAN POLICE.

A PICTORIAL ANALYSIS OF THE REPORT TO THE LEGISLATURE.

1. These gentlemen, finding the garroting business on the decline, resolve to become guardians of law and order, and enter the Metropolitan Police.

2. Policemen are but men, and when young and fascinating women happen to get into the police-stations, who can blame them if they are civil and gallant?

3. As to poor devils, houseless wretches, with no good looks, and steeped in poverty and misery, can a high-bred policeman be expected to cringe to such as these? No, no; let them eat the bread of sorrow.

4. If a rowdy who votes with the Republicans happens to stick his knife into his neighbor's midriff, the judicious Metropolitan policeman instantly discovers a fight between two small boys at the next corner and hastens to interfere on behalf of law and order.

5. But if a poor wretch of a Democrat steals a loaf for his starving family, the zeal and fury of the Metropolitan police know no bounds, and the fellow is lucky if he be not brained on the spot.

6. A high-minded Commissioner scorns the idea of accepting a house bought by the members of the Force; but somehow the house *is* bought, and the title-deeds are slipped into somebody's pocket without his knowledge and tremendously against his will.

7. The powers that be ask no favor; but when they want new clothes a friendly captain goes round with the hat, and as for the patrolman who declines to put in a quarter, he had better emigrate to California by the next steamer.

8. The consequence of which is, that the poor patrolman is unable to procure the food which his sick wife requires, and his children go without stockings and without new frocks.

9. The police service continues, however, to be admirably efficient, and quite a number of hack-carriages are actively employed on pressing police duty, as above depicted.

While somewhat extraneous to the Tweed Ring story itself, the anti-Catholicism of *Harper's Weekly* and Nast played a role by association with the Irish "problem" in the campaign against the Tweed Ring. In fact, neither Tweed, Nast or Oakey Hall was Catholic.

However, Pope Pius IX focused extra attention on Catholicism as a political force in his 1869 declaration that the Pope was infallible, and Nast used that as a focal point of attack primarily on the Church and secondarily on the Ring. The cartoonist took direct aim at the Pope in his November 27, 1869 cartoon entitled "Pilgrim's Progress in the 19th Century."

Although Nast was born Roman Catholic, he didn't observe the faith and became a Protestant after his marriage to Sarah Edwards in 1861. Before he was 21, he spent six months in Italy with Giuseppi Garibaldi, who was in the process of unifying the country by military force, and became Nast's first hero. It is conceivable that some of Nast's anti-Vatican feelings were stoked by his early experience in Italy.

While neither Nast nor Tweed cared much about religion personally, the fact that most of the Irish immigrants were Catholic—and were a threat to take over political control and jobs from the Protestant and anti-immigrant Nativist establishment (which include the four Harper brothers)—probably was the ultimate factor behind Nast's vitriolic cartoons.

The more apparent issue was the perceived threat of the Ring's using government money to fund Catholic schools and "buy" the Irish vote by doing so. Nast drummed on this theme in a number of cartoons, and in an 1871 book, *Miss Columbia's Public School or Will It Blow Over?*, which he illustrated.

July 29, 1871

January 22, 1870

July 29, 1871

The American River Ganges

Nast's most notorious anti-Catholic cartoon was "The American Ganges," whose visceral, divisive images stunned—or gratified—readers of the September 30, 1871 issue of *Harper's Weekly*. It departed from the flow of cartoons featuring the travails of Tweed, Hall, Sweeny and Connolly, but vividly associated them and Tammany Hall with overt threats to America's public schools from the Catholic Church.

It depicts Catholic bishops as a sizeable flotilla of hungry crocodiles (their miters transformed into toothsome jaws) invading America's shore from Rome to devour the nation's schoolchildren—white, black, American Indian, and Chinese. (The white children are prominent in front; the rest are in the background.) The public school building on the sandbank stands as a fortress against the threat of theocracy, but it has been bombarded and flies Old Glory upside down to signal distress. The blitzed ruin of a school is armed with a "Quaker gun," a painted log to camouflage the fact that it is defenseless. A second such weapon has fallen from its battlement onto the rocks below.

Watching insouciantly from atop the sandbank beside the school are Boss Tweed and Peter Sweeny, while Mayor Oakey Hall drops a despairing boy to his doom at the water's edge. In the right-background, a pair of Tammany thugs march Lady Liberty off to the gallows. Out of the mists of the waters in the left-background arises a combined St. Peter's Basilica/Tammany Hall, flying the papal flag (left) of tiara and crossed keys (looking suspiciously like a skull-and-crossbones) and an Irish flag (right) featuring a winged harp. The scene surrounding the building hints of the hills of Rome and the city's Tiber River, while a portion of an encircling colonnade—labeled "The Political Roman Catholic Church"—is about to enclose New York City.

Nast's inspiration for transforming the miters of the Roman Catholic bishops into the menacing jaws of crocodiles was a small cartoon by John Leech in the English publication, *Punch*, of September 6, 1851 (20 years earlier). Nast expanded Leech's single Irish cleric into an invading horde of crocodile-clerics, and added images related to American public schools, Tammany Hall, and the Catholic Church. In selecting a title referring to the Ganges River in India, considered sacred by Hindus, Nast may have remembered an article in *Harper's Weekly* from 1867 about the worship of crocodiles in India. The cartoonist would have realized that most of his American audience would associate the Ganges with religious superstition, which was one of the messages about the Roman Catholic Church he wished to convey.

The impact of "The American River Ganges" was immediate. Four days after the cartoon was in print, a long letter appeared in the September 24, 1871 issue of the *Herald* from "J. E. B.," who protested that the cartoon grossly misrepresented the Roman Catholic hierarchy in the United States. "It would be difficult to imagine an illustration which could be more insulting to the Catholic community than this picture. And it would be difficult to imagine one that is so bold and patent a lie."

On the same day, the *New-York Times* printed an editorial entitled "Pity the Poor Protestant." It accused the Irish-Catholic press of hysterically fomenting fears of a Protestant conspiracy against Catholics.

"A very active member of the cabal that treacherously seeks to oust Romanists from their natural and constitutional supremacy is one Thomas Nast, generally believed to be a Prussian. He is aided and abetted by a set of bloated Protestant millionaires, engaged in publishing Harper [and Brothers] periodicals. Next to the *Times*, which is credited with untold influence, our Catholic rulers fear the rebel Nast, who presents his incendiary ideas in such an attractive manner, that it overtaxes the ingenuity of the priesthood to contradict them. It doesn't do any good to keep their people from being able to read, because Nast's artful productions appeal even to those who can't read…"

"It was probably at this delicate moment, to judge from its place in Nast's scrapbook, that the cartoonist received a clipping of a printed portrait of himself, to which the sender had attached about the throat a tiny hangman's noose fashioned from thread. It was inscribed "A just doom for the pimp.""

THE AMERICAN RIVER GANGES,
THE PRIESTS AND THE CHILDREN.—[See Page 915.]

The Civil War Draft Riots

When the Civil War began in April 1861, New York City had a lot of Confederate sympathizers, called Peace Democrats by themselves and Copperheads or traitors by Unionists. Mayor Fernando Wood was a Lincoln-hating Copperhead who even suggested in early 1861 that New York City secede from the Union. Fernando Wood preceded Bill Tweed on Thomas Nast's list of true villains as shown below.

January 2, 1864

" The Chicago Platform"

October 15, 1864

Fernando Wood is in the center, along with fellow Copperheads Clement Vallandigham, Daniel Voorhees, Horatio Seymour and George Pendleton (left to right).

Many Irish immigrants, who were largely unskilled, supported slavery, both to ensure white equality and to protect them from job competition from free blacks. In contrast, the majority of German immigrants disapproved of slavery and supported the Union.

During the Civil War, Tweed and Nast each supported the Union cause in an important way. Tweed devised a financially innovative system for complying with President Abraham Lincoln's Conscription Act in the face of overwhelming opposition from potential draftees, who constituted his political base. He was responsible for enlisting more than 100,000 recruits in the 20 months after a major July 1863 draft riot in New York City.

Nast's devastating portrayals of Confederate soldiers and politicians in illustrations and cartoons, as well as his emotion-arousing, sympathetic depictions of Union forces, reportedly resulted in Lincoln's calling his pictures "the best recruiting sergeants on the side of the Union." Nast also played an important role in Lincoln's 1864 re-election campaign, where two of his cartoons were each transformed into thousands of campaign posters.

February 17, 1863

On Saturday, July 11, 1863, President Abraham Lincoln's Conscription Act became effective in New York City and a military draft began. Two days later, the Irish potential draftees started perhaps the worst riot in American history. It lasted four days until sufficient troops could be recalled from Gettysburg (after their victory there two weeks earlier) to squelch it. More than 100 people were killed, including at least 11 black men, and property damage was in the millions of dollars.

Thomas Nast saw the draft riots first-hand and vividly illustrated some of their terrifying scenes in the *Harper's Weekly* issue of August 1, 1863. One of the worst atrocities was the burning of the Colored Orphan Asylum located on the west side of Fifth Avenue between 43rd and 44th Streets, and running the length of the block to Sixth Avenue. It was home to between 600 and 800 black children, all of whom escaped before their residence of last resort was sacked and burned. Before he moved two miles north to accommodate his family needs, Nast had lived further west on 44th Street from late 1861 to mid-1862, so he knew the area well.

THE RIOTS AT NEW YORK—THE RIOTERS BURNING AND SACKING THE COLORED ORPHAN ASYLUM.—[SEE PAGE 494.]

HANGING A NEGRO IN CLARKSON STREET.

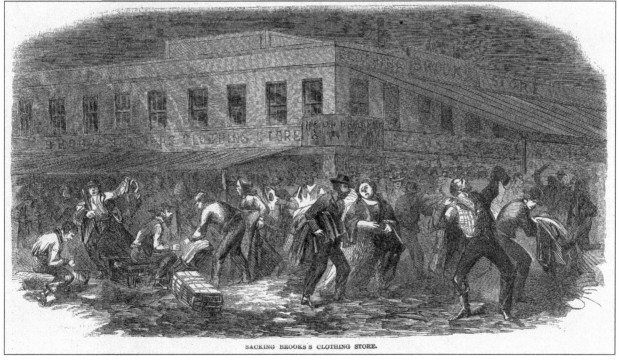

SACKING BROOKS'S CLOTHING STORE.

On the second day of the riot, Governor Horatio Seymour—also a Copperhead or Peace Democrat—tried to calm the rioters by addressing them as "My Friends." Five years later, when Seymour became the Democratic candidate for president in 1868—running against Nast's all-time hero, General Ulysses S. Grant—Nast vilified him with the "My Friends" quote and scenes from the riots.

"A MOB CAN REVOLUTIONIZE AS WELL AS A GOVERNMENT."

GOVERNOR SEYMOUR'S SPEECH TO THE NEW YORK RIOTERS.

MY FRIENDS,—I have come down from the quiet of the country to see what was the difficulty, to learn what all this trouble was concerning the draft. Let me assure you that I am your friend. [Uproarious cheering.] You have been my friends. [Cries of "yes" "yes"—"that's so"—"we are, and will be again."] And now I assure you, my fellow-citizens, that I am here to show you a test of my friendship. [Cheers.] I wish to inform you that I have sent my Adjutant-General to Washington to confer with the authorities there, and to have this draft suspended and stopped. [Vociferous cheers.] I now ask you as good citizens to wait for his return, and I assure you that I will do all that I can to see that there is no inequality, and no wrong done any one.—NEW YORK TRIBUNE, *July* 14, 1863.

October 31, 1868
The Colored Orphan Asylum is
burning in the left background.

THE HAND WE SHOOK SO OFTEN.

General Grant
April 14, 1866

Again, in the cartoon below (July 29, 1871) following the Orange Day riot of July 12, 1871, Nast reprised two horror scenes from the draft riots which took place eight years earlier, to make his point about Irish rioters.

The 1871 riot, coming four days after the first *New-York Times* disclosures about the Ring, became a public opinion tipping point in the Ring's downfall because it became apparent that Tammany Hall couldn't control its mob of core voters. (See pages 110-115.)

Bill Tweed, who by 1863 headed up Tammany Hall and was, in fact, Boss Tweed, played a leading role during and after the draft riots. Tammany was firmly pro-Union, but Tweed needed to protect his constituents as best he could. He accompanied Horatio Seymour as he traveled and spoke to various groups during the rioting and tried to calm them. Tweed's presence on the street was noted and praised, even by the *New-York Times*.

During the next month, Tweed and two New York City Republicans worked out a plan acceptable to President Lincoln and Secretary of War Edwin Stanton, whereby future draftees or enlistees were paid a $300 bonus from a municipal bond issue, and deferments were granted for key occupations or for family circumstances. Lincoln got 116,000 troops, and Tweed kept his constituents under control.

 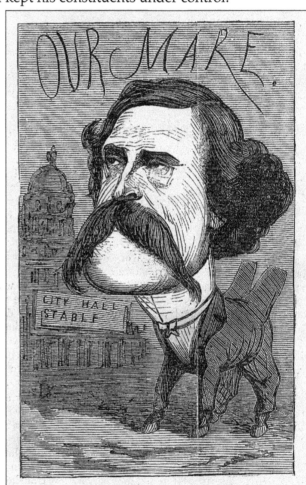

April 14, 1866

In addition, two of Tweed's future Ring associates played a key role in trying and sentencing dozens of looters, arsonists and even murderers. District Attorney Oakey Hall (later to be Mayor) and Recorder (presiding judge) John Hoffman (later to be Mayor, then Governor and potential presidential candidate) did a publicly applauded job in prosecuting and sentencing the culprits.

For the 20 months remaining in the Civil War, both Nast and Tweed were strong supporters of the Union cause.

In Boss Tweed's time, newspapers printed whatever they wanted, true or not. Moreover, some of their editors or owners, who simultaneously served in Congress or state governments, had political points of view that became indistinguishable from the "news" they reported.

The Tweed Ring took control of the press to the next level through direct payments for advertising, which included Mayor Oakey Hall's speeches and comments, as well as legal announcements. These were paid for at a dollar a line, when the normal rate was twenty to forty cents a line. Between January 1869 and September 1870, Hall approved vouchers for $2.7 million for newspaper payments; in 1875, after the Tweed Ring was long gone, the city paid $100,000.

In addition to the direct payoffs, on occasion Tweed also awarded city printing contracts to selected newspapers to assure their support. Finally, he had an "easy, back-slapping way with newsmen . . . quick to break out the glasses and cigars, or to give a newsman a few dollars for a favor," as Croswell Bowen put it in his 1956 biography of Oakey Hall.

The *North American Review* estimated that 54 daily and 26 weekly newspapers in New York City and State received advertising subsidies from the Ring for at least not attacking—if not actively supporting—its administration. Moreover, a number of reporters were paid directly—or with public payroll sinecure jobs—to write favorable stories. Conversely, Comptroller Richard Connolly was known to withhold payment of selected advertising claims until newspapers complied with his specific wishes to support bills in the state legislature or print specific stories.

Some of the papers were owned by the Ring. They had small circulations, but received large amounts of advertising dollars: for example the *Transcript*, which printed judicial opinions and abstracts, received over $500,000 with a circulation of only 2,000. The editor of the *Transcript*, Charles Wilbour, also held three city jobs and three similar county jobs, which paid him a total of $18,000 annually; in addition, he was president of Tweed's printing and stationery supply monopoly companies (see page 54). Another Ring newspaper, the *Leader*, was actually edited by Mayor Oakey Hall.

- *Herald*—James Gordon Bennett, Sr., the well regarded founder (1835) and editor, was a personal friend of Oakey Hall, who previously had done legal work for him. By 1867, James Gordon Bennett, Jr. was running the paper on a day-to-day basis, although his father didn't die until 1872. The *Herald* always supported the Democratic party. In the summer of 1870, the *Evening Free Press* broke a story that D. George Wallis, a senior editor at the *Herald*, held three sinecure positions at City Hall paying him a total of $15,000 annually. That went a long way towards cementing the *Herald's* loyalty to the Ring.

Manton Marble and
James Gordon Bennett, Sr.
from a July 11, 1868 Nast Cartoon.

- *Evening Post* — The *Evening Post* was published by well-known editor and poet William Cullen Bryant, who generally leaned Republican but was 76 in 1871, and possibly not making key decisions any longer. Bryant had been in charge of the paper for about 40 years, but had given authority to a new business manager, Isaac Henderson, who bore an unsavory reputation. Editor Charles Nordoff was fired after he criticized Tweed, and the paper subsequently attacked the *Times* and *Harper's Weekly* for their anti-Ring positions. After the *Times* disclosures, the *Post* editorialized "If we were dishonest or disingenuous partisans we should probably do as the *Times* and *Harper's Weekly* do, and our praise and our blame would presently count for no more than theirs with honest and intelligent men."

William Cullen Bryant
April 14, 1866

- *World*—Manton Marble, owner and publisher, acquired the *World* in 1862, when he was only 27. He was a close adviser to fellow Democrat Samuel Tilden, especially during Tilden's presidential campaign in 1876.

Marble attacked the Ring in 1869, but turned around in the next year after receiving payoffs. The *World's* ad revenue from City Hall jumped from $7,500 in 1869 to $43,500 in 1870.

Nast captured that perfectly in the *Harper's Weekly* issue of November 12, 1870, when Marble supported Hoffman, Hall and Tweed in their winning election races, calling them "Good and Honest Men," while playing Cupid shooting arrows at Tammany Ring dollars. At the bottom of the globe (the *World*) are Marble's pre-payoff words: "Down with the shameless corruption of the Ring, O. Hall, W. M. Tweed." Nast's pun: "It's Love That Makes The *World* Turn Round" is one of his absolute best.

"It's Love that makes the *World* turn Round."

- *Sun*— Publisher Charles A. Dana learned the newspaper business at the *Tribune* under Horace Greeley. During the Civil War, he served with distinction in the War Department in the Republican Lincoln administration. He became partial owner and editor of the *Sun* in 1868 and supported Democratic Tammany Hall, although the *Sun's* motto was "It Shines for All.". Aged 52 in 1871, Dana had a reputation for being perverse and cynical. Nast emphasized his short stature when caricaturing him.

After the *Times* disclosures in July 1871, the *Sun* responded by attacking *Times* editor Louis Jennings with false charges about his prior employment with the *London Times*, as well as a "tedious monotony of slander, disregard of truth and blackguard vituperation."

Right: This extract from a March 29, 1873 cartoon shows:

- Whitelaw Reid, who succeeded Horace Greeley at the *Tribune*

- The diminutive Charles Dana of the *Sun*

- James Gordon Bennett, Jr. who succeeded his father at the *Herald*

Left: This November 1, 1873 pre-election cartoon shows a perplexed "Spotty Sun" and "Battered World" after John Morrissey, who was competing with "Honest John" Kelly to become Tweed's successor, told them: "Stand by Boys; I'll show you what muscle can do" (vs. bribes and payoffs). Boss Tweed, now out of power, is shown with his moneybag head pinned under the block behind Morrissey.

Horace Greeley, founder (1841) and publisher of the *Tribune*, was an outstanding, if erratic, editor. He was candid, provocative, and consistent on many important issues, including principled opposition to the extension of slavery beyond the existing boundaries of the institution after 1844.

However, Greeley also was known for his unrestrained language—for example, using the word "liar" with some frequency. He also changed editorial positions on occasion, as Nast enjoyed pointing out in late 1871 and 1872 when Greeley was a favorite target. By 1871, when Greeley was 60 years old, he had effectively installed Whitelaw Reid as managing editor, although he still contributed editorials on an almost daily basis.

The *Tribune* had the largest circulation of any American newspaper—about 301,000 claimed, and 251,000 according to G. P. Rowell's *American Newspaper Ratebook and Directory* for 1870. (Rowell was the most prominent advertising agent of his time.) Most leading newspapers published daily, semi-weekly, and weekly editions: the Tribune's circulation was 39,000 daily; 20,000 semi-weekly; and 192,000 weekly, according to Rowell. About 40% of the subscribers lived in New York State.

Greeley was responsible for training Charles Dana (*Sun*) and Henry Raymond and George Jones, founders of the *Times*, among many other journalists. He never hesitated to advise anybody, including President Abraham Lincoln.

In late 1869, Mayor Oakey Hall, probably with a few drinks in him, concluded a speech to the New England Society: "Here (in New York City) you enjoy extensive freedom—**freedom in newspaper abuse**; freedom to gamble in Wall Street; freedom in marriage; freedom in divorce; free lagers; free rights; free love!"

Greeley's response in the *Tribune* was classic: "New York must be delivered from the thralldom of the Hall family. **It is wearied of Tammany Hall, Mozart Hall, all the political halls, Oakey Hall and alcohol.**"

At that time, Greeley was critical of the Ring. An October 18, 1869 Tribune editorial stated, "The three men who manipulate the Democratic party in this city for their individual aggrandizement and profit, and who form what is popularly termed the Tammany Ring, are, it is well known, Peter B. Sweeny, William M. Tweed and Richard B. Connolly."

How Thomas Nast depicted Horace Greeley on April 14, 1866.

Thomas Nast never trusted Horace Greeley and his influential *Tribune* to join his and the *Times'* crusade against the Ring. As early as the issue of June 24, 1871 (available June 14)—before the *Times* first disclosure about the Armory frauds on July 8—Nast pictured Greeley "plowing toward the White House" in 1872, aided by former Republican governor Reuben Fenton of New York. Greeley, who had a farm in Chappaqua, N.Y., had published a book called "What I Know About Farming."

"WHAT I KNOW ABOUT FARMING."

H. G. Plowing toward the White House.

Greeley, of course, knew that Tweed and the Ring were promoting Governor John Hoffman for the presidency in 1872. As a liberal Republican, Greeley should have joined the attack on Tweed, but refrained from doing so until after the second round of *Times* disclosures on July 22. He probably wanted to avoid Tammany's displeasure, so that he would have Democratic support if Hoffman's nomination failed, and he was able to put together a fusion ticket against Nast's hero, President Ulysses S. Grant.

Greeley's link-up with Tammany Hall actually did happen a year later after Greeley won both the breakaway Liberal Republican, as well as the Democratic, nominations to run against Grant. (See page 273.)

After the *Times* July 1871 disclosures—in the cartoon (below left) from the August 12, 1871 issue of Harper's Weekly—Nast skewers a weeping Greeley with Comptroller Richard Connolly, Mayor Oakey Hall, Boss Tweed and Peter Sweeny looking on. Greeley had co-signed the $100,000 bail-bond to get former Confederate President Jefferson Davis out of Fortress Monroe, VA prison in May 1867, an "act of kindness" for which Nast never forgave him, and which explains the title of the cartoon: "Not a Bailable Case." (See page 68). Connolly, literally on his knees begging for support, is holding a $10,000 "city fan" over ailing "Mare" Hall, while Tweed and Sweeny peep over a low barrier in the rear. This $10,000 fan refers to charges that Greeley had accepted certain concessions from the city administration.

NOT A BAILABLE CASE.

THE GREAT AMERICAN FARMER TROUBLED WITH THE MILK OF HUMAN KINDNESS AGAIN.

"*We have scrupulously refrained from the intemperate and indiscriminate style of attack in which the* TIMES *has of late profusely indulged, because words thus used lose their force, and because we did not have proofs to warrant charges which, nevertheless, we have often believed to be true.*" —*N. Y. Tribune,* July 21.

The following week, August 19, Greeley appears totally befuddled about the *Times'* disclosures in the extract from "WHO IS INGERSOLL's CO? N.Y. *Tribune.*" (A detailed explanation is on page 130.)

"WHO IS INGERSOLL'S CO?" N.Y. TRIBUNE.   MR. INGERSOLL: "ALLOW ME TO INTRODUCE YOU TO MY CO?"

TWO GREAT QUESTIONS.

In March 1817, brothers James and John Harper, aged 22 and 20, started a printing company called J. & J. Harper. Brother Wesley joined in 1823 and the youngest brother, Fletcher, in 1825. By that year, the firm had become the largest book publisher in the country. (It continues today as Harper Collins Publishing, part of News Corporation.)

The firm name was changed to Harper and Brothers in 1833. In June 1850, the company started *Harper's New Monthly Magazine* with Henry Raymond as managing editor, a year prior to his co-founding the *New-York Times*. (*Harper's Magazine* also continues today as an independent publication.)

On December 15, 1855, Frank Leslie brought out the first issue of *Frank Leslie's Illustrated Newspaper*. Leslie was born in England and learned the newspaper trade at the *London Illustrated News*. After coming to this country in 1848 at the age of 27, he spent eight years as a newspaper engraver and promoter, before succeeding with his new illustrated weekly.

Harper & Brothers responded with *Harper's Weekly*, just over a year later, with the first issue dated January 3, 1857. Under Fletcher Harper's supervision, its target audience—as a self-styled "Journal of Civilization"—was the upper and upper-middle classes.

In contrast, *Leslie's* catered to the lower-middle and lower classes, and covered topics like boxing, dog-fighting, and "low-life" theatre that Harper's generally disdained. By 1870, *Harper's Weekly* had a regular circulation of about 100,000 while *Frank Leslie's Illustrated Newspaper* had a norm of about 70,000.

According to Joshua Brown in *Beyond the Lines* (p. 275), "*Leslie's* stance toward the Ring scandal characteristically teetered until the finality of Tweed's downfall was indisputable . . . . Although *Leslie's* covered his subsequent trial (1873), it seemed to lavish the most attention on Tweed once he became a fugitive." Because his normal circulation probably included many more lower-income Tweed supporters than *Harper's Weekly's* readership, it was understandable why Frank Leslie chose to play it safe until the definition of "safe" changed from pro-Ring to anti-Ring.

Harper's Weekly, with a normal weekly circulation of 100,000, and the *New-York Times*, with a total circulation of 59,000 (35,000 daily, 4,000 semi-weekly, and 20,000 weekly, according G. P. Rowell), worked almost in tandem after August 1870 to bring down Boss Tweed and his Tammany ring. However, the relationship between the Harper brothers and the *Times* management began more than 20 years earlier.

In the 1840's, Harper & Brothers was the leading book publisher in the country. On occasion, Henry J. Raymond, the founding editor of the *Times*, read manuscripts for the firm. When *Harper's New Monthly Magazine* began publication in June 1850, Henry Raymond was its editor, and remained so until 1856, five years after he and George Jones started the *New-York Daily Times*. Raymond was given his approximate 20% interest in the *Times* in exchange for his editorial services.

Jones and Raymond originally became acquainted when both worked for Horace Greeley on his *New York Tribune* in the 1840's—Raymond a reporter and editor, and Jones in the business office. Jones later became a banker in Albany. Jones, who was responsible for raising all the money to start the paper, put up $25,000 and became publisher of the *Times*; his former banking partner, Edward Wesley, also put up $25,000. The remaining initial funding came from three investors in Albany, and two in Aurora, N.Y. (E. B. Morgan and Christopher Morgan), in response to solicitations from Jones.

Henry Raymond

October 24, 1868

George Jones

November 6, 1869

Jones probably got to know Fletcher Harper, Sr., the youngest of the four Harper brothers, as a potential initial financial backer of the *Times*. In 1853, Fletcher Harper, Jr. bought into the *Times* and entered its business department, where he worked under Jones.

When Thomas Nast attacked the Tammany Ring in 1867, 1868 and 1869, the *Times* usually did not participate, although it could be critical on occasion. As late as April 1870, Tweed steered a new charter for New York City through the State Legislature; while Nast attacked it (see pages 81-83), the *Times* praised it, as well as Mayor Oakey Hall's appointment of Tweed as Commissioner of Public Works. Both developments vastly increased the Ring's capability for fraud as the *Times* later came to recognize and regret.

Henry Raymond unexpectedly died in June 1869; ironically, Oakey Hall was one of his pall bearers, along with George William Curtis, the long-time editor of *Harper's Weekly*, and Horace Greeley. George Jones stepped into Raymond's shoes as chief executive of the paper.

However, Jones' ability to attack Tweed and the Ring was limited by his executive committee. One member was James B. Taylor, who was part-owner of Tweed's New York Printing Company, a 2000-employee operation which handled all of the city's printing. Another member was Leonard Jerome, who had joint real estate holdings with Tweed; Tweed was by then the third-largest real estate owner in the city. (Jerome's daughter Jennie became Winston Churchill's mother.)

Unfortunately for Tweed, Taylor died suddenly of typhoid fever on August 22, 1870. After that, Louis Jennings, 33, a British-born hard-hitting editor who Jones had put in charge earlier that year, was free to attack the Ring. Jones encouraged him to do so, even through 5% or so of the *Times* revenue, which came from ads from City Hall advertising, was bound to disappear.

In July 1871, the *Times* received proof of the Tweed ring's fraudulent bookkeeping from two separate "whistle-blowers". Its publication of the disclosures literally blew the cover off the Ring.

August 19, 1871

After that the *Times* fed off and praised Nast's cartoons, and Nast often got ideas from commentary and editorials in the *Times*. George William Curtis, the long-time editor of *Harper's Weekly*, also chimed in with timely editorials.

Tweed did his best to stop the attacks. Nast was offered and turned down as much as $500,000 ($10 million in today's dollars) to go to Europe until after the November 1871 election. Jones reportedly turned down ten times as much to sell his stake in the *Times* to Tweed.

Next, Tweed (through an emissary) reportedly tried to buy Henry Raymond's widow's 34% ownership of the *Times*. In a close call, George Jones arranged for E. B. Morgan, one of his original minority partners from Aurora, N.Y., who already owned 7%, to buy Mrs. Raymond's shares before Tweed could act. If Tweed had obtained them, he could have arranged for one of his crooked judges to shut down the paper.

Still another attempt to stifle the *New-York Times* was made by Mayor Oakey Hall. As *Harper's Weekly* put it on September 9, 1871: "Mayor Hall, exasperated by his inability to answer or buy off the *Times*, suddenly remembered that he had been unfaithful to a sacred religious trust."

Fourteen years earlier, the *Times* had bought and built on a property, which previously had been occupied by the Old Brick Church, after the church moved further uptown. New York City, which owned the property, gave the *Times* a quit-claim deed, signed by the Mayor and other officials, in exchange for a payment of $50,000. Hall's attempt to repossess the property was considered an attack on freedom of the press by other newspapers and, consequently, was abandoned although not until after passage of a resolution in favor of it by the Board of Aldermen.

Even more outrageous was a piece of legislation called the Code Amendment, which was originally suggested by Mayor Hall, drawn up by Judge Albert Cardozo, and passed by the state legislature. It would have allowed courts to punish by fine and imprisonment, without trial by jury, "the free and public expression upon the conduct of judicial tribunals." Any act of the Ring, approved by its crooked judges, could not be criticized by the press without the paper and its editor being subject to the mercy of those same judges.

Fortunately, Governor John Hoffman, backed by most of the press including the pro-Tammany Democratic *World*, vetoed the Code Amendment. In this scene from "Hash," a July 1, 1871 cartoon, Judge George Barnard says to Emperor Tweed, "What is to protect me from slander?" Maybe it even influenced his total break from the Ring when he issued an injunction two months later, which cut off the Ring's ability to issue further payments. (See pages 106-107 and 140.)

THE FLAG OF TRUCE.
FROM THE ENEMY.

Harper & Brothers was the largest publisher of school books. In response to Nast's cartoons, Tweed threatened to take that business away and give it to his New York Printing Company. Fletcher Harper convinced his two older brothers (James Harper had died in 1869) to stay the course in spite of the probable loss of about $50,000 of textbook sales, which Nast captured so well below in his cartoon of May 6, 1871

THE NEW BOARD OF EDUCATION.

SOWING THE SEED, WITH AN EYE TO THE HARVEST.

Undoubtedly, the Nast-Curtis-Fletcher Harper combination at *Harper's Weekly* and the Jones-Jennings combination at the *Times* worked closely together. Nast's pictures and the *Times'* disclosures ultimately brought the Ring down. It's a vivid story as Nast portrayed it.

In 1858, Tweed began building his political machine as a result of his election to the recently restructured and empowered Board of Supervisors for New York County. Devised as a reform measure, the revamped governing body consisted of 12 members—six Democrats and six Republicans—who were expected to keep an eye on one another. Tweed's first successful experiment in political muscle-flexing came during the 1859 mayoral campaign, when he and his associates successfully bribed a Republican supervisor named Peter Voorhiis with $2500 to skip the next meeting at which election inspectors were to be appointed. The strategy worked well: 550 of 609 inspectors selected were Democrats.

However, it was not enough to stop the mayoral triumph of Fernando Wood, the former two-term Tammany Hall mayor now running on the splinter Mozart Hall ticket. That put Wood in charge of New York City when the Civil War began.

By 1863, Tweed held the rank of chairman of the General Committee of Tammany Hall and grand sachem of the Tammany Society, making him the first person to hold the two top leadership positions in that political organization. A major source of Tweed's power came from his control over the nomination process: in exchange for office, politicians turned over their patronage-granting privileges to him, thereby making both appointed and elected officials beholden to the "Boss." He also began consolidating power from his new and deceptively innocent-sounding position of deputy street commissioner (1863-1870), where his patronage authority was direct. Under the intoxicating growth of the Civil War economy (1861-1865), all manner of imaginative new projects in jobbery and corruption would spring into being, including the new courthouse. In fact, Tweed gained virtual political command over the city government, its patronage, and its ballooning budget, as well as the development of future possibilities. By the late 1860s, the sky seemed to be the limit.

Tammanyite Matthew Breen later recalled Tweed's shrewdness "in locating his men on the political checker-board, so as to entrench himself and add to his power." By that process, Tweed "originated a political junta which grew year by year in influence … and was the germ of a combination that became almost invincible."

First, his friend George Barnard was nominated for city recorder (judge), and advanced in 1860 to the state supreme court (a lower appellate court), where he would remain until his impeachment 12 years later.

Peter B. Sweeny, who would be publicly regarded as the sinister mastermind and "brains" of the Tammany Ring, was elected in 1857 as the district attorney for New York County. He was appointed in 1866 by Mayor John T. Hoffman as the city chamberlain, soon after gained the position of county treasurer, and in 1870 was appointed president of the City Parks Commission by Mayor A. Oakey Hall.

The installation in 1867 of Richard B. Connolly as city comptroller added the third principal player. Over a dozen years older than Tweed, Sweeny, and Hall, Richard "Slippery Dick" Connolly had ties with Tammany Hall dating back to 1839. His accounting and auditing skills made him the logical choice for massaging the numbers—perhaps the most sensitive position of all.

The election in December 1868 of Oakey Hall to replace Governor-elect John Hoffman as mayor (inaugurated on January 1, 1869) completed what many, including cartoonist Thomas Nast, considered the four pillars of the Tweed Ring-- Tweed, Sweeny, Connolly, and Hall.

Looking back in 1876, journalist Theodore P. Cook, a reporter for the *Utica Observer*, explained how the Tweed Ring had secured its support:

"Tweed's policy was to buy off with offices all the powerful opponents whom he could not bully or bribe into submission. ...But the "Ring's" belief in its invincibility rested on some substantial ground. Usually when it wanted a man, it stretched forth its hand—and he came. For instance, near the close of the legislative session of 1869, three Republican senators were needed to insure the passage of the bill known as the New York tax levy. The bill was under debate until late in the evening, with the general understanding that "negotiations" were pending. Tweed, Connolly, and Sweeny were gathered in a room. The "Boss" remarked: "I think five horses apiece will draw 'em; I know that six will." A "horse," in their parlance, meant $5000. "Put on six horses," said Tweed. Within an hour the sum of $30,000 was paid to each of the three Senators, and they went back to the Senate-Chamber and voted for the tax levy. With such means at their command, and such corruptible elements surrounding them, is it surprising that Tweed and his associates grew to have boundless faith in themselves?"

After the eventual fall of the Tweed Ring, *Harper's Weekly* editor George William Curtis reminisced in *Harper's Monthly* (April 1874) about Boss Tweed:

"He did not believe that there was any risk. Tweed was the most striking illustration of a very common faith—belief in the Almighty Dollar. He is the victim of a very touching fidelity which every good American will surely be the last to flout. His creed was very simple; it was that money would buy every thing … Certainly his confidence was not surprising. He had proved his creed. He had seen money work miracles. He had seen himself, a man of no cleverness and no advantages, rising swiftly by means of it from insignificant poverty to the control of a great party. It had made him master of one of the great cities of the world. It had secured for him Governors, Legislatures, councils, and legal and executive authorities of every kind. He invested in land and judges. He bought dogs and lawyers. He silenced the press with a golden muzzle and money made his will law.

"Here was a man who wanted nothing that money could not buy: was it strange that he had unbounded faith in it? Every form of virtue was to him mere affectation, a more or less ingenious and tenacious "strike" for money. If a man spoke of honesty, patriotism, self-respect, the public welfare, public opinion, truth, justice, right, Tweed smiled at the fine phrases in which the auctioneer, anxious to sell himself, cried "Going! Going!" Argument, reason, decency; they were meaningless to him. If an opponent held out, he simply asked, "How much?" The world was a market. Life was a bargain.

THE "BRAINS"

That achieved the Tammany Victory at the Rochester Democratic Convention.

"In Albany he had the finest quarters at the Delavan, and when he came into the great dining room at dinner-time, and looked at all the tables thronged with members of the Legislature and the lobby, he had a benignant, paternal expression, as of a patriarch pleased to see his retainers happy. . . And he never doubted that he could buy every man in the room if he were willing to pay the price. So at the Capitol, where sits the Legislature of a noble commonwealth of four millions of souls, he moved about with an air of fat good nature, like the chief shepherd of the flock. If he stood at the door of the Assembly looking in, it is easy to fancy him saying to himself, the State pays these men two or three hundred dollars for four months' service; I will give them better wages. He did not doubt that it was a fair transaction. What is the State? It is only four millions of people, he thought, who are all trying to be rich—struggling, cheating, by hook or by crook, every man for himself, and the devil take the hindmost, to be rich. These men would be fools not to take my money. And he smiled his fat smile, and paid liberally for all that was in market."

In his memoirs (1899), Tammanyite Matthew Breen described William M. Tweed in much gentler terms. According to Breen, Tweed was a man of

"rather commanding presence, standing fully five feet eleven inches in height, and weighing nearly, if not quite, three hundred pounds. His complexion was slightly florid, his features large, and there was always a merry twinkle in his eye when in the company of those he knew to be his friends; a warmth in his greeting, and a heartiness in the grasp of his hand, which were reassuring to those properly introduced to him. He had a sympathetic heart, and those who knew him intimately knew that his deeds of kindness and charity were almost numberless. He was a man, too, of generally correct habits. While of a social disposition, and fond of entertaining his friends he scarcely ever partook more than a sip of wine when extending hospitalities, and never permitted strong drink to get the best of him; neither did he have the tobacco habit. He was scrupulously careful concerning his attire, while never striving to make a show of dress. He was always suave and polite in manner, and while clinging to his friends with hooks of steel, was vigorous and most determined in his conflicts.

There was nothing boastful or cowardly in his make-up, as was shown by the manner in which he faced, single-handed, the fierce public denunciation of the Ring of which he was the actual head and front."

In the May 19, 1871 issue of the *New-York Times*, George Alfred Townsend, journalist and author writing under the pseudonym "Gath," provided a highly subjective snapshot of Boss Tweed at the peak of his power as "The Ruler of New York":

"I have known Tweed for very many years. He is a man without shame, and very nearly without fear. A newspaper attack will make Dick Connolly think that a vigilance committee's going to hang him straightaway, and he will cringe and writhe in pitiable terror … Sweeny feels a newspaper attack like a man of education and worldly wisdom, who has lived long enough to feel that the worldly opinion of the world is the highest felicity; but, unwilling to give up his bad power, he can only sit and mope and have a mental spell of sickness every time he is admonished that no one respects him. But Bill Tweed, or "Tweedy," as they call him, is perfectly callous; nothing impresses him; he has fits of good nature, spells of licentiousness, a good deal of gluttony, and most of the lower tastes kept well in check; but for all he is a powerful business man, always at work, never wearied out, never thoughtful, stirring from morn till midnight, doing a great part of his work himself, a fair judge of agents, a big brutal nature, equal to the most brutal situation and animated with the same spirit which drives a mill or runs [A. T. Stewart's department store]—confidence, economy, energy, enterprise. "

Samuel J. Tilden, chairman of the New York State Democratic Party, was instrumental in orchestrating Boss Tweed's fall from power in 1871-1872. Tilden built on the appreciation and respect he garnered for his efforts by being elected governor in 1874 and securing the Democratic presidential nomination in 1876. In Tilden's campaign biography of the latter year, author Theodore P. Cook, a reporter for the *Utica Observer*, remarked on the source of Tweed's success:

"Tweed owed his success more to his physical than to his mental resources. His bulky figure conveyed at first sight an impression of fat weakness, of flabbiness, which impression was modified by his firm, swift gait, and altogether dissipated by his keen piercing eyes, his sharp nose and his implacable lips.

He never looked or acted as if he were tired. He would come up as fresh at midnight as at noon. At his office in Duane Street, …where a dingy sign bore the inscription "William M. Tweed, Attorney-at-Law," he might be found often when the crowd thought he was out of town. There sometimes word would be brought to him that trouble was brewing at a distant point, somewhere perhaps in the Nineteenth or Twenty-second Ward, miles away from his office. Within an hour or two he was at the scene of the alleged revolt against his power. His sinister smile, his shrewd glance, his omnipresence frightened and subdued the enemies who were of his own class. His untiring activity enabled him to learn their plans, to cope with them successfully, to frustrate and tame them. If he had been a lazy man he could not have been the 'Boss'."

Boss Tweed controlled at least 12,000 jobs and 60,000 votes through patronage alone, (according to Alexander B. Callow, Jr. in *The Tweed Ring*). Callow estimated that one-third of the jobs went to men who did little or no work (sinecures), or to fictitious names whose checks were cashed by the Ring. Even holders of paying jobs were subject to Ring assessments.

Political, business and personal friends, along with their relatives, were rewarded with real and/or phony positions. Peter Sweeny, who became Commissioner of Public Parks in April 1870, directly controlled about 4,000 jobs. Tweed, in his capacity as Deputy Commissioner of Public Works prior to April 1870 and as Commissioner after that, could offer work to at least that many uneducated Irish laborers in return for their support at the polls.

One of Tweed's principal income sources was The New-York Printing Company which he established and controlled. All of the municipal printing for blank forms, citizenship applications, ballots, etc. went through it at exorbitant prices—over $2.8 million in 1870 alone.

Subsequently, The New-York Printing Company absorbed three of its larger competitors and several smaller ones. Insurance, transportation, and other private corporations subject to municipal or state regulation, effectively were forced to pay Tweed's unconscionable prices for their printing needs, or face his legislative consequences.

In addition, Tweed was the majority owner of the Manufacturing Stationers' Company which furnished all the stationery and office supplies used by the municipal government, public schools and other public institutions. It consistently billed the City Treasury $10,000 for $50 or so worth of supplies (according to Abram S. Genung in his 1871 pamphlet *The Frauds of the New York City Government Exposed*).

Moreover, the president of these two companies, Charles Wilbour, held six sinecure positions paying him $18,000 a year: $3,000 as Stenographer to the *County* Bureau of Elections, $2,500 as Stenographer in the Superior Court, and $3,500 for "examining accounts he has never seen," according to Genung. He received the same salary for the same positions from the *City*, as he did from the *County*.

Cornelius Carson, secretary of both companies, earned $6,000 as *County* Chief of the Bureau of Elections and $3,500 for examining the same "unseen accounts" as Wilbour, and also received comparable salaries from the *City*.

New York City, even in the post-Civil War period, had an unsanitary and unsafe environment, ripe for large scale corruption. Its unpaved streets were choked with dust in the summer, snow in the winter, and horse droppings all year round. Homeless children, prostitutes and men who depended on thievery for a living were conspicuous almost everywhere.

The Board of Supervisors had the authority to levy taxes for city expenses with the concurrence of the state legislature. One 1858 project created a commission to explore the possibility of creating a new city courthouse. By 1861, the supervisors persuaded the legislature to let them take over the courthouse project from the state commission. The supervisors also obtained the authority from the legislature to lease courtrooms, armories and a jail, as well as to issue bonds to cover their debts and other financial obligations as might seem opportune.

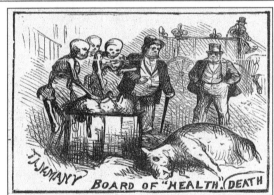

The courthouse project continued for more than ten years and became the most blatant example of the Ring's dishonesty. Originally budgeted at $250,000, it ended up costing tax-payers over $13 million. All of the marble in the courthouse came from a Vermont quarry owned by Tweed.

Its full exposure in 1871 was the focal point of the *New-York Times* disclosures and some of Nast's cartoons, and led to the voter revolt that resulted in Tweed and his cohorts being overthrown.

All sketches from January 22, 1870

Along with bribery, patronage and illegal naturalization, control of the ballot box assured the Ring's perpetuation in power. After a combination of Nast's cartoons and the *New-York Times* disclosures in the summer of 1871 upset the Tammany applecart, a Municipal Reform Meeting was held at Cooper Union on September 4. Congressman Robert B. Roosevelt—uncle of future president Theodore Roosevelt and a staunch but honest Democrat—delivered a key speech detailing three ways in which vote fraud was committed.

Repeaters

"By a combination of certain Democratic and Republican office-holders in this city, the votes of the people no longer express their will. They are falsified in three different ways, so that no matter how honest the mass of voters might be, the corrupt Ring would apparently be retained in power. To effect this, three forces are brought into play. There is the use of repeaters at the polls, the manipulation of ballots as they are deposited, and the false counting of them in making up the canvass. Precisely how these schemes are managed I will explain to you.

"Heretofore there has been a registry of all legal voters in this city. I can only speak of the past. I cannot tell what Tammany will do hereafter, and now that the registry law has been repealed we may be sure that matters will not be improved. There are three registers to supervise these lists, three inspectors to receive the votes, and three canvassers to count them. One of each of these boards was a Republican, and could stop all frauds if he pleased, but as the parties to be defeated were only those Democrats who were opposed to Tammany, he shut his eyes with resolute determination.

"To begin with, gangs of repeaters were organized whose first duty was to have their names recorded in as many districts as possible, usually from a dozen to fifty; and it was curious with what childlike innocence the Republican register would receive the names of 100 men who assumed to reside at the private dwelling of some leading Tammany Ward politician, or who pretended to camp out on some vacant lot. So the repeaters were enrolled, and I have had lists of them offered to me for sale at so much a vote when Tammany did not need them.

"On election day, these men went to the polls in gangs with their captains, and marched from district to district like companies of soldiers. If one of them were challenged, the result depended upon the locality; in a disreputable neighborhood, the challenger was knocked into the gutter, and probably locked up by the police for disturbing the polls. In a district where this would not answer, the accused was taken before the police magistrate, who let him out on bail, the necessary bail being also on hand for the purpose; the repeater was usually back at the polls, and hard at work—before the challenger—and no one ever heard of such a case being brought to trial afterward.

"In another way were these repeaters used. Many people, especially wealthy Republicans, do not vote. It is the duty of every man to vote; this is one of the obligations he assumes in demanding liberty, and rather than have the duty neglected, Tammany sees that it is performed.

"Toward the latter part of the day, it will be found that certain persons who are registered have not voted, and it then belongs to the polling officers to copy such names on slips and pass them to the proper parties outside; and it would horrify if not amuse some of our wealthy millionaires to see what ragged-clothed, bloated-faced, and disreputable individuals represented them at the polls, and performed for them a public duty which they had neglected. This is repeating. I have given you but a hurried sketch of it; the votes polled by it count up tens of thousands.

"But, successful as it was, it had its defects. The repeaters began to imagine they were their own masters; they thought they held the power because they were the instruments of power. To use a political term, they undertook to set up shop for themselves. Still repeating, when kept in its place, is not disapproved by our Ring rulers."

November 5, 1870 (See pages 90-91.)

Ringing the Ballots

"The manipulation of ballots—'Ringing' the ballots, as it is appropriately called—is a very beautiful operation, and it is said by those who have tried it to be perfect. It is now the favorite plan; it is simple, inexpensive and effective. When one of you good, innocent Republicans, we will suppose, is going to the polls to vote the wrong ticket or support the wrong man, as you are so fond of doing, your unwise intentions are quietly frustrated. The inspector holds in his hand the ballot you ought to deposit, and when he receives yours quietly substitutes one for the other, and drops yours on the floor before he puts his in the box. This is a simple slight-of-hand trick, easily learned and readily applied.

"If, however, you are suspicious, and watch the official, or if the latter is awkward and inexperienced, a man near by pushes against you or the policeman seizes you and accuses you of having voted before. Of course, ample apologies are immediately tendered for the rudeness, the inspectors are indignant that so respectable a gentleman should be insulted, they abuse the rough or the policeman, you are shown out with great respect; but your ballot went down on the floor, and the substitute got in the box.

"Repeating is expensive, false counting is troublesome, our Tammany men are not experts at arithmetic, and figures are often troublesome, as our amiable Comptroller will admit at this moment; but "Ringing" ballots is a complete success. It is only necessary to buy a Republican inspector, and a small place or a few hundred dollars will usually do that."

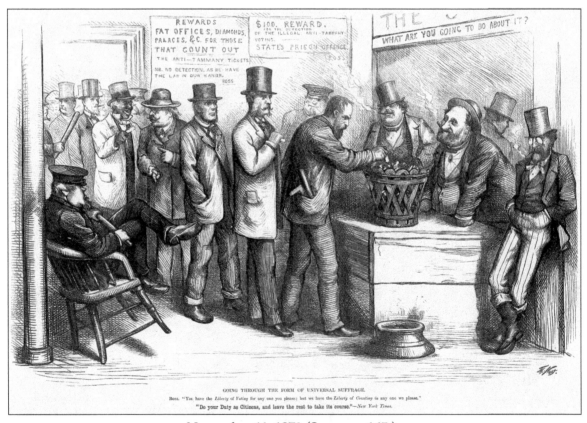

November 11, 1871 (See page 165.)

False Counting

"The third plan is false counting. This is done generally by transferring the figures bodily. For instance, if Jones, the Tammany candidate, gets 100 votes, and Smith, the opposite candidate, receives 200; the 200 of Smith are transferred to Jones, who gives his 100 to Smith. This is an exquisitely simple process, but in practice it is said to work badly, and great complaint is made of it by those who have tried it. In the first place, the candidates are often too nearly equal to give Tammany its just preponderance or to overcome some persistent opposition in a district where this plan cannot be worked, for it is found utterly impracticable in some districts. Its defects can sometimes by cured by a false count. That is to say, the votes are counted by tens, one canvasser taking them up and counting ten, when he calls "tally," and slips a piece of elastic around the bundle. Of course, he has only to take five votes instead of ten, and call "tally" to augment greatly the chance of his favorite. In one instance, this was done so enthusiastically that the Tammany candidate had received fifty "tallies," or 500 votes, and had a large quantity yet uncounted, when the poll-clerk felt it advisable to inform the canvassers that there were only 450 names on the registry."

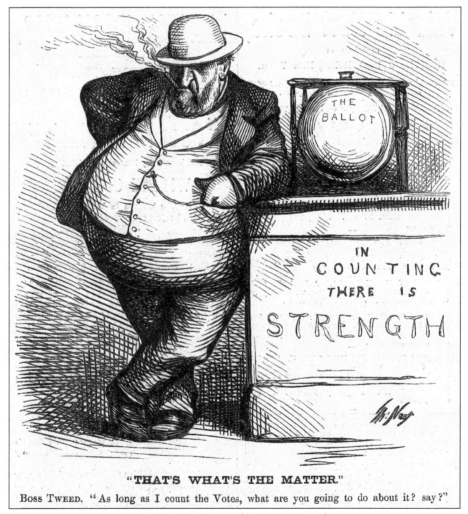

"**THAT'S WHAT'S THE MATTER.**"

Boss Tweed. "As long as I count the Votes, what are you going to do about it? say?"

October 7, 1871 (See page 148.)

The February 1866 issue of *Phunny Phellow* contained the artist's first full-page caricature of a specific Tweed Ring figure, John T. Hoffman (1828-1888), the new mayor of New York City. Hoffman, a lawyer, had joined Tammany Hall in 1854 and its ruling general committee in 1859. The next year, he won election as the youngest recorder (judge) in New York City's history. In that position, he garnered bipartisan support for his competence and severity in trying and sentencing participants in the bloody Civil War Drafts Riots of 1863. Building on that popularity, he won the first of two consecutive terms as mayor of New York City in December 1865.

Nast's *Phunny Phellow* cartoon was published in mid-January 1866, two weeks after Hoffman took office. With the new mayor's elegant bearing, massive chin, and distinctive handlebar moustache, he would become an appealing front man for the developing Tweed Ring; first as mayor, and then as governor (1869-1873). However, in early 1866, Nast presented him in a positive fashion, as "Our New Mayor. May he sustain his reputation!" With City Hall on the right, Hoffman was shown ordering a motley crew of Irish-American draft rioters to prison.

In the April 14, 1866 issue of *Harper's Weekly*, 18 of Nast's caricatures frame his fanciful illustration of the Grand Masquerade, a ball held at the Academy of Music. At the bottom-center of the cartoon is Hoffman as an equine figure—"Our Mare"—in formal attire, positioned in front of the "City Hall Stable" (below, right).

John Hoffman

In the October 27, 1866 issue of *Harper's Weekly*, Hoffman again appears as the "mare," this time being ridden by President Andrew Johnson during the latter's disastrous campaign tour known as the "Swing 'Round the Circle." The pair gallop through City Hall Park, apparently on the way to the city's famous gourmet restaurant, Delmonico's. An over-line informs viewers that "This Same Mayor Is Running for Governor"—a major ploy in Tweed's master plan, which was frustrated when the incumbent Republican governor, Reuben Fenton, defeated Hoffman. The panel is one of several which Nast depicted in "Andy's Trip."

The next year, Congressman Fernando Wood challenged Hoffman for the mayoralty, and Nast accepted a commission to produce a wood-engraved handbill/poster supporting Hoffman's reelection. In it, "Mare" Hoffman, a sleek racehorse, was contrasted with Wood, a hobbyhorse handled by editors Horace Greeley of the *New York Tribune* and James Gordon Bennett Jr. of the *New York Herald*. Entitled "December Races 1867. Mayoralty Stakes," the poster has "For Mayor" on the left side and "John T. Hoffman" on the right. The text below the images identified Wood as one who "enters himself" in the race "to Carry Everybody's Purse" and Hoffman as "The People's Entry … by Honesty, out of Lady Tammany, to Carry the True Democracy and Win." In *Harper's Weekly*, editor George William Curtis gave a tepid endorsement to Hoffman, advising Republicans that they held the balance of power between the selection of an honorable man with unfortunate political allies (Hoffman) and an infamous scoundrel (Wood). Hoffman was reelected by a landslide.

1866: Horace Greeley vs. Tammany Hall

Thomas Nast had to have been uncomfortably aware of the widespread corruption existing in New York City politics long before it showed up in his cartoons. It is difficult to believe that the subject had not come up in conversations with his editor at *Harper's Weekly*, George William Curtis, who was a well-known crusader for good-government reforms. Furthermore, the cartoonist's close association with James Parton, a historical biographer and first cousin of Nast's wife, Sarah, must have provided a highly useful stimulus. Parton introduced the topic of government malfeasance in the metropolis to an international audience through an anonymous and controversial 51-page essay entitled "The Government of the City of New York," which appeared in the October 1866 issue of the *North American Review*. Despite later descriptions to the contrary, it consisted mainly of eyewitness reportage of the Common Council in action, rather than introductions or excoriations of the leading Tammany Hall conspirators (who were not yet fixed in the public mind). Parton introduced the subject by stating:

"We have undertaken to write something about the government of the city of New York, and yet we have fallen into a discourse upon stealing. The reason is that after having spent several weeks in investigating our subject, we find that we have been employed in nothing else but discovering in how many ways, and under what a variety of names and pretexts, immature and greedy men steal from that fruitful and ill-fenced orchard, the city treasury."

According to Parton, the problem was not that the politicians controlling the city government stole on occasion, but that they did "nothing but steal; for even the most useful or necessary public work is sanctioned by it [the city government] only so far as it affords promise of gain to politicians." He emphatically concluded, "The thieves must be driven out, if it costs a bloody war; and it will cost a bloody war if they are not." Parton's influential piece was widely reviewed and reissued in pamphlet form, but did not appear under his own name until it was published—unaltered—in his 1871 book, *Topics of the Time*.

George William Curtis editorialized on the anonymous essay in the *Harper's Weekly* issue of November 3, 1866. Curtis judged the *North American Review* article to be "the most vigorous, shrewd, and able assault yet made upon our civic iniquity." Perhaps it was no coincidence that Nast's first reference to a current Tammany Hall situation came in the following issue of *Harper's Weekly*, dated November 10, 1866. In it, the cartoonist contrasts the congressional candidates in neighboring districts of New York City, Horace Greeley, editor of the *Tribune*, and John Morrissey, a former boxer and current Tweed protégé at Tammany Hall.

The circular symbol of the "Ring" — a serpent biting its tail — appears for the first time below Morrissey's cigar. It has a double meaning: a boxing ring and the Tammany Ring. In heavily Democratic New York City, Republican Greeley lost, giving the popular Tammany Democrat the first of two terms in the U.S. House of Representatives (1867-1871).

The Candidate of the Blood-thirsty Radical Faction in the
Fourth Congressional District. (GREELEY.)

The Conservative Candidate of the Peace Democracy in the
Fifth Congressional District. (MORRISSEY.)

In a post-election editorial in the *Tribune*, Greeley blamed Tweed—still largely invisible to the public—for his electoral defeat, for corrupt rule in the city, and for the recent suicide of a young officeholder.

"We wonder if our readers know the terrorism of Tammany Hall. Look at the men who control it. William M. Tweed, rich with the plunder of a hundred jobs, fat, oily, and dripping with the public wealth—the head and center and front of every job that has disgraced New York for ten years. In a little while he has risen from obscurity to wealth and power ... His chief confederate is Peter B. Sweeny [head of the Public Parks Department]... Sly, patient, hidden, never seeing the sun—the man who arranges the wires and shifts the scenes and intrigues—Sweeny is known as the Mephistopheles of Tammany. Then we have [Mayor] John T. Hoffman, who is kept by Tammany Hall as a kind of respectable attaché ...

"No one can hold a place under Tammany without being compelled to 'stand and deliver' a portion of his pay whenever Mr. Sweeny or Mr. Tweed fancies the party needs some money" [a common patronage practice called "assessment"]. This is the strength of Tammany Hall. Its leaders hold the [city] Treasury as Rob Roy and his thieves hold the Highland Passes. Whoever comes their way must pay toll, for Tammany must live and its leaders must revel in wealth. [Quoted in Matthew Breen, *Thirty Years of New York Politics* (1899), pp. 129-30.]"

The cartoon that is generally regarded as the opening shot of Nast's anti-Tammany campaign appeared in the *Harper's Weekly* issue of February 9, 1867. In it, the artist gave New Yorkers a bare-knuckle view of their government at work, borrowing both the cartoon's title—"The Government of the City of New York"—and its ironic over-line—"A Chance To Steal Without The Risk Of The Penitentiary"—directly from Parton's article in the previous October's *North American Review*. The illustration stands as Nast's earliest effort to confront the theme of the general corruption of urban government; his first cartoon for *Harper's Weekly* focused specifically on police malfeasance. (See pages 26-27.)

In the same issue of *Harper's Weekly*, a corresponding commentary on "How New York Is Misgoverned" discussed the rapid deterioration of order and decorum in the city's political administration. It delineated recent "horror stories" of bribes, extortion, overpayment for public services, and other misgovernance, as well as described a melee that erupted over election of the council president.

> "An attack on the President [of the Common Council] by a disappointed member, with an inkstand as the weapon of assault, brought to light the fact that the President himself was not unprepared for the fray. That dignitary instantly produced his pistols; the crowd rushed over the barriers into the thick of the struggle; the police, forewarned of the impending conflict, presented themselves in solid phalanx, and before any blood worth mentioning had been shed the chief combatants had been taken into custody."

The reporter pleaded for the New York State Legislature to intervene with a sweeping reform of New York City government. "If the Legislature does not come to our aid, we shall soon have arrived at the condition which our artist [i.e., Nast] has depicted on another page." The author also urged delegates to the upcoming state constitutional convention to reinstate a tax qualification for voting. (They did not.)

The shape of Nast's Common Council cartoon is the arch of a theatrical stage, which the cartoonist had employed several times in previous years for particularly dramatic effect. Four months earlier, Parton had described the Common Council's chamber, arranged with members' desks in two semi-circles; presumably, Nast paid the scene a visit for atmosphere and background color. At the top of the illustration's design is a bare-fisted prizefighter, representing the connection between that illegal blood sport and urban politics (many boxers served as "shoulder-hitters"—enforcers of the will of political bosses), and particularly the election of John Morrissey, who would take his seat in Congress in early March 1867. The relationship is further symbolized by the framed portrait of a boxer dog hanging on the wall (upper-left).

Across the space of the page, projectiles fly, a minie ball appears to be striking the council president's desk, and a smoking bomb lobs overhead. The hazy, tavern-like atmosphere of the scene reflected Nast's abhorrence of the excessive use of alcohol and tobacco, and the violence and dissipation he associated with those habits. On the right, the throne of the presiding officer is decorated with Nast's early attempt to sketch the Tammany Tiger, and on the wall above the chair hangs a "Steal Ring" comprised of a snake swallowing its own tail. Two of the inkwells are chained to their desks to deter theft or their use as weapons.

Significantly, Nast links the city's political corruption with a rousing rendition of the "Irish problem"—i.e., the perceived ill effect of immigrant Irish Catholics upon the morality of American politics and society. The figure seated at a desk in the center-foreground and the boxer in the wall portrait (center-background) are stereotypical Irish.

1867: St. Patrick's Day: Another Irish Riot

An even more critical depiction of New York City's Irish Catholics came in Nast's savage sequel to "The Government of the City of New York." Published in the postdated April 6, 1867 issue of *Harper's Weekly*, "St. Patrick's Day 1867/The Day We Celebrate" was available to readers by March 27, nine days after the city's annual festivities honoring Ireland's patron saint. The cartoon was prompted by a violent clash in lower Manhattan on Monday, March 18, between members of the Brooklyn Irish Societies and New York City police officers. Established by the Republican-controlled state legislature in 1857 to undermine the political authority of New York City's Democratic mayor, Fernando Wood, the Metropolitan Police Department was unpopular with much of the city's large immigrant-Irish community. (The police force returned to city control after passage of a statewide referendum in November 1869, spearheaded by Tweed's Tammany Hall.)

According to the *New-York Times* of Tuesday, March 19, the fracas erupted when members of the Third Division of the Ancient Order of Hibernians forcibly removed a driver whose truck was inadvertently blocking the parade. A policeman who intervened to halt the altercation "was knocked down and severely injured by being trampled upon by the infuriated assailants." A police squad arriving to protect their fellow officer were similarly "knocked down, trampled on, and kicked," resulting in "several ugly scalp wounds and bruises." One of the parade marshals inflicted "a severe and dangerous wound" by striking his saber on a policeman. Finally, additional police were able to collect their injured comrades and drive away the rioters, who then reorganized and joined the parade.

Basing his illustration on the *Times* report, Nast mobilized his emotions and well-trained imagination. The cartoonist conjured up adversarial overtones that in likelihood had nothing to do with the actual event. The illustration sports such screaming lines as "RUM," "BRUTAL ATTACK ON THE POLICE," "IRISH RIOT," and "BLOOD," and presents a crazed mob of ape-like Irishmen encircling the injured police, who are attacked with broken shillelaghs, bricks, sword, and even a pointed flagpole.

Nast did not originate the stereotype of the violent, simian Irishman, but he may have carried it further than any caricaturist before him. It seems fair to say that by early 1867, the cartoonist was bracing for a holy war against urban crime on all fronts.

1868-9: Capturing New York State

On July 4, 1867, Mayor John Hoffman laid the cornerstone for an imposing new Tammany Hall on East 14th Street, which would be selected as the site for the following year's National Democratic Nominating Convention. To effect better control over city politics, Tweed entered state government himself by winning election to the state senate in November 1867, and reelection two years later. Taking office on January 1, 1868, the "Boss" was soon installed in a large, opulent, seven-room suite on the second floor of the Delavan House in Albany, with attendants on the city payroll guarding access.

According to Matthew Breen, the rumors at the time were that this turn of events was to have been followed in 1872 by Hoffman's election as president of the United States, Mayor Oakey Hall's election as governor, and Tweed's selection by the state legislature to one of New York's seats in the U.S. Senate. Connolly would become city comptroller, and Sweeny (who disliked the limelight) would remain "the power behind the throne."

The Grand Caricaturama

For the year extending from June 1867 to June 1868, Nast was on a sabbatical of sorts from *Harper's Weekly*, attending to his "Grand Caricaturama" (a stage presentation of 33 large, tempera paintings of American historical scenes from Plymouth Rock to the presidential election of Ulysses S. Grant), working at "serious" history painting and book illustration, and providing cartoons in April-June 1868 for a short-lived weekly called *Illustrated Chicago News*.

20. SOUR APPLE TREE.
Music. Air—Fierce Flames—"Il Trovatore"

In May 1867, the month before the Grand Caricaturama opened, *Tribune* publisher Horace Greeley co-signed a $100,000 bail bond to get former Confederate President Jefferson Davis out of Fortress Monroe, VA prison. Nast would rather have seen Jeff Davis hung from a sour apple tree, as a popular song urged. In this painting, Nast vividly portrayed Greeley's turbulent rescue of Davis while the frustrated sour apple tree, with noose attached, protested in the background

1. THE ARTIST'S DREAM.
Music. Air—I dreamt I dwelt in Marble Halls.

33. AU REVOIR
Music. Air—Make me no gaudy Chaplet.

Grand Caricaturama images reproduced with the generous permission of
Macculloch Hall Historical Museum, Morristown, N.J.

Meanwhile, Mayor John Hoffman continued to be the "front man" for the caricaturist and for almost everyone else. The New York State Democratic Convention convened on September 2, 1868, at Twaddle Hall in Albany and nominated Hoffman for governor. The following day, an editorial in the *New-York Times* noted that his nomination was "a prudent one. Mr. Hoffman is the strongest man the Democracy could present. Personally unobjectionable, able, and with a patriotic war record, he may be expected to run ahead of the National ticket." He was considered a valuable link to German-Americans in the state's Hudson Valley region (even though he was actually of Finnish stock on his father's side). On September 4, the *Times* assured its readers that although Hoffman was the "Grand Sachem of Tammany, he is uniformly regarded as its ornament rather than its tool."

The following week, Mayor Hoffman began his gubernatorial campaign with a trip to Buffalo. In his absence, the acting mayor was Thomas J. Coman, president of the Board of Aldermen and a Tammany loyalist. Coman teamed with Sweeny and Connolly to sign a group of fraudulent warrants (i.e., written authorizations of payments) approved by the city treasury. In fact, during the nine weeks between Hoffman's nomination and his election as governor, the same trio authorized greatly padded expenditures of over $3 million by utilizing new state laws permitting old (and often fictitious) "adjusted claims" to be paid by the issuance of bonds.

In the September 19, 1868 issue of *Harper's Weekly*, editor George William Curtis endorsed the Republican gubernatorial nominee, John Griswold. "If the people of the State are anxious to extend the operations of this Ring they will vote for Mr. Hoffman." The next week, Curtis ridiculed how Hoffman was stumping the state chastising the extravagant expenditures and high taxes enacted by the Republican-controlled state legislature, while as mayor he had presided over a similarly free-spending and taxing regime. Curtis furthermore noted that as Grand Sachem of Tammany, the mayor was complicit in additional extravagances.

> "Modesty forbids Mr. Hoffman to declare that he, as the candidate of a party which, by his lips, so lustily denounces corruption and shouts aloud for economy, is the very head of the most enormous system of public corruption and extravagance in the country... The modesty of representing Jefferson Davis as an apostle of loyalty to the Union is surpassed only by that of the grand sachem of Tammany presenting himself as the apostle of economy and retrenchment."

The ground was now well prepared for Nast's cartoon, in the October 10, 1868 issue of *Harper's Weekly* (in print September 30), "A Respectable Screen Covers A Multitude Of Thieves." Hoffman appears in formal attire on the principal panel of a four-unit folding screen shielding a scene of wholesale pilferage from the city treasury. Inscriptions on the screen include "High Taxes Make High Rents," "City Hall Steal Ring," and "Notice to the People We (The Ring) Would Like to Move this Nice Screen to Albany N.Y." The Ring commandment above the scene of theft—"Thou Shalt Steal as Much as Thou Canst"—hangs over references to bloated building projects for a courthouse, city hall, and Harlem bridge.

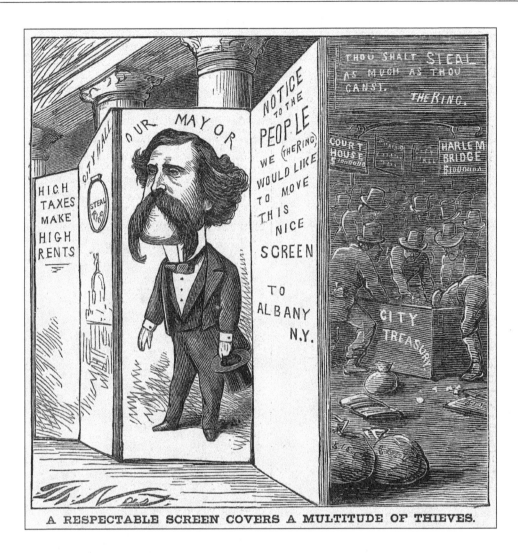

A RESPECTABLE SCREEN COVERS A MULTITUDE OF THIEVES.

On October 11, even though the *New-York Times* had approved Hoffman's nomination, the paper complimented Nast's Hoffman cartoon and another, in the same issue, on the abuse of civil rights, and encouraged his continued efforts at political satire.

"It is a work which well deserves careful examination, and even if taken by itself it would prove that Mr. Nast has it within his power to make a great and enduring reputation as a delineator of men and manners peculiar to our own time. The sketches of New-York life under Democratic rule may not be entirely welcome to the Tammany chiefs, but the great body of citizens will sorrowfully admit that they are not in the least exaggerated. Mr. Nast ought to continue these pictorial satires on local and national politics…"

The artist's caricature, though, was not enough to thwart the Tammany candidate. Although Tweed had failed to place Mayor John Hoffman in the governor's mansion in 1866, Hoffman probably was aided by enough voter fraud in the 1868 election to give him a 3% margin of victory.

Boss Tweed and his Tammany Hall associates kept a very low public profile during the 1868 presidential campaign. However, Thomas Nast's back-page cartoon of Horatio Seymour, the Democratic presidential nominee, as guilt-ridden Lady Macbeth, in the September 5, 1868 issue of *Harper's Weekly*, may contain **the artist's first attempt to sketch Boss Tweed for publication**. Barely visible in the background (left) are two figures lurking in the shadows, including (far left) an obese, bearded man wearing a Scotch plaid cap and kilt. The artist's first recognizable rendition of Tweed would not appear for over a year.

The substance of the cartoon refers to Seymour's "My Friends" speech to the Irish draft rioters in July 1863, which Nast used to demean Seymour on many occasions. (See page 36.) Nast's hero, General Ulysses S. Grant, won the presidency relatively easily.

Time, midnight. — Scene, New York City Hall.

LADY *******. "Out, damned spot! out, I say!......Here's the smell of the blood still: all the perfumes of Democracy will not sweeten this little hand. Oh! oh! oh!"

Boss Tweed's first acknowledged appearance in a Nast cartoon was a modest role in "The Democratic Scape-Goat" (*Harper's Weekly*, September 11, 1869). He is the portly individual in monkish habit standing before the throne of the "Democratic National Executive Committee," which is marked with a sign "Reserved Chair For Mr. Tweed." A poster from the "Tammany Association" (of the Seventh Ward) harshly denounces the alleged inabilities and poor performance of August Belmont as National Democratic Party chairman, blaming him for the party's defeats in the three previous presidential elections. Nast emphasizes Belmont's Jewish identity by depicting him as a scapegoat, an animal on which the Jewish high priest symbolically placed the sins of the Jewish people on the Day of Atonement ("Yom Kippur"). (During the 1872 presidential campaign, Nast portrayed Chairman Belmont as Shakespeare's mean-spirited moneylender, Shylock, a Jewish stereotype; Belmont backed Horace Greeley, who Nast fiercely opposed.)

In this cartoon, Tweed seems to be inciting a Tammany thug and an angry group of Irish supporters to drive Belmont into the wilderness. At the time, the Tammany boss may have been plotting to remove both Belmont and the state chairman, Samuel J. Tilden, in order to smooth the advance of Hoffman toward the Democratic presidential nomination in 1872. Nothing came of the effort to oust the men, apparently because Tammany strategist and city chamberlain Peter Sweeny, having returned from an overseas vacation in mid-September, argued for calm, and the matter was dropped.

THE DEMOCRATIC SCAPE-GOAT.

"The Twentieth Ward Jackson Club, presided over by Mr. THOMAS COSTIGAN, adopted the following Resolution, on motion of Mr. JOHN DELANY, at their meeting last evening: *Resolved*, That the farther continuance of Mr. AUGUST BELMONT in the chair of the National Democratic Executive Committee is fraught with great peril to the existence and Salutary Influence of the party; that, inasmuch as he is lethargic in the performance of his official duties, wavering in his political faith, and distasteful to THE IRISH SECTION OF THE DEMOCRACY, that he be forthwith requested to vacate his position."

Sweeping Democratic successes at the polls in the New York State elections of November 1869, indicated that Tammany had free rein to do pretty much as it pleased. Although Nast later would relish the opportunity to portray the ponderous Tweed as leader of the Tammany Ring, the artist's earlier cartoons tended to give equal or greater importance to Sweeny, following the public perception of the moment. The lead editorial in the January 22, 1870 issue of *Harper's Weekly* argued that Sweeny was the "Dictator of Tammany Hall" and the real "Governor of New York." According to editor George William Curtis, State Senator Tweed was Sweeny's "lieutenant," and Governor Hoffman's inaugural message was "merely a solemn presentation of Mr. Sweeny's opinion and intentions." A similar viewpoint was reiterated in the lead editorial of February 19, 1870.

In the *Harper's Weekly* issue of December 4, 1869, Nast personified President Ulysses S. Grant as the shipwrecked Robinson Crusoe (from Daniel Defoe's 1719 classic novel) coming upon an ominous sign in the form of a "Footprint on the Land of Peace" (a reference to the Republican president's campaign slogan in 1868, "Let us have peace.").

The wet imprint marked "Democratic Victory/New York State" belongs to "the Tammany Tribe." On the lower third of the page, in an inset circular, the artist introduces Peter Sweeny as "Peter the Great/ Chief of the Tammany Tribe." Sweeny wears a feathered headband inscribed "Steal Ring" and a necklace of shrunken skulls and a ferocious Tammany Tiger head. To the left is a scene of his fellow savages "At Their Fiendish Work," scalping the police and burning various city andstate administrative boards, while to the right Grant/Crusoe sadly beholds the embers, skulls, and empty treasury "After the Feast."

The Economical Council: The "Big Four" Meet Thomas Nast

On December 8, 1869, Pope Pius IX (pontificate, 1846-1878) of the Roman Catholic Church convoked an ecumenical council at the Vatican to affirm the doctrine of Papal Infallibility and to confront such contemporary notions as rationalism, liberalism, and human progress. The December 25, 1869 issue of *Harper's Weekly* contained a Nast satire, "The Economical Council, Albany, New York," in which Governor John Hoffman appears as the pope, "Pius Hoffman I," and Peter B. Sweeny as the papal secretary of state, Cardinal Giacomo Antonelli. The two men are receiving emissary bishops from Tammany Hall, suitably attired in ecclesiastical copes and miters, while "Repeater Guards" (i.e., perpetrators of vote fraud) in traditional Vatican Swiss uniforms unpack vast tribute of "Public Money" and "Hard Cash" from "Tax Payers and Tenants."

This is the earliest of Nast's drawings to portray the four Tammany Ring leaders together in a single picture. In addition to Sweeny, William M. Tweed—state senator, county supervisor, and deputy street commissioner—is readily identifiable on the right with a Tammany Tiger head on his "Big Six" miter; next to him (left) is Richard "Slippery Dick" Connolly, the city comptroller; and, two figures to the left of Connolly stands Mayor Oakey Hall (without the eyeglasses which would become a trademark of his caricature).

Other recognizable men in the cartoon include: George W. McLean (between Connolly and Hall), Tweed's nominal superior as street commissioner, who holds a frayed push broom; Jay Gould (left) and Jim Fisk (right), business moguls and Tammany allies, wearing miters bearing the title "Erie" in reference to their control of the Erie Railroad. On the left of Gould is William Henry Vanderbilt, who, along with his father, Cornelius, was engaged in a losing struggle with Gould and Fisk for control of the Erie Railroad.

The pictorial design hinges on Governor/Pope Hoffman's two symbolic keys identified as the "Tax Levy," referring to tax authorization bills prepared by the New York City's comptroller (Connolly) and presented for passage by the state legislature to pay for the city's bloated budgets. In Albany, the city tax bills would grow and ripen through the winter and spring, acquiring all manner of additions to suit the various whims of New York City members. As was customary, legislation to extend and increase the city's power to tax itself was delayed until the last possible moment before the end of the session, when it was least likely to receive the critical attention that it merited. Under the skillful management of Connolly, the levies could always be adjusted even after there was any review or revision.

Two days after the appearance of the "Economical Council," the *Sun* (December 17, 1869) drew attention to Nast's "Remarkable Cartoon," arguing that "in point of design and artistic skill, [it] probably exceeds any of his former works … The likenesses are excellent…"

An editorial in the same December 25, 1869, issue of *Harper's Weekly*, "A Truly 'Democratic' Policy," commented on Governor Hoffman's pointed denunciations of the practice of governing the city from Albany, and doubted that the Tammany chiefs were as "painfully exercised" about good government as they were about maximizing their own patronage and plunder. Editor George William Curtis expressed concern that thus far the principal expressed objective of the new leadership's policy was to reverse the previous state legislature's ratification of the Fifteenth Amendment to the U.S. Constitution, which stipulated that the right to vote not be abridged on account of race, color, or previous condition of servitude (i.e., slavery).

Tammany Hall opposed the Amendment because it feared that it could not control the black vote, and might lose elections as a result. The resolution withdrawing New York's assent was introduced by State Senator William M. Tweed, and passed both houses shortly thereafter. However, enough state legislatures ratified the proposed amendment for it to become part of the Constitution on March 30, 1870.

Shadows of Forthcoming Events

Nast's first major effort of 1870 was a mosaic of urban menace, dirt and exploitation, calculated to rivet the attention of longsuffering New Yorkers. Published in the January 22 issue of *Harper's Weekly*, "Shadows of Forthcoming Events," subtitled "The Fruits of the Democratic Victory" (in the November 1869 elections), consists of two pages of multiple vignettes. The violent imagery and rhetoric of the scenes are emphasized by the quotation under the subtitle, "Crowns Got By Blood Must Be By Blood Maintained." The centerpiece is a fiendish, masked Irishman called "King Mob," who sits on the back of the murdered female personification of "Suffrage" atop a barrel of rum (associated with Irish immigrants). The fearsome monarch's hat sports the Irish symbols of shamrock and clay pipe, and a reference to the foundation of the Tweed Ring's power: "Tammany Hall," "City Hall," and "Alcohol." (Attributed to Horace Greeley. See page 42.)

Note: This cartoon appeared horizontally on two facing pages of Harper's Weekly. The two columns on the far right are shown completely only on page 79, and the two on the far left are shown completely only on this page.

On the lower left-center, the cartoonist imagines a jubilant mass meeting in Central Park to advance the Democratic national ticket of Hoffman for president and Tweed for vice president in 1872. On the lower-center, a circle of statues of the Tweed Ring foursome surrounds an equestrian statue of Governor Hoffman on his "high horse." On the lower right-center, the park is home to Tammany Hall, a horseracing course, and a public bar. In the panel to the right of "King Mob," the artist toys playfully with the nostalgic notion that the "Merry Old Times" of the city's Volunteer Fire Department might be revived—with Boss Tweed in his Big Six/Americus uniform (vintage 1850) leading the way. Other segments highlight how the corruption, indifference, and indolence of Tammany rule threatens the public health, sanitation, schools, safety, and morality. In cahoots with the Tweed Ring is the city's Roman Catholic Church (upper-right).

Note: Some of the small vignettes in this cartoon have been enlarged so Nast's details can be appreciated. (See pages 25, 29 and especially 55.)

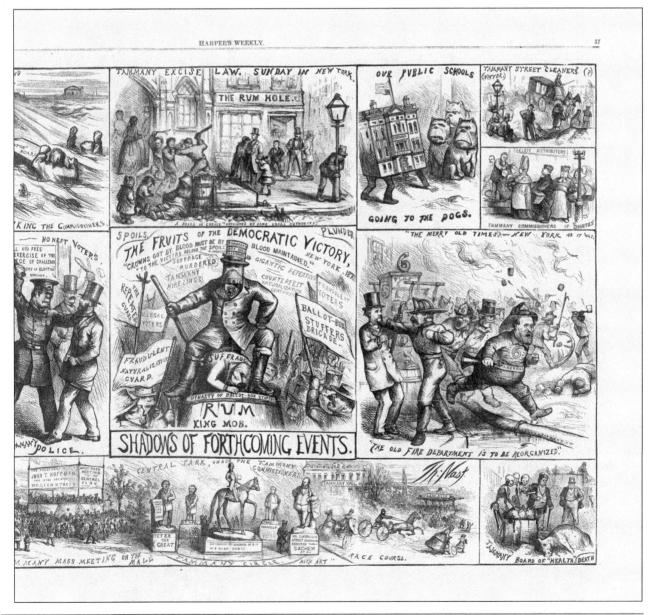

Except for a pervasive sense of governmental corruption in New York City and Albany, there was little in the way of particular issues for the cartoonist to address in the winter and spring of 1869-1870. In the absence of any hard news touching on what might going on behind the closed doors of the Tammany Ring, and no substantive financial reports from Comptroller Connolly over a period of more than thirty months, Nast was forced to build a case on intuition, innuendo, and historical parallel until the summer of 1871. Nevertheless, he persisted over a period of three years, developing his argument gradually, with increasingly effective use of wit, caricature, and emotional force.

Throughout 1870, the cartoonist continued to develop his cast of characters, almost as if he were auditioning actors for the role of leading villain. Nast and the rest of the press settled initially on the dark, brooding figure of Peter Sweeny, the city chamberlain (treasurer) and president of the Public Parks Commission. For example, an editorial in February 26, 1870 issue of *Harper's Weekly* referred in its headline to the proposed new charter for New York City as the "Sweeny Charter," even though after its passage (in April) it would thereafter be known as the "Tweed Charter" (see page 81). Journalist Theodore Cook, Samuel J. Tilden's campaign biographer, described Sweeny as "a well-read and well-bred lawyer ...the most quiet, unobtrusive, and cultured man in the 'Ring.'"

Effective caricatures usually have a dynamic interaction with reality, whereby the distorted likeness depends upon a general awareness of what the subject actually looks like—physical features, movement and gestures, and deportment in public. **Nast soon decided that in terms of stature and visual potential for mischievous menace, Bill Tweed as a target would provide the greatest opportunity for artistic development and effectiveness**. The cartoonist's instinct was borne out by events, for by April 1870 Tweed was demonstrably the "master of the situation."

However, as if to hedge his bets on the matter of the Tammany Ring leadership, in the April 16, 1870 issue of *Harper's Weekly*, Nast provided a full-page drawing of Peter Sweeny as an intimidating slave-overseer with "Diamonds" and "Gold" in his pocket and a cat-o'-nine-tails lash under his arm. In a burlesque of Hiram Powers' famous sculpture (1843) of an enchained, nude, female Greek slave, Nast presents Sweeny keeping close watch over "The Greek Slave," a grizzled and dispirited Irish immigrant chained to a "Tammany" ring encircling a "Democract" [sic] stump upon which is a ballot box topped by "Rum" and "Whisky" bottles.

Subsidiary vignettes illustrate "Inducements to Leave the Old Country" (upper-left); a new arrival "Landed and Branded" with the label "Democrat" (upper-right); "Slaves" (lower-left) doing hard labor on the streets of New York City; "The Slave Drivers," Tammany thugs whipping voters to stuff the ballot box (lower-center); and, "Masters" (lower-right), the Tammany/Democratic leaders celebrating at an elegant party. (See page 19 for enlargement of these vignettes.)

THE GREEK SLAVE.

In early April 1870, State Senator Tweed introduced a "reform" charter for New York City—probably the work of Sweeny and Hall—which promised to provide home rule for the metropolis and independence from the state legislature, and to strengthen the office of mayor; eventually, Mayor Hall received the authority to make every major appointment in the city government.

Samuel J. Tilden, chairman of the New York State Democratic Committee, was one of the few strenuous opponents of the measure. On April 4, 1870, he testified before the State Senate Committee on Cities, which Tweed chaired. Tilden warned that the city government proposed under the charter "is not a popular government; it is not a responsible government; it is a government beyond the control and independent will of the people." Privately, Tweed threatened to depose Tilden as state chairman of the Democratic Party, but no action was taken.

On the following day, the "Tweed Charter" passed easily and was signed into law on April 6 by Governor Hoffman. It was later estimated that Tweed and his associates spent between $600,000 and $1 million to buy legislative support for the 1870 charter, although those figures may be too conservative. In 1875, journalist Charles F. Wingate stated in the *North American Review* that a "good authority" had asserted that Tweed's expenses had been between $1.2 and $1.3 million for passage in both houses of the state legislature.

In contrast to the point of view of Nast and *Harper's Weekly*, at the time of its passage there was much praise for home rule and the enhanced efficiency promised by the new city charter. In its April 8, 1870 edition, the *New-York Times* enthused, "Senator Tweed is in a fair way to distinguish himself as a reformer." (Less than six months later, the *Times* reversed itself completely.)

Another important supporter of the "Tweed Charter" was the Citizens' Association, headed by former mayor and leading industrialist Peter Cooper. It is likely that turncoat Tammany Republican Nathanial Sands, who was secretly on Tweed's payroll for $75,000 while serving as Secretary of the Citizens' Association, played a key role in gaining this support.

A related law passed on April 12, 1870, abolished the current Board of Supervisors, on which Tweed sat, and created a new body consisting of the mayor, the city recorder, and the Board of Aldermen, with the authority to approve county expenditures. On April 26, after more bribery, the annual tax levy for the city became law. Among the riders attached to the tax bill was the establishment of a "Board of Special Audit" comprised of the mayor (Hall), city comptroller (Connolly), and president of the newly created Public Works Commission (Tweed), which met one time (May 5, 1870) to race through authorization of direct payment of all claims against the County of New York which predated the passage of the levy.

To protect Connolly in office, the position of comptroller was made appointive rather than elective, and his term was extended until January 1, 1875. (This provision backfired against the Ring in September 1871 when Hall was unable to fire Connolly.) Moreover, in the event of the mayor's departure from office by "death, removal, or resignation," the mayoral authority was transferred to the comptroller.

Of the $6,312,500 worth of vouchers the Board of Special Audit approved for payment in 1870, more than 90% were later alleged to have been fraudulent. Most accounts pending were for work ostensibly done on the new courthouse, but were subsequently revealed to have been enormous kickbacks.

It was discovered that calculated interest due officials for bogus claims had been charged on the basis of pre-dated warrants (i.e., written authorizations of payments), and that some of the cost of bribing lawmakers to keep the system running smoothly was assessed against participating contractors who inflated their bills as they were directed at any given time.

The suggested inflated payoff for members of the Tweed Ring began at about 10% of value received in 1867, and rose incrementally to about 65% by 1870 and even higher in 1871. When anticipated income failed to meet expectations, imaginary projects, suppliers or contractors were invented. Thus liberated from public scrutiny, Tweed and his associates must have assumed they had devised and perfected a loom for spinning straw into gold. Under the tax levy of 1871, increases of up to 2% on the aggregate value of taxable property helped fund the fraudulent payments.

Tweed's debut as the star of Nast's satirical production came in the April 16, 1870 issue of *Harper's Weekly*, available to readers on April 6, the same day Governor Hoffman signed the new Tweed-sponsored charter for the government of New York City. "Senator Tweed in a New Rôle" presents the Tammany boss as Hamlet's unfaithful mother, Gertrude, in the confrontational bedroom scene of Shakespeare's drama (Act III, Scene IV). Carrying the new charter and wearing a Tammany tiara, Tweed/Gertrude was about to push into the state legislature when the Hamlet figure, perhaps representing outraged public opinion, demands confession of and contrition for the sin. To the crying Boss/Queen, Hamlet demands, "Assume a virtue if you have it not." For the first time, Tweed's emerging taste for gigantic diamonds is reflected in a Nast cartoon by the jeweled ornaments at the boss's neckline and waist.

In addition to the city charter, the tableau depicts Tammany's triumph (on March 28) in outmaneuvering an insurgent faction called the "Young Democracy," which had been plotting since New Year's Day to oust Tweed as head of Tammany Hall. Instead of Polonius, (whom Hamlet mistakenly killed thinking him the hated king), the body behind the drapery (lower-right) is that of Sheriff James "Jimmy" O'Brien, the leader of the rebel Democrats figuratively extinguished by Tweed. The tapestry by which the bulky O'Brien is partially obscured shows the realm's titular king, Governor Hoffman, watching the massacre of the Young Democrats by Tammany braves on the altar of "New York City Treasury and Fat Offices." The tapestry vignette is labeled "Democratic Fight Over The Sacking Of N[ew] Y[ork]" and is intended to parallel Shakespeare's play within a play from *Hamlet's* Act III, Scene II.

Fifteen months later, in July 1871, O'Brien became the key informant against the Tweed Ring, turning over devastating incriminating evidence to the *New-York Times*. However, this is the only time that Nast actually drew O'Brien, and he showed only the lower half of his body.

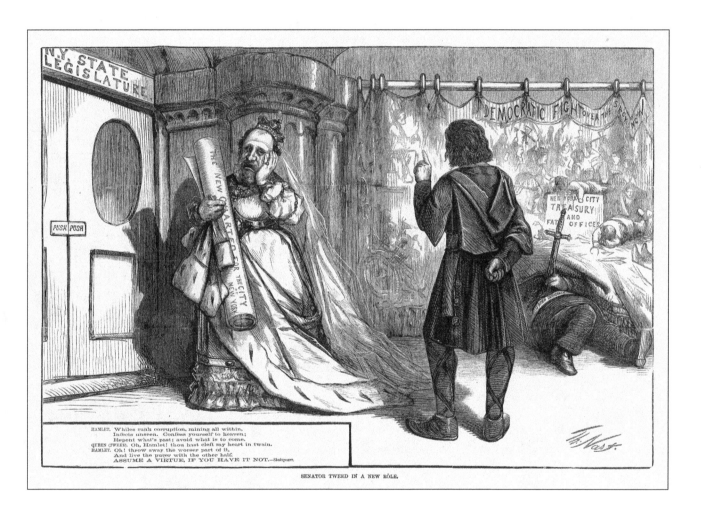

SENATOR TWEED IN A NEW RÔLE.

A city election on May 17 was the first modest test of the vast new powers Tweed had wrung from the state legislature under the charter "reform" of the preceding month, and Tammany's slate of judges and aldermen had been elected easily. Nast's most sweeping condemnation of Tammany Hall to date appeared seven weeks later in the June 4, 1870 issue of *Harper's Weekly*. His bleak warning reached readers on May 25, barely a week after the election.

The cartoon's title, the motto taken from the official seal of New York State, is slyly lettered so it can be read either "New York Excelsior" or "New Cork Excelsior," the latter suggestive of an Irish-Catholic takeover. It also mimics the title of Henry Wadsworth Longfellow's 1849 poem, "Excelsior," from which the heroic imagery of "A youth who bore, 'mid snow and ice, / A banner with the strange device, / Excelsior!" is, here, inverted into an ominous presence. Nast depicts a devilish figure girded by a "Tamm[any]" belt, which holds a pistol and dagger, and who has climbed to the highest precipice of a mountain promontory ("excelsior" is Latin for "ever upward"). The character's pointed goatee, spiraling locks of hair forming horns, and cape resembling bat-like wings, are all reminiscent of traditional illustrations of Lucifer. He hoists aloft a pole, topped by the deadly symbol of a skull and cross-bones, from which a banner bears a long list of political and moral vices.

Distant lightning on the center-right directs the viewer's gaze to the lower hills. In the foreground (lower-right), labeled "KKK in the South," a figure hangs from a tree in front of three standing figures in silhouette. On the hilltop above them, famed eighteenth-century robbers Dick Turpin and Jack Shepard hang from gibbets. On the far right, two figures hanging from a double gallows within a stockade represent criminals executed in San Francisco in the 1850s by citizens' Vigilance Committees.

This picture of Tammany's malevolent rule perhaps had its root in a personal experience of Thomas Nast's, which occurred over a year prior to publication of the "Excelsior" cartoon. To conclude the presentation of the colors at a gathering of the Seventh Regiment of the New York National Guard, of which Nast was a member, Mayor Oakey Hall handed the New York State flag to "the designated official, exclaiming at the same time, 'Excelsior.'" [*Herald*, April 20, 1869] That evening may have been the occasion Nast recalled two decades later concerning a good-natured encounter with Mayor Hall. "'I have read your handwriting on the wall,' said Oakey Hall affably when he met the artist at a military reception. 'You will read it again,' was the equally affable reply." [*Oakland Evening Tribune*, March 8, 1888.]

In the lead editorial of the same June 4 issue of *Harper's Weekly*, George William Curtis asserted that in passing the new charter, "the city was literally bound and delivered to the Ring." The editor charged that massive vote fraud made the recent election "the most unblushingly corrupt that was ever known." He asserted that the Democratic ascendancy threatened to undo the Fifteenth Amendment (adopted March 30, 1870) and other federal measures aimed at protecting black civil rights. At the same time, diarist George Templeton Strong observed that the judiciary in New York was beginning to stink like horse urine.

In the first half of 1870, Boss Tweed had scored a series of impressive victories: defeat of the rebel Young Democracy (March), passage of the new city charter (April), and Tammany success in elections for aldermen and judges (May). In addition, with the "Tweed" charter, he had become Commissioner of Public Works and a member of the Board of Special Audit, and his antagonistic superior on the Street Commission, George McLean (caricatured on page 77), was legislated out of office.

When Tweed had returned to Manhattan from Albany in April, an enthusiastic crowd saluted him with a torchlight parade, and his full-length portrait was placed in the Board of Supervisors' meeting room. As Tweed's first biographer, Denis T. Lynch, wrote (1927), "The Boss may be pardoned, when in the early summer of 1870, he began to assume the grand manner in public."

After "Excelsior," Nast did not touch on Tammany Hall for almost five months. During most of that period, the *New-York Times*, which had labeled Tweed a "reformer" in April 1870, continued to treat the Boss with kid gloves. Publisher George Jones wanted to follow the lead of Nast and *Harper's Weekly* in pursuing the Tammany Ring, but apparently was cautious because of a new addition to the newspaper's three-member board of directors, James B. Taylor, a Republican businessman. Taylor was one of Tweed's minority partners in the immensely profitable New York Printing Company which, not surprisingly, received almost all the city government's printing business, as well as that from private companies which were subject to municipal regulations (like transportation and insurance.).

The *Times'* policy changed after Taylor abruptly died of typhoid fever on August 22, 1870. Less than a month later, liberated from Taylor's support of Tweed, Jones and his managing editor, Louis John Jennings, removed the gloves and went after Tammany with all the editorial power they could muster.

The New-York Times.

Starting with "The Democratic Millennium" in the September 20, 1870 issue, a series of furious, bitterly ironic editorials made it plain that the *New-York Times* was taking a new hard line against Tammany Hall. The opening salvo was a blistering consideration of the Tweed Ring's affect upon the condition of the Democratic Party as its State Convention prepared to meet in early October in Rochester:

> "Could any party long survive under the gigantic abuses which cause this city to be a by-word wherever the true state of affairs is known? The Democratic organization staggers under the load which Tammany has placed upon it. We see the Tammany leaders in league with the harpies who have plundered Erie [Railroad] shareholders. Mr. Tweed … is silent about the wholesale misappropriation of the public funds which goes on under his eyes. The injustices for which he and his friends are responsible cry aloud for redress, and they will someday bring about the disgrace and fall of all who are concerned in them. Let the Rochester Convention construct its delusive platform as it may, it can never shake off the odium which Tweed & Co. have fastened on the very name of Democracy. The whole confederation will one day be buried beneath the ruins of a system which is regarded with indignation by all men who have not sacrificed honor for private gain."

The next day, a second lead editorial entitled "Mr. Tweed and His Friends" elaborated on the trouble, and, in the process, handed Nast the substance for his next cartoon:

> "What these men have done in this City, the Democrats would do in the State, and what they would do in the State they would do all over the country if they had the opportunity. And yet the people are now invited to support the Democrats in the approaching elections. They are asked to make Mr. Tweed autocrat—for that after all is what it comes to. Has Governor Hoffman ever dared to disobey the commands which proceeded from the man who today does almost as he likes with public property in this City?"

A week later, on September 28, a third editorial lead called "King Tweed and His Subjects" lamented the apathy of Republicans and of a supine public disposed to submit "to the first audacious man who chooses to impose upon them." Living under this particular monarch was compared to "thralldom of an Eastern potentate" when the latter wanted money:

"They simply levied a requisition and the people had nothing to do but submit. This is what we should call living under a despotism, and so it is—but our own plight is scarcely any better. New York is immensely overtaxed, and every year thousands of people are driven out of it because they cannot afford to live within its boundaries. The northern towns of New-Jersey are filled with refugees from this City. We have the worst-paved and the worst-lit City in the universe and yet taxes are wrung from us to an amount scarcely known elsewhere. Of the money thus raised, a large sum goes into the hands of Tweed and his associates, and there it sticks... There was never so extravagant, so unprincipled, or so degraded a government seen in the United States as the Democratic government of this City, and Mr. Tweed himself would scarcely take the trouble to deny the fact. Public opinion matters very little to a man of his description ... We must go back to the worst days of Rome or Venice to find any parallel..."

The following day's message ("Why Attack Mr. Tweed?") concluded with an appeal to the voter: "We can, at least, prevent the projected election frauds if we try. Shall we still bend the neck to the yoke of this Tweed rabble—or rise, as becomes free men, and shake it off?" (In fact, Tweed was so confident of election victory that year, he actively discouraged adherents from committing fraud at the polls.) Two days later the paper declared ("The *Times* and the Ring," October 1, 1870):

"We have the satisfaction of entering upon the second stage in our assaults upon the 'Ring.' The first was marked by several overtures to us on the part of Tammany to keep silent—'for a consideration.' This having failed, the second arm of Tammany is to be brought into play—namely the arm of ruffianism."

The *Times* continued to write as though it might be in possession of incriminating details, but was not yet going to share them with readers; instead, the tension would continue to mount. Addressing "All Honest Democrats" on October 8, 1870, Jennings assured readers that the Ring thieves were not at all sophisticated. The editorial writer almost seemed to be abandoning commentary to cartoonists and those who might follow a simpler visual train of thought.

"There is nothing inscrutable about the career of these gentlemen. No deepness of insight, or power of analysis, or broadness of comprehension is needed to fathom their motives. Nobody who comes to the consideration of them need prepare himself for his work by study or observation. Anybody who can guess why a pig wants to get into a potato-field ... or a cat to creep into a cup-board ... or why dogs hang around slaughter-houses, is competent to write an exhaustive essay on New York City politics, and paint the whole Tammany Ring with the hand of a master. So we do not invite any respectable citizen to spend his precious time accounting for them..."

The Tammany Kingdom (Ring-Dom)

In October 1870, after spending almost five months covering the Franco-Prussian War and other topics in his cartoons, Nast returned to his anti-Tammany theme, commenting on the alleged administrative impotence of Governor John Hoffman and the supposed intent of Tammany to rig the upcoming elections for governor and mayor. The "Tammany Kingdom: The Power behind the Throne" in the postdated October 29, 1870 issue of *Harper's Weekly* (available, October 19) portrays Hoffman sitting uneasily on the Tammany throne. **For the first time in a Nast cartoon, Boss Tweed is indisputably a more prominent figure than Peter Sweeny, although their combined names imply a certain equality or interchangeableness.**

The "K" in "Kingdom" is crossed so it can be read as "Ring-dom." Behind the throne (left) is the rotund figure of the Boss, wearing a cap marked "Sweed" and bearing the sword of "Power," and the city chamberlain (right), adorned with a hat labeled "Tweeny" and gripping the executioner's axe.

Behind Tweed, financier Jim Fisk holds an "Erie Bill"—doubtless, the "Erie Classification Bill" signed under duress by the governor (May 1869), which proposed to lock Fisk, Jay Gould, Tweed, and one other director into positions on the railroad's board for five years, no matter how they might defraud their stockholders. In the weeks before Nast's cartoon appeared, the *Times* had been referring to "King Tweed" and his subjects, and to Hoffman's fear of reforming the latter's corrupt judiciary. George William Curtis's editorial in the October 22 issue of *Harper's Weekly* concentrated on the governor's accommodation of Tweed on the Erie Bill, and on Hoffman's status as the Boss's intended presidential candidate in 1872.

The *New-York Times* of October 21, 1870, welcomed Nast back to the contest, lauding "his highly effective cartoons," singling out "The Tammany Kingdom" as a "masterly sketch … of a very clever tableau," and hoping that *Harper's Weekly* would "continue to aid the anti-Tammany crusade by such powerful weapons" as Nast's cartoons. "The Tammany Kingdom" elicited similar praise from the *Commercial Advertiser and the Tribune*. Writing in the latter, editor Horace Greeley remarked, "Mr. Thomas Nast, who has done brave service heretofore in the cause of honest government, deals another good blow this week by his picture of 'The Power Behind the Throne.' …We commend it to the attention of politicians generally, and the supporters of Governor Hoffman in particular."

The following issue of *Harper's Weekly*, November 5, 1870 (published October 26), exhibits Tweed as "Our Modern Falstaff Reviewing His Army" of thugs, convicts, and fraudulent voters. Based on Shakespeare's *Henry IV* (Part I, Act IV, Scene II) and an illustration by John Gilbert, Nast's inspiration came from an editorial in the October 11 *New-York Times*, which compared the Tammany Ring's gang of repeat voters with Falstaff's rag-tag army. The Shakespearean setting of "A public road near Coventry [England]" has been replaced in Nast's sketch by "The Tammany Ring Inn—Sweed, Tweeny & Co." The Boss and his associates (left-right)—Sweeny, Hall (now wearing a monocle), Gould, Fisk (with an Erie Railroad hat), and (foreground) a diminutive Hoffman as a page holding Tweed's sword—cast jaundiced eyes at the potential poll-workers. The man at the far left is Alderman Theodore Allen, who the *World* (October 27, 1870) referred to as "the notorious chief of the pickpockets and thieves."

The corresponding explanatory note in *Harper's Weekly* commented that:

"Only those who have not visited our city in recent times, since it fell under the domination of the Ring, need to be informed the municipal authorities maintain a vast army of loafers, ostensibly for service under the Department of Public Works, but really for political purposes, and chiefly for repeaters work on election-day."

On October 27, the day after the cartoon's publication, the *Times* doffed its cap to the artist and acknowledged the cartoon's paternity in the *Times* previous editorial, "The Paradise of Repeaters." The editor concluded, "Mr. Nast will add much to his reputation with cartoons such as this."

According to journalist Charles F. Wingate (*North American Review*, 1875), the pair of Nast satires just presented, "The Power Behind the Throne" and "Our Modern Falstaff," may have provoked Boss Tweed into his reputed famous tribute to the cartoonist: **"I don't care a straw for your newspaper articles; my constituents don't know how to read, but they can't help seeing them damned pictures."**

Regardless of Nast's success in getting under Tweed's thick skin—not an easy feat—Tweed got the last laugh in the calm before the storm. Sweeping victories in the elections on November 8, 1870, provided the final coup in an extremely successful political year for Tammany Hall. Hoffman was reelected governor and Hall was reelected mayor; Tammany's entire slate of congressional candidates won, and it captured the offices of county clerk, country sheriff, all of the coroners, and 19 of the 22 seats on the school board.

Also, in the final days of October 1870, the first of five annual almanacs showcasing Nast's work went on sale. "Nast's Illustrated Almanac for 1871" contained a set of "Historical Sketches" purporting to relate the "Landing of the Pilgrims" and concerned in part with the Tammany "Indians" and their relations with the "Puritans" of New York. An intense, acerbic little portrait of "A War Chief" depicted Tweed with a Big Six volunteer fireman's hat and megaphone. Another sketch showed two vindictive Tammany braves squaring off against a pair of Cavaliers, at the right, including apparently Nast's only image of Hoffman's Republican opponent, Stewart L. Woodford.

OUR MODERN FALSTAFF REVIEWING HIS ARMY.—[See Page 714.]

FALSTAFF.—My whole charge consists of slaves as ragged as Lazarus, and such as indeed were never | the villains march wide between the legs, as if they had fetters on; for, indeed, I had the most of them out
soldiers, but discarded serving-men and revolted tapsters. No eye hath seen such scarecrows. Nay and | of prison.—*Shakspeare, slightly varied.*

Nast's first anti-Tammany Ring cartoon of 1871, appearing in the January 14 issue of *Harper's Weekly*, was a broad burlesque of Tweed and Sweeny as "Clown" and "Pantaloon," two popular figures from classic British pantomime, who are, here, industriously depleting the safe labeled "Public Treasury." For Christmas 1870, Tweed received publicity for giving $50,000 to aid the poor in his old district, the Seventh Ward, during that particularly severe winter. Consequently, Nast portrays him taking money with his left hand and giving some of it away with his right hand.

The Boss is costumed after the fashion of comedian George Fox in the popular homegrown pantomime of "Humpty Dumpty" (1867-1868), for which Nast had drawn the programs. This attire also provided a perfect vehicle for optimum display of an enormous diamond stickpin, which had become a regular Tweed accessory. In fact, it is difficult to tell whether he refers to the charitable donation or the jewel, when he says "Let's Blind them with this, and then take some more." This picture of "Tweedledee" and "Sweedledum" is based on an eighteenth-century verse, or an even older nursery rhyme, about two very similar individuals. (Lewis Carroll more famously incorporated the two characters into his book, *Through the Looking-Glass and What Alice Found There*, published in December 1871).

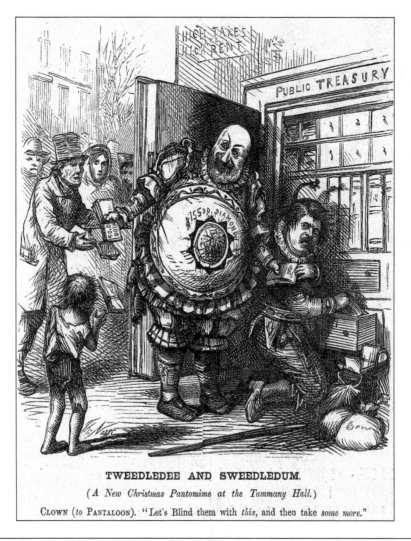

TWEEDLEDEE AND SWEEDLEDUM.

(*A New Christmas Pantomime at the Tammany Hall.*)

CLOWN (*to* PANTALOON). "Let's Blind them with *this*, and then take *some more*."

After the resounding Tammany victories in the November 1870 elections, the *Sun* suggested facetiously that a collection be taken to erect a statute in honor of Boss Tweed. Proposals eventually ranged from a large Indian with war paint and feathers, to young Tweed as a volunteer fireman with a crouching tiger, to a Roman senator in a toga. Of the latter, the intended honoree objected to that "style of coat," saying it would make him seem as if he were ready to take a bath.

Quickly the spoof became a serious project. Tweed allowed it to proceed for a while, perhaps to test his associates for their friendship, as indicated by how much each of them might be prepared to contribute. By March 13, however, the project had gone far enough for Tweed, and in a letter to the fundraising organizer and chairman, Edward J. Shandley, a police justice, the boss pulled the plug:

> "Statues are not erected to living men, but to those who have ended their careers, and where no interest exists to question the partial tributes of friends . . . I claim to be a live man, and hope (Divine Providence permitting) to survive in all my vigor, politically and physically, some years to come . . .

> "I hardly know which is the more absurd, the original proposition, or the grave comments of others, based upon the idea that I have given the movement countenance. I have been about as abused as any man in public life; but I have never yet been charged with being deficient in common sense. . ."

Nast's response appeared in the April 1, 1871 (April Fool's Day) issue of Harper's Weekly. It portrays Judge Shandley as Shakespeare's sprite, Puck, offering the winking head of an ass to the cringing Tweed as the former states. "Allow me to immortalize you, Boss." Playing the expected role, Tweed emphatically rejects the proffered honor. In a delicious background detail (upper right), financier Jim Fisk, owner of the Grand Opera House and Tweed's close friend and business associate, executes a neat pirouette while dressed in a ballerina's tutu.

THE REHEARSAL.

SHANDLEY (*as Puck*). "Allow me to immortalize you, Boss!"
TWEED (*realizing his part*). "I most emphatically and decidedly object to it. I am not deficient in common-sense."

Emperor Tweed

During the Franco-Prussian War (July 19, 1870–May 10, 1871), Napoleon III, the French Emperor, was captured after the French defeat at the Battle of Sedan on September 2, 1870. Paris fell on January 28, 1871, with an armistice signed the same day, and the Treaty of Frankfort formally ended the war on May 10, 1871. In the midst of the war, in August 1870, the French emperor had taken his 14-year-old son, Louis, the Prince Imperial, to the frontlines. That incident provided cartoonist Nast with an emphatic metaphor for the impending fate presumably awaiting the corrupt Tammany Ring.

In "The Baptism of Fire," published in the postdated April 22, 1871 issue of *Harper's Weekly*, Tweed, as Emperor Napoleon, tries to shield Governor Hoffman, as the prince imperial, from bursting shellfire from the "Christian Church," "The Press That Can't Be Bought," "Political Reform Meeting" (which took place at Cooper Institute in New York City on April 6), "Connecticut," and "Rhode Island" (the latter two indicating rising criticism in nearby states). Hoffman's presidential hobbyhorse has tipped over. Sweeny grimaces anxiously from between Tweed's legs, an alarmed Jim Fisk (in his uniform as colonel of the Ninth Regiment New York National Guard) dives for cover, while "Mare" Hall gallops away. Although the Tammany Society was a Democratic Party organization, a few "Tammany" Republicans assisted the Tweed Ring in its corrupt dealings. Here, three of them are fleeing in the background (left-right) Nathaniel Sands, tax assessor and Board of Education member, Henry "Hank" Smith, a police commissioner, and Tom "Torpedo" Fields, a ward leader.

"THE BAPTISM OF FIRE."
EMPEROR TWEED AND THE PRINCE IMPERIAL.

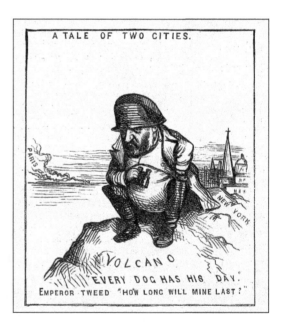

Ten weeks later, Nast again depicted Tweed as Napoleon. It may be that Nast knew something about the damaging disclosures soon to be published in the *New-York Times*. The introductory panel to a potpourri of vignettes entitled "Hash—Or A Tale of Two Cities" (New York and Paris), printed in the July 1, 1871 *Harper's Weekly* (published June 21), features Tweed as Napoleon III (again wearing the hat of Napoleon I) sitting on a volcano. In the background, Paris is in flames (an allusion to the violent overthrow of the Paris Commune in May 1871), while the foreground caption reads: "Every Dog Has His Day. Emperor Tweed 'How Long Will Mine Last?'" The title of the cartoon derives from Charles Dickens's novel, *A Tale of Two Cities*, about London and Paris during the French Revolution. (See pages 106-107.)

The Irish were known to hold most of the appointive jobs while German immigrants received slim pickings. A *New-York Times* listing in September 1869 showed 1,025 patronage jobs filled by Irish immigrants vs. 46 for the Germans—a 22 to 1 ratio vs. about a 2 to 1 ratio for population.

The German immigrants, who were sometimes referred to as "Dutch," tended to vote Democratic. If they could be induced to vote for the Republican reform party and against Tammany Hall, they would hold the balance of power in the election.

Using a see-saw as a catapult in "How To Knock Them Higher Than A Kite," Nast portrays that vividly in this cartoon from the April 29, 1871 issue of *Harper's Weekly*. The Irish have "All the Fat Offices" as a base for their power. In addition, this Irish stereotype is rooting for the French, who the "Dutch" beat in the Franco-Prussian War just three months earlier when Paris fell.

Nast is urging "Our Fritz" to tip the balance of power, which "Fritz" ultimately did. (See page 141.) When the see-saw shifts, the Tammany Ring goes flying into space, while "Our Fritz" asks "How is this for HIGH?" The figure cheering behind "Our Fritz" is probably Nast himself.

HOW "TO KNOCK THEM HIGHER THAN A KITE."

YOUNG AMERICA (*to "Our Fritz"*). "Don't stand there all day looking on; but come and help."

In December 1870, Harper's Brothers put in a bid to publish textbooks for the New York City public schools, but the *New-York Times* reported on April 23, 1871, that Tweed had taken great exception to several recent Harper's Weekly cartoons, especially "The Power behind the Throne," "Our Modern Falstaff," and "Tweedledee and Sweedledum." Of the latter, *The Times* reported:

"It was a very striking cartoon and caused considerable comment in the City at the time. When the paper was shown to Mr. Tweed, he is reported to have said: 'That is the last straw that breaks this camel's back.' And he immediately sent word to his subservient tools in the Board of Education to reject all bids made by the Harpers. This was two or three days after the appearance of the cartoon.

"After the above statement of facts, the public will not be surprised when informed that it is the intention of the Ring to *have books of instruction prepared by its favorites, and to be printed exclusively by the New-York Printing Company*, an association composed of the leading members of the Ring. The plans for this gigantic swindle have not been matured, but the fact that such a plan has been broached is an augury that it will be successfully and profitably carried out."

The Board of Education resolution proposing that Harper's textbooks be banned from the public schools was proposed by Tammany Republican Nathaniel Sands. Nast may have known that, and it may be why Sands was depicted prominently in so many Ring cartoons. In any event, the resolution was rescinded the day after the election.

The threat of removal of Harper's textbooks from the city schools prompted Nast to respond with the cartoon, "The New Board of Education," in the May 13, 1871 issue of *Harper's Weekly*. It shows Tweed, Sweeny, and Hall forcibly taking over a classroom, threatening a boy, seizing his book, pitching Harpers' texts out the window, and demonstrating discerned truths on a wall placard: "Hoffman Will Be Our Next President," "Sweed Is an Honest Man," "Tweeny Is an Angel," and "Hall Is a Friend of the Poor."

THE NEW BOARD OF EDUCATION.
SOWING THE SEED, WITH AN EYE TO THE HARVEST.

On April 7, 1871, five days prior to publication of "The Baptism of Fire," (see page 94), a violent physical assault on Smith M. Weed, a Republican state legislator in Albany, led to the forced resignation of his assailant, James Irving, a Tammany Hall alderman and a strapping bully. (Nine months later on January 1, 1872, Irving contributed to another uproar in his final New York City Alderman's meeting, when he struck a small boy who was trying to serve him with a writ ordering him to step down in favor of his elected replacement.)

The situation created a serious problem for the Tammany Ring, which needed one more vote in the State Assembly to rescue key elements of its program for that session. On Saturday morning, April 15, Tweed purchased the services of Assemblyman Orange S. Winans, of Dunkirk, Chautauqua County. Winans had been elected as a Republican member in 1870, but as a 30-year employee of the Erie Railroad, he was probably subject to the dictates of its top management, Jim Fisk and Jay Gould; Boss Tweed was also a director and shareholder. According to the *New-York Times*, the alleged inducement was a $75,000 bribe and a guaranteed promotion.

On April 16, the *Times* labeled Winans "a venal knave" and a "hideous moral deformity" who should become "an object of contempt to all men..." His statement to the Assembly that he would vote with the Democrats because they deserved a constitutional majority (the call for a special election having been previously defeated, including a nay vote by Winans) was met by his fellow Republicans with jeers and exclamations of "Shame," "Traitor," and other epithets. The following morning, April 17, the editorial page of Greeley's *Tribune* carried the following mock advertisement:

"For Sale or to let for Business Purposes—a Member of the Assembly. Rent for the season, $100,000, or will be sold cheap for cash. Possession as soon as the Tax Levy and Election Bills are passed, the present lessee having no further use for the property. Inquire of William M. Tweed, Albany, or O. S. Winans, on the premises."

Nine days later (April 26), in the *Harper's Weekly* dated May 6, 1871, Nast dealt with the subject. Winans, clad in rags, branded with the words "Traitor," "Corruption," "Treachery," and "Bribe," stands cowering between the "Republicans" and the "Tammany Ring." The latter group includes (left-right) turncoat Republicans Nathaniel Sands, and Tom Fields, Governor Hoffman, Boss Tweed, and, in the rear, lawyer David Dudley Field and his Erie client, Jim Fisk. The Republicans collectively say "He sold himself." and the Tammany Ring says "We bought him."

In fact, Winans was treated as a leper. His wife left him and his neighbors ostracized him. He fled from his home and disappeared forever.

Nast produced a second satire at the same time for the May issue of *Phunny Phellow*. It was a double-page image showing Tweed purchasing Winans in the "Uncle Sam Political Auction Sale Rooms" over the title "Every Man Has His Price: This Kind of Slavery Not Yet Abolished." Nathaniel Sands of the Board of Education and Police Commissioner Hank Smith are included in the lot of Tammany Republicans acquired by Tweed.

MAKE ROOM FOR THE LEPER.

For added context, the same issue of *Harper's Weekly* supplied three additional items: a large portrait of Winans from a photograph; a paragraph on his extreme unpopularity with the Republicans of his district, who on April 22 demanded his resignation; and the full text of a ten-stanza poem by Nathaniel Parker Willis entitled "The Leper," which had once been a popular verse for schoolhouse recitation. It began:

> "Room for the leper! Room!" And as he came
>
> The cry passed on—" Room for the leper! Room!"
>
> …
>
> And onward through the open gate he came,
>
> A leper with the ashes on his brow,
>
> Sackcloth about his loins, and on his lip
>
> A covering, stepping painfully and slow,
>
> And with a difficult utterance, like one
>
> Whose heart is with an iron nerve put down,
>
> Crying—"Unclean! Unclean!"

Under the Thumb

Four days after the Winans incident of April 15, while Nast was hard at work on his "Leper" cartoon, editor George William Curtis scrambled to insert in the *Harper's Weekly* published that Wednesday, April 19, a paragraph under "Notes," which evidently planted the seed for the cartoonist's first great symbolic cartoon of his anti-Tammany campaign:

> "We hope that New York Republicans have now learned the folly of making bargains with the Ring. ...Meanwhile, we invite the attention of men every where to the fact that the New York Democrats, **under the thumb** (emphasis added) of Mr. Tweed, gravely proposed to dissolve the Legislature, because the Republicans in a party caucus, decided they could not support certain bills which they not only believed to be injurious to the public interest, but intended merely to help the Democratic party."

Curtis's phrase "under the thumb" must have struck a chord with Nast. The artist had previously employed a similar idea for the November 1862 cover of the monthly *Phunny Phellow*, "Showing How General Butler Has the Crescent City Under His Thumb." It concerned the controversial rule of General Benjamin Butler (May-December 1862) after the Union first occupied New Orleans during the Civil War. Much less forceful a drawing than Nast's later anti-Tweed cartoon, the earlier sketch shows Butler from top to toe and the city on a low table, receiving the "back of his hand" for good measure.

As the cartoonist tackled the same idea for the June 10, 1871 *Harper's Weekly* (published May 31), the concept was distilled to the absolute essence of the Tammany Boss's gargantuan fist, thumb, and huge diamond cufflink reading "William M. Tweed." **In the caption, Nast for the first time associates Boss Tweed with the cynically defiant taunt, "Well, what are you going to do about it?"** The cartoonist's unerring introduction of his deadliest provocation to the embattled citizens of New York City was one of the masterstrokes of his career.

The *New-York Times* picked it up a month after Nast's "Under the Thumb" cartoon, and it was soon generally, although falsely, considered to have been a direct quote from Tweed (usually) or another Tammany Ring leader. Even Nast's biographer, Albert Bigelow Paine, credits Tweed with the fatal words, "Well, what are you going to do about it?" (page 164). In fact, the catch phrase had been coined by William Evarts, former senator, secretary of state, and attorney general, at an anti-Ring protest meeting at Cooper Institute on April 6, 1871:

> "And yet I speak now of a party to which I do not belong [i.e., Democratic Party]. I think that the present managers and administration of that party, now in power in the city, do boast of their corruption and do despise honest men. [Applause.] They say, 'What are you going to do about it?' [Laughter.] I think they will find out what we are going to do about it. [Great applause.]" —(*New-York Times*, April 7, 1871, page 1.)

While Nast wanted to drive home the point that the Tammany Ring was a great evil, he wanted to avoid implying that its reign was invincible. As historian Thomas Leonard has pointed out in his *Power of the Press* (page 116), when Nast chose to represent Boss Tweed as a monarch or emperor, the cartoonist selected a figure associated with failure and/or a violent death—e.g., Napoleon III, Richard III, Queen Gertrude (Hamlet's mother), or Caligula. With "Under the Thumb," Nast punched home the idea with masterful economy.

Concentrated on a single boxwood block barely larger than four-and-one-half inches square, the cartoonist epitomizes the subjugation of Manhattan with Tweed's thumb, and contrasts it to the foreground view of free, prosperous, mercantile New Jersey, with its public school prominent on a hilltop, bustling factories, belching chimneys, railways, shipping, church, and residential homes. Nast must already have been thinking of relocating with his family to Morristown, New Jersey, which he did later that summer.

UNDER THE THUMB.

The Boss. "Well, what are you going to do about it?"

During the quiet before the coming anti-Tammany storm, the cartoonist contributed a wonderfully funny satire to the June 17, 1871 *Harper's Weekly* (published June 7). The tableau casts Tweed and his merry men creeping furtively through woods to capture the White House in 1872 for Governor John Hoffman. The American Indian motif is based on the Tammany Society's designation of their leaders as "sachems," meaning Indian chiefs, and their head as the "grand sachem."

The cartoon's title is a clever backhanded slap at Horace Greeley, the *Tribune* editor who had just returned to New York from a speaking tour through the South during which he floated his own trial balloon for the Democratic presidential nomination. The "On to Washington!" title mirrors the daily headline of Greeley's *Tribune* during the early summer of 1861, which urged Union troops "Forward to Richmond," the Confederate capital. After the Union rout at the First Battle of Bull Run on July 21, 1861, "On to Richmond" became a sarcastic phrase for reckless and unjustified optimism.

On the White House portico, President Ulysses S. Grant imperturbably reads a newspaper and puffs a cigar, unaware of (or unconcerned about) the approaching war party. The president's reelection poster—"Let Us Have Peace For Another Term"—is plastered on the front column. On the left, the equestrian statue of Andrew Jackson is Nast's visual metaphor for the system of partisan patronage or "spoils" (which the cartoonist wanted replaced with a merit-based government bureaucracy).

The Tammany procession is led by the impetuous Jim Fisk, donned in a plumed colonel's hat and "Erie" belt, and armed with tomahawk and dagger. He is restrained by Peter Sweeny, who has grabbed Fisk's foot after dropping the front handle of the wheeled platform bearing Hoffman, who appears as a cigar-store Indian. Grand Sachem Tweed strenuously pushes from behind, followed by Mayor Oakey Hall, who wears a jester's cap and appears on the verge of kissing the Boss's foot. Comptroller Richard Connolly is conspicuously absent from the picture.

Among others in the main group: Manton Marble, editor of the *World*, the bearded figure to the side of the platform; Sinclair Tousey, owner of the American News Company, the man with a goatee standing over Tweed by the tree; John McCloskey, the Roman Catholic archbishop of New York, beside Hall; behind McCloskey, lawyer Thomas G. Shearman, counsel to Gould; on the right of Shearman, Judge George Barnard; and financier Jay Gould protecting the rear with a rifle. The caricatures of Tousey, McCloskey and Shearman (a founder of today's Shearman and Sterling law firm) are firsts and rare for Nast.

On the day following publication (June 8), the *New-York Times* called attention to Nast's latest shot at the Ring:

> "*Harper's Weekly* ought to be in everybody's hands. The current number contains one of Nast's best drawings—a drawing which would alone suffice to gain a large reputation for its designer. …The likenesses of the principal figures are drawn with Nast's peculiar skill."

ON TO WASHINGTON!

As mentioned in the explanation of the previous cartoon, "On To Washington," Horace Greeley had recently returned to New York from a speaking tour through the South during which he floated his own trial balloon for the 1872 Democratic presidential nomination. Two weeks after that cartoon, in the July 1, 1871 issue of *Harper's Weekly*, Nast published two cartoons dealing with John Hoffman's need to capture the Southern vote if he seriously wanted to be president. The South was still under military rule, the Ku Klux Klan was causing trouble, and many former Confederates still embraced the "Lost Cause" of the Civil War. The "New Departure" slogan of the Northern Democrats was intended to reflect the reality that the results of the Civil War were final and the Confederate cause was extinct.

In "Some Are Born Great; Some Achieve Greatness," Hoffman thoughtfully points out to Tweed, with Sweeny looking on, how difficult it will be to sit on two stools at once—the Lost Cause of Jeff Davis, whose stool says "Not Lost"—and the Lost Cause of the Ring's "New Departure," whose stool says "Lost." Tweed, stumped, replies with an irrelevant: "If you were blessed with my figure, you could manage it."

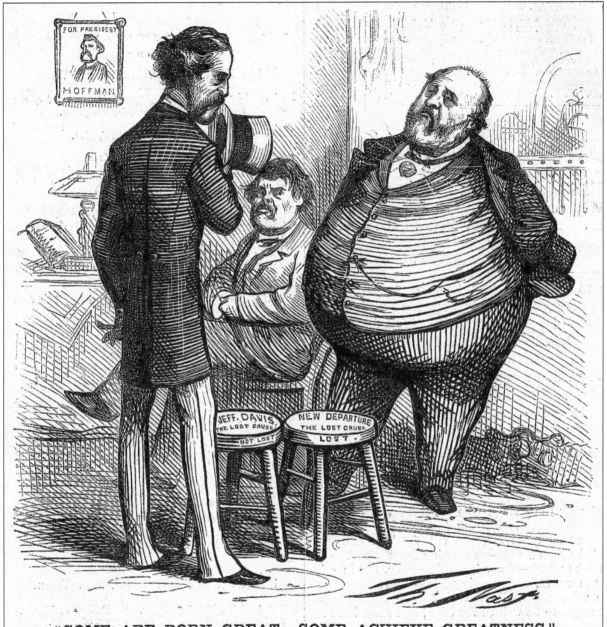

"SOME ARE BORN GREAT; SOME ACHIEVE GREATNESS."

HOFFMAN. "It will be very difficult to sit on both of those Stools at once. You know the Proverb, Boss?"

BOSS TWEED. "If you were blessed with my Figure, you could manage it."

Nast's second cartoon in the July 1, 1872 issue, which is entitled "Hash—or, a Tale of Two Cities," is just that: hash. Its ten sketches cover a lot of geographical and political ground, primarily in New York and Paris. The first cartoon, Emperor Tweed, was explained on page 94. The other two cartoons on the top and the one on the bottom right show the riotous conditions in France, after the conclusion of the Franco-Prussian War. The cartoon on the upper right shows the Ring leaders proclaiming "We will make New York into the Paris of America," but cower as the spirit of Ben Franklin points out: "All good Americans when they die go to Paris." The "Barbarous Germans," who won, show their magnanimity towards children in the bottom left, in contrast to the "Civilized French" who are burning and killing.

Nast's next two panels, second from the top, deal with the Lost Cause. With Tweed pushing Hoffman for the 1872 Democratic presidential nomination, Hoffman faced the same quandary as Greeley: Should Hoffman and Tammany look for backing from the Southern Democrats? Clement Vallandigham, a Copperhead (Southern sympathizer, traitor) leader during the Civil War, is playing a "new organ" (on the left) saying he accepts that the Civil War (the Lost Cause) is really lost. In the background, Tweed and Hoffman are discussing the situation with ex-President Andrew Johnson, a Tennessean who favored the South after the war and consequently was impeached and almost forced from office. Johnson advises what today's politicians would call a trial balloon: "Let him (Vallandigham) play those tunes and we will see if they will take." A group of Irish listen to the tunes, without and within Democratic headquarters. On the right opposite panel (second from the top), Jeff Davis is playing the Bonnie Blue Flag, a Confederate song, on his organ and not accepting that the Lost Cause is really lost. Ku Klux Klan members are dancing to the tune.

Embracing both panels is "The new rebellion among the Democrats." Meanwhile, in the small center box marked "New Departure," (the Ring's program which accepted the Civil War results), a figure that looks like Tweed is jumping ship.

Nast's third panel from the top delivers a subtle but meaningful message: Governor Hoffman, supported by owner/editor Manton Marble of the *World*, had broken away from the Ring on what was an important judicial issue at that time even though it is obscure today. Hoffman is carrying a "Flag of Truce from the Enemy" showing his veto of the Code Amendment. His veto is supported by the flags of "The Press" and "The Bar" in the right upper background.

One of three proposed amendments to the Legal Code of Procedure, all of which had been passed by the state legislature, would have allowed courts to punish by fine and imprisonment, without trial by jury, "the free and public expression of opinion upon the conduct of judicial tribunals" (May 1, 1871 minutes of the American Bar Association in New York). Hoffman's veto, at the urging of the ABA, put him outside Emperor Tweed's fortress, and even outside Tweed's friendly pickets—Nathaniel Sands and Tom Fields—doing guard duty in the trenches. Judge George Barnard, "Emperor" Tweed's corrupt judicial enabler, animatedly asks the Boss: "What is to protect me from slander,?" now that the amendment was vetoed. Peter Sweeny, Oakey Hall and Jim Fisk (left to right) are behind Barnard.

Finally, in the lower miniature panel, an Irishman with a tin cup and the Pope in his lap, is collecting for the holy "prisoner."

Nast's title of "Hash" is well taken because he touches so many themes in this cartoon. However, the issues of whether Hoffman should embrace Southern Democrats, and Hoffman's anti-Ring veto, were important for the Ring's future before the effect of the *Times* disclosures made them rhetorical.

HASH—OR, A TALE OF TWO CITIES.

On July 4, 1871, the Tammany Society held an Independence Day celebration at its headquarters, Tammany Hall, on 14th Street. Boss Tweed delivered a 525-word welcome, which was reprinted verbatim in the next morning's *New-York Times*.

Nast illustrated the main points of Tweed's talk with a page of 25 scenes in the July 22, 1871 *Harper's Weekly* (published July 12). Entitled "The Glorious Fourth: Address of Grand Sachem Tweed at the Tammany Wigwam," the first image is of Tweed with a rubber-ball body and feathers in his hair. The initial capital letter "F" of the text is fashioned into a gibbet from which a ballot box hangs, symbolizing the death of voting rights from vote fraud.

As Tweed's speech continues on the page, it is interspersed with 24 more drawings, which belie the corresponding claims and promises of the oration. For example, Nast illustrates the speech excerpt, "the purpose of keeping alive the patriotic fires," with a picture of Tweed and Sweeny (and perhaps Hall and Connolly in the background) burning the female personification of Justice alive at the stake. Other vignettes include Tammany raiding the New York Treasury, robbing a representative taxpayer, transferring public schools, land, and funds to the Roman Catholic Church, and taking over the federal government.

The middle vignette on the far right is entitled "Mr. Tweed's Next Castle." It shows the Executive Office Building in Washington, which was located next to the White House. Once again, with Hoffman as President, Tweed would be pulling the strings from behind the scene and the screen (Hoffman) as Nast subtly portrays the scenario.

"Something That Will Not 'Blow Over'"

In early July 1871, the Loyal Order of Orange, an organization of Protestant Irish-Americans in New York City, requested a parade permit from the city government. They intended to display their ethnic and religious pride by commemorating the 1690 victory of William of Orange, the new Protestant king of England, over the deposed James II and his mainly Catholic supporters at the Battle of the Boyne. The city's Irish- Catholic associations lodged protests in order to halt the parade, arguing that the celebration offended Catholic Irish-Americans, and citing the Protestants' behavior on the previous year when the marchers taunted Irish- Catholic street crews with insulting songs and curses.

On July 10, Police Superintendent James J. Kelso followed an order from Mayor Oakey Hall to deny the permit on the grounds that the parade would threaten public safety, as well as the fact that obscene or violently derogatory language or gestures in public were misdemeanors. Irish Catholics praised the decision, and the police chief had the further support of Boss Tweed. Irish Protestants objected, demanding equal treatment with Catholics, whose St. Patrick's Day parade Mayor Hall attended, and for whose charities and schools Tammany Hall allocated public funds. Protestants warned that cancellation of the parade would strengthen the position of violent Irish nationalists, like the Fenians. Governor John Hoffman, in consultation with Mayor Hall and Boss Tweed, reversed the decision, letting the parade proceed as planned.

Irish Catholics were divided over how to respond, but some drilled in military units in case of trouble. The governor ordered 5000 members of the New York National Guard to safeguard the marchers and keep the public order. One member of the Guard's Seventh Regiment was Private Thomas Nast, whose vantage point at 24th Street and Eighth Avenue allowed him to sketch scenes of the ensuing melee for *Harper's Weekly*. The parade began down Eighth Avenue from 29th Street at 2 p.m., with the Orangemen surrounded by the guardsmen. Cheers for the Protestants clashed with jeers from the Catholics, many of who began throwing rocks, bottles, and other projectiles. Guns were fired on both sides, and a confusing battle scene unfolded. Despite the bloody clash, the parade reformed and continued forward to Cooper Union, where the marchers disbanded at 4 o'clock.

The Orange Day Riot resulted in 60 civilians and two guardsmen killed, and over 100 civilians, 22 policemen, and one Orangeman injured. Irish Catholics hanged Governor Hoffman in effigy, called the riot "Slaughter on Eighth Avenue," and turned out 20,000 strong for the funerals of their slain.

The Orange Day Riot occurred on July 12, four days after the first of the *New-York Times* exposures of Tweed Ring Corruption. **Mayor Hall had dismissed the *Times* initial July 8 allegations, claiming they would soon "blow over."**

The July 29, 1871 issue of *Harper's Weekly* (published July 19) contained a description of "The Tammany Riot" which began by blaming Tweed, Hall and other Tammany leaders for not restraining their Irish-Catholic supporters. **In order to condemn the entire Ring, Nast incorporated Hall's memorable phrase into his cartoon's title: "Something That Will Not 'Blow Over'." He was to use the phrase several times in future cartoons.**

"Something That Will Not 'Blow Over'"

The central arching design fills a space marked by the curving horizon of "The Promised Land. U. S. A." stretching from California to Washington, D.C., to New York. It portrays an enraged mob of stereotypical Irish-Catholic ruffians charging a single unarmed Irish-Protestant parade marshal, as Uncle Sam draws his sword to defend him. Real and symbolic world figures, including (left to right) Queen Victoria, John Bull, King Victor Emanuel of Italy, Emperor Franz Josef of Austria, and Tsar Alexander II of Russia, turn away in fear and disgust. A line above the central scene asks pointedly, "Has No Caste, No Sect, No Nation, Any Rights That the Infallible Ultramontane Roman Irish Catholic Is Bound to Respect [?]" The use of "infallible" alludes to the 1869 announcement of the doctrine of Papal Infallibility, while "Ultramontane" refers to those supporting papal supremacy within the Catholic Church. By contrast, Nast includes among the besieged world figures a banner for two prominent liberal Catholics who rejected papal supremacy, Fathers Dollinger and Hyacinth.

Coincidentally, the July 1871 Orange Day riot occurred almost eight years to the day after the Civil War draft riots began in New York City. Above the hypocritical phrase "Live and Let Live" are fallen bodies, while images of a lynched black man and the burning Colored Orphan Asylum revive memories of the bloody 1863 riots. (See pages 34-35) On the upper-left of the central picture an American flag flies inverted (a symbol of distress) near a demolished public schoolhouse. It is paralleled on the upper-right by a flag promoting Tammany Hall, Irish-Catholics, and papal supremacy. The center panel on the right shows "The Unconditional Surrender" of Tammany Ring officials, who grovel before ape-like Irish-Catholics. The Tweed members are (clockwise from front left): Sheriff Matthew Brennan, Sweeny, Connolly, Hoffman, Tweed, Hall, and Kelso. Sweeny, Tweed, and Hall appear to bless Kelso, each with a right hand on his head, as the chief truckles to the Hibernian mob. A parallel image on the left shows most of the same group fawning on their knees before Columbia, who draws her sword. Brennan and Kelso are absent, replaced by Tom Fields in the back.

At the bottom center, the Tweed Ring sits in chains, guarded by two rioters, while surrounded by an Irish-Catholic crowd who jeer "Well, What Are You Going To Do About It?"—the question attributed by Nast (with poetic license) to Tweed when the corruption charges against him and his cohorts surfaced. The cartoon reverses the role of the Greek slave(s) and their masters. (See page 80).

Harper's Weekly took out a boldface advertisement in the city's daily newspapers drawing attention to "The Late Riot" and to a "Splendid Double Page by Thomas Nast." An editorial note in the *New-York Times* of July 20 recommended that: "Everybody should see, and seeing, retain Nast's great 'Riot Cartoons' on the New Number of *Harper's Weekly*." The artist's work helped nearly double the circulation of the July 29 issue of *Harper's Weekly* to 186,000 from the previous week's distribution of 100,000. On the other hand, an editorial in July 29 issue of *The Irish People*, a New York weekly, criticized *Harper's Hell Weekly* for "doing its very utmost to upset the laws and Constitution of this country" and for "insulting Irishmen and their religion."

At the bottom of "Something That Will Not 'Blow Over'" there are two seven-verse poems constituting a dialogue of sorts between Columbia and the Irish-Catholic "Pat." No authorship is shown, but it is highly unlikely that Nast himself wrote them. (They are reprinted on pages 114-115.)

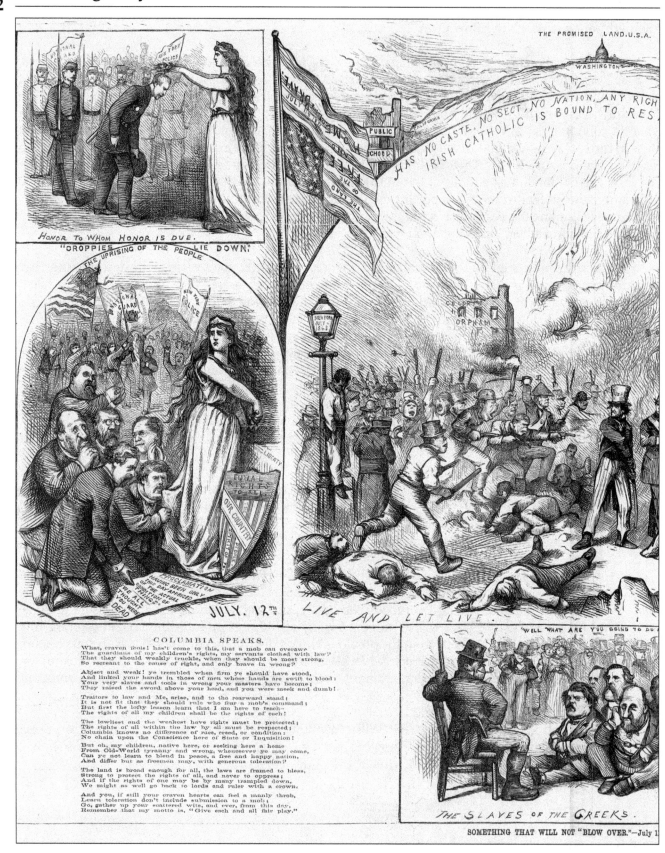

THE PROMISED LAND, U.S.A.

HONOR TO WHOM HONOR IS DUE.

"CROPPIES LIE DOWN!"

THE UPRISING OF THE PEOPLE

JULY 12TH

LIVE AND LET LIVE.

HAS NO CASTE, NO SECT, NO NATION, ANY RIGHT IRISH CATHOLIC IS BOUND TO RES

COLUMBIA SPEAKS.

What, craven fools! has't come to this, that a mob can overawe
The guardians of my children's rights, my servants clothed with law?
That they should weakly truckle, when they should be most strong,
So recreant to the cause of right, and only brave in wrong?

Abject and weak! ye trembled when firm ye should have stood,
And linked your hands in those of men whose hands are swift to blood;
Your very slaves and tools in wrong your masters have become;
They raised the sword above your head, and you were meek and dumb!

Traitors to law and Me, arise, and to the rearward stand;
It is not fit that they should rule who fear a mob's command;
But first the lofty lesson learn that I am here to teach—
The rights of all my children shall be the rights of each!

The lowliest and the weakest have rights must be protected;
The rights of all within the law by all must be respected;
Columbia knows no difference of race, creed, or condition;
No chain upon the Conscience here of State or Inquisition!

But oh, my children, native here, or seeking here a home
From Old-World tyranny and wrong, whencesoever ye may come,
Can ye not learn to blend in peace, a free and happy nation,
And differ but as freemen may, with generous toleration?

The land is broad enough for all, the laws are framed to bless,
Strong to protect the rights of all, and never to oppress;
And if the rights of one may be by many trampled down,
We might as well go back to lords and ruler with a crown.

And you, if still your craven hearts can feel a manly throb,
Learn toleration don't include submission to a mob;
Go, gather up your scattered wits, and ever, from this day,
Remember that my motto is, "Give each and all fair play."

"WELL, WHAT ARE YOU GOING TO DO

THE SLAVES OF THE GREEKS.

SOMETHING THAT WILL NOT "BLOW OVER."—July 1

COLUMBIA SPEAKS

What, craven fools! has't come to this, that a mob can overawe
The guardians of my children's right, my servants clothed with law?
That they should weakly truckle, when they should be most strong,
So recreant to the cause of right, and only brave in wrong?

Abject and weak! ye trembled when firm ye should have stood,
and linked your hands in those of men whose hands are swift to blood:
Your very slaves and tools in wrong your masters have become;
They raised the sword above your head, and you were meek and dumb!

Traitors to law and Me, arise and to the rearward stand;
It is not fit that they should rule who fear a mob's command;
But first the lofty lesson learn that I am here to teach—
The rights of all my children shall be the rights of each!

The lowliest and the weakest have rights must be protected;
The rights of all within the law by all must be respected;
Columbia knows no difference or race, creed, or condition:
No chain upon the Conscience here of State or Inquisition!

But oh, my children, native here, or seeking here a home
From Old-World tyranny and wrong, whenceever ye may come,
Can ye not learn to blend in peace, a free and happy nation,
And differ but as freemen may, with generous toleration?

The land is broad enough for all, the laws are framed to bless,
Strong to protect the rights of all, and never to oppress;
And if the rights of one may be by many trampled down,
We might as well go back to lords and ruler with a crown.

And you, if still your craven hearts can feel a manly throb,
Learn toleration don't include submission to a mob;
Go, gather up your scattered wits, and ever, from the day,
Remember that my motto is, "Give each and all fair play."

PAT'S COMPLAINT

Oh, have ye heard the tidings? It's disgusted quite I am!
Our boasted rights and freedom is all a fraud and sham;
The Orangemen parade the day with banners, drums, and guns,
To overawe ould Ireland and her poor, down-trodden sons.

Sure those noble-minded gintlemen, O'Kelso and O'Hall,
Had forbid thim bloody Orangemen that they should march at all,
Lest in their pride and madness they might, belike, waylay
And slaughter ivery Irishman they met upon their way.

It was, d'ye see, a splendid plan whereby to kape the peace,
Without the need of calling out the soldiers and the p'lice;
For if thim coward Orangemen would just kape out of sight,
There'd be no provocation to massacre and fight.

But now they'll go parading down in all their rage and pride,
With soldiers and policemen to guard on ivery side;
And ivery son of Ireland must hide his peaceful head,
And skulk away in cellars in terror and in dread.

Sure it's a shameful spectacle to see thim furren beats
Parading up and down all day and blockin' up the streets;
And to think that native citizens of Irish blood and birth
Must quail before these minions, the scum of all the earth!

But sure the worm will turn against the foot by which 'tis crushed;
And shall the voice of Irishmen for evermore be hushed?
Ah, even these proud oppressors, who tread us down to-day,
Will find their goaded victims may turn at last at bay!

By a traitor's proclamation we're bid to stand aloof,
But I'll claim a freeman's privilege to climb upon some roof:
And I'll get behind a chimly, and from where I can't be seen,
Heave a brickbat at the Orange, in honor of the Green.

Shakspeare on the Late Riot

On July 26, two weeks after the Orange Day Riot, the August 5, 1871 issue of *Harper's Weekly* hit the newsstands. It included Nast's "Shakspeare on the Late Riot," featuring Tweed as Richard III (left) and Fisk as Falstaff (right).

In the left panel, Tweed/Richard has awakened from a nightmare in which the ghosts of his misdeeds had visited him (Act V, Scene III), and in which he had a premonition of the loss of his steed in battle ("A horse! A horse! My kingdom for a horse!"). In the background, "Mare" Hall (left) now lies dead, surrounded by a trio of sullen (perhaps Irish-American) bystanders, while peeping out from behind the drapery (right) is Peter Sweeny, glaring in fright, his hair tousled; behind him is Richard Connolly. Although Boss Tweed's large diamond pin glistens and his Tammany Tiger medallion growls, his "Irish Rule" scepter seems about to slip from beneath his crown.

In the right panel, Nast concludes the exercise with a bit of comic relief: a view of financier Jim Fisk as Sir John Falstaff in a wild bit of alcohol-bolstered bravado found in Shakespeare's *Henry IV* (Part I, Act II, Scene IV). The caricaturist's composition of Jim Fisk and the barroom onlookers was clearly inspired by English artist John Gilbert's illustration of the scene, in which Falstaff gestures wildly with legs wide apart, wielding a battered sword in his upraised hand. Fisk, a good friend of Tweed's, was the commanding officer of the Ninth Regiment of the New York National Guard. Because the financier was also a theatrical producer and the headquarters of his Erie Railroad was in an opera house, the Ninth Regiment was commonly called the "Opera Bouffe" (comic opera) unit. They had joined other National Guard units on July 12 to protect the Orangemen who paraded down Eighth Avenue.

In reality, the portly Fisk had abandoned his elegant uniform on that fiercely warm day, when he found himself struggling to catch up with his men, and he was forced to take command with a borrowed sword. When shots were fired, and bricks descended from the houses, some of the men of the Ninth lost their composure, causing Colonel Fisk to be upended by a terrified crowd running for cover. Fisk's ankle was dislocated, and his sword was chipped. He was carried unceremoniously to a doctor's office, where the ankle was reset. Bandaged and supplied with a cane, Fisk hobbled his way painfully through various additional adventures, eventually beating a haphazard path to the Hudson River, where he caught a tugboat for New Jersey. He found sanctuary in the beach resort town of Long Branch, where he reportedly regaled skeptical saloon patrons with tales of his courage and daring during the Orange Day Riot.

Harper's Weekly couldn't stop ridiculing the elegant and pretentious Fisk's behavior. In addition to Nast's cartoon, it printed a 27-verse satire called "The Flight of Fisk" in the same August 5, 1871 issue (which is printed in its entirety on the pages following the cartoon.)

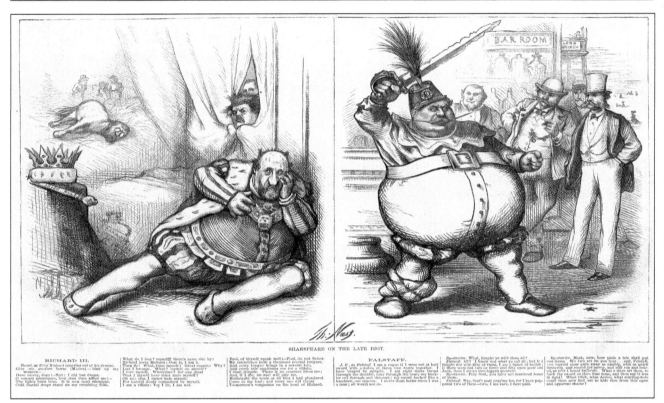

SHAKSPEARE ON THE LATE RIOT.

Also in the *Harper's Weekly* issue of August 5, (below right) Nast followed up "Something That Will Not Blow Over" with "Now We Go Up, Up and Now We Go Down, Down." The sub-title "Every grog-shop is taking down Governor Hoffman's portrait and hanging up Hall's" is self-explanatory. Hall had denied the permit for the Orange Day parade, but the governor, in consultation with Hall and Tweed, reversed the decision.

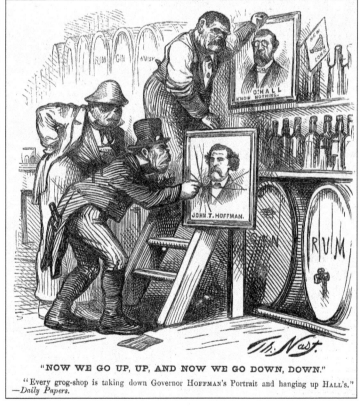

"NOW WE GO UP, UP, AND NOW WE GO DOWN, DOWN."

"Every grog-shop is taking down Governor HOFFMAN's Portrait and hanging up HALL's."
—*Daily Papers.*

THE FLIGHT OF FISK

Jim Fisk arose from dreams of wrath,
In purple-dyed sublimity,
And took his usual morning bath
With soap and equanimity.

Then, girding him for cruel war,
He buckled round his puny form
His bright, expensive cimetar,
And donned his first-class-uniform.

He was to lead the Ninth without
Or horse or light artillery,
And Mayor Hall had called him out
For "qualities ancillary."

But as the Ninth moved forward, then
He did not lead the column, for
He'd been compelled to leave his men—
That's what they looked so solemn for.

'Twas not another Erie vote,
Appointment of a lover, nor—
He'd gone to stop his Jersey boat
By order of the Governor.

But hearing now through rolling drums
Their voice, he joins them speedily,
Reflecting deeply as he comes
Upon the Riot Tweed-ily.

No sabre de mon pére he wore,
No coat, which was improperer;
Thermometer at 94—
He'd left them at the Opera.

No matter now, the line was dressed
Just opposite the Armory,
While close upon the soldiers pressed
Of rioter a "swarmery."

These bore a scowling aspect, which
No London rough or navvy knew;
And now Fisk saw three thousand *sich*
Come rushing down the avenue.

A moment, and the row broke out,
The rumpus and the rioting,
Sticks, bricks, and bullets flew about,
All nervous folk disquieting.

Without his hat, without his sword,
He rushed into the thick of it,
Till, in a moment, he was floored,
And very, very sick of it.

His comrades coming to his aid,
And finding him quite quakery,
His manly person straight conveyed
To a convenient bakery.

But such determined strength of mind,
Such resolution, still, is his,
Though crippled, he ne'er looked behind—
His case was like Achilles's.

And taking his foot, re ran—
What stanch, unyielding will he had—
More rapidly than any man
That's mentioned in the Iliad.

His comrades' voices rent the air—
"For ankle smashed what speed it is!
"They shouted, "Ce n'est la guerre,
Mais c'est superbe, indeed it is!"

Oh, where was then his coach-and-four?
Why should he not have sent for it?
He saw instead an open door,
And instantly he went for it.

On through the hall into the yard
He sped with strange temerity;
But here a fence his progress barred,
And checked his high celerity.

An empty barrel stood at had
(There seems no kind of doubt of it),
With which our hero quickly planned
A way of getting out of it.

For still resolved to hurry hence,
He with one hand the barrel held,
And leaping on it, jumped the fence
In manner quite unparalleled.

Fence after fence, yet unappalled,
He leaped them rather quieter,
And through a basement window crawled
To come upon a rioter.

A dressing he received from Pat,
But this was not inimical—
Old coat, old pantaloons, old hat,
Which made him pantomimical.

A New Departure now he ruled—
How blest to make a ride of it;
A passing cab contained Jay Gould!
And so he got inside of it.

Thence to the Hoffman House they drove;
But as the mob still harried him,
To Sandy Hook our downy cove
A steamer quickly carried him.

At last, supported by his friend,
His wits beclouded, waxy, dense,
Long Branch he reached, the happy end
Of all his morning accidents.

And now 'twill be the final sum
Of all incomprehensibles,
If Fighting Fisk should not become
Field-Marshall of the Fencibles.

Who struck the blow that laid Fisk low
Remains a hidden mystery;
His name, bedad, a Mac or O,
Will ne'er be writ in history.

But happily this thing is plain:
To keep whatever pledge he meant,
He did not seek to strike the Braine
Of that intrepid regiment.

County Auditor James Watson, who reported directly to Comptroller Richard Connolly, was in charge of actually paying the vouchers for every expense item. The vouchers were approved for payment by a signature from Connolly and/or Mayor Oakey Hall or even Boss Tweed himself.

Watson had served time for debt fraud in the Ludlow Street jail in the 1850's, the same jail in which Tweed was later imprisoned and died. After his release, he worked as a collector under three different sheriffs; a sheriff could keep all the fees he collected in lieu of salary. In 1863 Watson was appointed County Auditor at a salary of $1,500 a year.

Watson lived well but relatively modestly compared to almost all the other payoff participants. However, he splurged on fast horses as an active hobby. A sleighing accident on January 24, 1871 left Watson critically injured by a collision with a runaway horse, and his death three days later led to the Ring's downfall. Tweed and others kept a vigil at Watson's home to prevent the dying man from disclosing any compromising information. Tweed, Sweeny, Hall and Connolly all served as pall bearers.

Previously, in May 1869, the New York State Legislature had approved a Tammany plan for widening and straightening Broadway from 34th Street to 59th Street. It was a massive scheme for graft in which James Watson was closely involved.

Less than a month after Watson expired, a Nast cartoon in the March 4, 1871 issue of *Harper's Weekly* (published February 22), entitled "Gross Irregularity Not 'Fraudulent,'" shows "Sweed" and "Tweeny" as architects struggling grimly to solve a design problem. The Boss (whose hair appears as devil's horns for the first time) laments, "To make this *look straight* is the hardest job I ever had. What made Watson go sleigh-riding?" In the background (right), Mayor Hall dutifully sweeps away the dirt from the discarded public works project. On the wall (left) hangs a portrait of Governor Hoffman labeled "Our Next President."

"GROSS IRREGULARITY NOT 'FRAUDULENT.'"

Boss Sweed. "To make this *look straight* is the hardest job I ever had. What made Watson go sleigh-riding?"

To the left of Hoffman's picture is a square above the disclaimer, "Not Used In This Office," above "S.T.A." (Sweeny Tweed Architects). Nast, of course, is punning by contrasting the crooked roadway with the square.

Seven months later, in the *Harper's Weekly* issue of September 30, Nast came up with a hangman's noose and the gallows as "The Only Way to Get Our Tammany Rulers on the Square." That cartoon came in the wake of the *Times* disclosures and the blatant theft of some of the evidence relating to them. (See page 137.)

THE ONLY WAY TO GET OUR TAMMANY RULERS ON THE SQUARE.

After the Tweed Charter was approved by the well-bribed New York State Legislature in April 1870, Boss Tweed, Comptroller Richard Connolly and Mayor Oakey Hall established themselves as a Board of Audit to approve and pay all liabilities against the County or City (effectively the same entity) of New York. They set up a complex system of vouchers, authorizations and checks that, taken individually, looked to be perfectly normal.

Some of the money for these expenses came from tax revenues but a significant share also was raised from the sale of bonds. "Slippery Dick" Connolly issued enough bonds to double New York's debt from $36 million to more than $73 million between January 1869 and January 1871.

In addition to County Auditor James Watson, the other key bagman was Elbert A. Woodward, who was chief clerk to the Board of Supervisors at a salary of $1,500 a year. He primarily functioned as Tweed's assistant and expeditor of fraudulent payments for the Ring. Unlike Watson who had served time in jail, Woodward started as a sort of errand boy for the Board, receiving tips in lieu of a salary.

Beginning in May 1870, Watson and Woodward rounded up 190 old bills going back up to two years, which had not been paid. The majority of them were for work on the new County Courthouse, a 120,000 square foot building which had recently opened on Chambers Street. (Today it houses the New York City Board of Education.)

These bills were marked up to total $6.3 million. Most of it ended up in one of three bank accounts belonging to Woodward, furniture-maker James Ingersoll, or plasterer Andrew Garvey. Many of the other recipients apparently signed their checks over to Woodward, who deposited them in his own bank account. In some cases, Woodward probably forged their endorsements.

Woodward, Watson, Ingersoll, Garvey and a few other contractors like plumber John Keyser and chair-maker George Miller then paid off Tweed, Connolly, Sweeny (always through his brother James) and Hall, after keeping what they were owed for goods, services and/or their share of the graft proceeds. Tweed's share was 25%, Connolly's 20%, and Sweeny's 10%. Watson and Woodward participated to a lesser extent; Hall probably did too, although more indirectly.

After May 1870, every contractor who submitted a bill to the City or County was instructed to increase the amount—at first by 55%, later by 60%, and finally by 65%. Watson then paid the full amount to Ingersoll, Garvey, Miller or another cooperating contractor, who kept their allotted amounts and kicked back the difference in cash or by bank deposit as directed.

In the issue of September 2, 1871 (available August 23), and subsequent to the *Times* disclosures of the Ring's actual accounts a month earlier, *Harper's Weekly* devoted two pages to sketches of "Summer Palaces of the Ring" by artist Theodore R. Davis. The massive Connecticut estates of Boss Tweed in Greenwich and Woodward, Ingersoll, Garvey and Keyser in Norwalk are pictured, as well as described in accompanying text. (See pages 124-125.)

The *Times* reported the contractors' incomes for 1869 and 1870:

James Ingersoll for furniture and carpets	$5,663,647
Andrew Garvey for plastering and repairs	$2,870,464
John Keyser for plumbing and repairs	$1,231,818

In the same issue, Thomas Nast drew Tweed's Greenwich home, using the Davis sketch as his inspiration, as part of a cartoon called "The Tammany Lords and Their Constituents." Tweed, Connolly, Sweeny and Hall are all raising a toast to "the Rich Growing Richer."

THE BED OF ROSES.

"THE RICH GROWING RICHER, THE POOR GROWING POORER."

"—WE DRINK TO OUR CONSTITUENTS. MAY THEY LIVE LONG, SO THAT WE MAY PROSPER."

HOME OF "THE BOSS," GREENWICH, CONNECTICUT.

J. H. KEYSER.   E. A. WOODWARD.   J. H. INGERSOLL.

E. A. WOODWARD, NORWALK, CONNECTICUT.

J. H. INGE

SUMMER PALACES OF THE TAMM

AMERICUS CLUB HOUSE, GREENWICH, CONNECTICUT.

A. J. GARVEY.

GARVEY'S STABLE.

CONNECTICUT.

Page 818 AND CARTOON ON PAGE 812.]

J. H. KEYSER, NORWALK, CONNECTICUT.

Jimmy O'Brien, at 30 a year younger than Thomas Nast in 1871, was an ambitious Irish-born friend and associate of Boss Tweed, who rebelled against him. First, he founded Young Democracy, an alternative political party which was crushed in March 1870 (see pages 82-83). Elected Sheriff of New York County in 1867 with Tweed's backing, he became angry when Tweed refused to pay him $350,000 for unjustified expense vouchers.

In January 1870, O'Brien obtained a job in Comptroller Richard Connolly's finance department for William Copeland, an acquaintance of his who needed a favor. Copeland observed the fraudulent bookkeeping going on and, with O'Brien's encouragement, secretly made copies of incriminating payment records. He brought them to O'Brien in late 1870.

In January 1871, O'Brien, who no longer was Sheriff, tried to use Copeland's transcript of the Ring's ledgers to blackmail the Ring into paying his $350,000 claim. Reportedly, Tweed and Connolly wanted to do so, but Sweeny initially opposed giving into extortion because he despised O'Brien and believed there would be more such attempts in the future. Ultimately, County Auditor James Watson was designated by the Ring leaders to negotiate with O'Brien, but Watson died in his sleighing accident before that could happen. In March 1871, Copeland was fired for "political reasons," as he described his exit; probably, Connolly came to believe that he was the leaker who provided O'Brien with his ammunition.

After Watson's untimely death on January 27, 1871, Connolly promoted bookkeeper Stephen Lynes to take over Watson's secret ledgers and fraudulent payment responsibilities. To replace Lynes, he hired a bookkeeper named Matthew O'Rourke. O'Rourke had been a newspaper reporter of military affairs and was familiar with military expense accounts.

O'Rourke quickly spotted extraordinary irregularities in rents, repairs, carpentry and furniture in "Armories and Drill-room" accounts. Huge sums were paid to Ingersoll & Co., or endorsed to Ingersoll & Co. by contractors like George S. Miller, or paid to Andrew J. Garvey.

O'Rourke copied some of the fraudulent entries before he quit his job in disgust on May 19. In early July, he turned them over to George Jones of the *Times*, and was promptly hired by Jones to work with Times reporter John Foord and Editor Louis Jennings to incorporate them into a news story published on July 8, 1871.

"More Ring Villainy—Gigantic Frauds in the Rental of Armories. Exhorbitant Prices Given for Regimental Headquarters—Stable-Lofts at a Premium
— Thousands of Dollars paid for Bare Walls and Unoccupied Rooms—Over Eight Per Cent of the Money Stolen."

This was the first disclosure about the Ring's finances with actual proof of its fraudulent activities, although it referred only to armory expenditures, not the new courthouse. Under "Armories and Drill Rooms" were entries for non-existent repairs and rents in excess of $500,000.

All the money was paid or endorsed to Ingersoll & Co. Furniture-maker James H. Ingersoll was a close friend and business associate of Tweed, who fronted for the Ring. Nast knew Ingersoll too because both men were members of the Seventh Regiment. In fact, it almost certainly was Ingersoll who, in early 1871, offered Nast as much as $500,000 ($10 million in today's dollars) to go to Europe until after the forthcoming November election took place.

NEW-YORK, SATURDAY, JULY 22, 1871.

THE SECRET ACCOUNTS.

Proofs of Undoubted Frauds Brought to Light.

Warrants Signed by Hall and Connolly Under False Pretenses.

THE ACCOUNT OF INGERSOLL & CO.

The following accounts, copied with scrupulous fidelity from Controller CONNOLLY's books, require little explanation. They purport to show the amount paid during 1869 and 1870, for repairs and furniture for the New Court-house. It will be seen that the warrants are drawn in different names, but they were all indorsed to "INGERSOLL & CO."—otherwise, J. H. INGERSOLL, the agent of the Ring. Each warrant was signed by Controller CONNOLLY and Mayor HALL. What amount of money was actually paid to the persons in whose favor the warrants were nominally drawn, we have no means of knowing. On the face of these accounts, however, it is clear that the bulk of the money somehow or other got back to the Ring, or each warrant would not have been indorsed over to its agent.

We undertake to prove whenever we are afforded the opportunity, that the following account is copied literally from the Controller's books, and forms a part of the documents to which the public is entitled to have access.

The dates given for the work done are obviously fraudulent. For example: On July 2, 1869, a warrant was drawn for furniture supplied for County Courts and offices, from Oct. 18 to Nov. 23, 1868, for $42,560 64. On July 16—fourteen days afterward—another warrant was drawn for $94,058 13 for furniture supplied to the same offices from Nov. 7 to Dec. 31. That is to say, the bill was fully paid by the *first* of these two warrants down to Nov. 23. And yet a fortnight afterward another warrant was drawn paying the bill over again from Nov. 7. It is obvious that the fictitious dates were not remembered by the City authorities when these warrants were drawn. Many similar cases will be observed in the figures given below.

It will be seen that on one day furniture is supposed to have been supplied to the amount of $129,469 48—at least a warrant for that sum was signed by HALL and CONNOLLY in favor of C. D. BOLLAR & Co., and indorsed by INGERSOLL & Co.

1869.   **INGERSOLL & CO.**   **1869.**

Date of Warrant.	Character of Work.	Date on Which Work was Supposed to be Done.	Amount Drawn.
July 2.	Paid for Furniture in County Courts and Offices from Oct. 18 to Nov. 23, 1868		$42,560 64
July 16.	Paid for Furniture in County Offices from Nov. 7 to Dec. 31, 1868		94,038 13
Aug. 4.	Paid for Furniture in County Offices July 19, 1868		53,206 75
Sept. 7.	Paid for Furniture in County Offices Aug. 30, 1868		60,334 71
Sept. 8.	Paid for Furniture in County Courts and Offices Sept. 22, 1868		42,901 47
Oct. 22.	Paid for Iron Railing, Cases, Stairs, &c., Check in name of M. W. Davis, indorsed by Ingersoll & Co., July 29, '68.		63,201 16
Oct. 23.	Paid for Carpets, &c., in Co. Courts and Offices, Check in name of J. A. Smith, indorsed by Ingersoll & Co., Aug. 10, '68.		27,154 55
Oct. 28.	Paid for Furniture in County Courts and Offices Dec. 28, 1868		28,032 11
Nov. 5.	Paid for Carpets, &c., in Co. Courts and Offices, Check in name of J. A. Smith, indorsed by Ingersoll & Co., April 6, '68.		36,422 10
Nov. 17.	Paid for Carpets, &c., in Co. Courts and Offices, Check in name of J. A. Smith, indorsed by Ingersoll & Co., Jan. 20, '68.		32,617 12
Nov. 16.	Paid for Carpets, &c., in Co. Courts and Offices, Check in name of J. A. Smith, indorsed by Ingersoll & Co., July 29, '68.		23,185 90
Nov. 19.	Paid for Furniture, &c., in County Courts and Offices, Oct. 18, 1868		10,494 61
Nov. 24.	Paid for Furniture, &c., in Co. Courts and Offices, Check in name of C.D.Bollar & Co., in'd by Ingersoll & Co., Aug.17,'68.		33,826 81
Dec. 3.	Paid for Furniture, &c., in Co. Courts and Offices, Check in name of C.D.Bollar & Co., in'd. by Ingersoll & Co., Nov. 9,'68.		32,632 38
June 8.	Paid for Furniture, &c., in Co. Courts and Offices, Check in name of C. D.Bollar & Co., in'd. by Ingersoll & Co., May 8, '69.		129,469 48
June 15.	Paid for Carpets, &c., in New Court-House, Check in name of J. A. Smith, indorsed by Ingersoll & Co., April 16, 1869.		73,605 97
June 8.	Paid for Furniture, &c., in New Court-House to April 8, 1869.		90,923 40
Dec. 16.	Paid for Furniture, &c., in County Court-rooms and Offices, April 26, 1868.		54,343 57
Jan. 11.	Paid for Furniture in Armories and Drill-rooms, Nov. 12, 1868.		38,906 71
Jan. 19.	Paid for Furniture in same, Dec. 3 and 22, 1868.		31,801 95
Feb. 27.	Paid for Furniture in same from Jan. 13, 1869, to Feb. 9, 1869.		55,791 56
April 26.	Paid for Furniture in same, March 11, 9186.		39,544 68
June 5.	Paid for Furniture in same, Nov. 17, 1868.		26,325 26
Sept. 20.	Paid for Furniture in same, May 26, 1869.		30,116 26

• • •

1870.   **INGERSOLL & CO.**   **1870.**

June 24.	Paid for Cabinet-work in Court-house, Jan. 9, 1870.	$49,083 30
June 27.	Paid for Cabinet-work in County Buildings and Offices, March 29, 1870.	85,163 29
June 30.	Paid for Cabinet-work in County Court-house, April 2, 1870.	59,932 01
Aug. 1.	Paid for Cabinet-work in County Court-house, Oct. 8, 1869.	69,537 68
Aug. 9.	Paid for Cabinet-work in Armories and Drill-rooms, April 16, 1870.	77,949 58
Mar. 26.	Paid for Repairs in Armories and Drill-rooms, Aug. 26, 1869.	49,742 45
Mar. 31.	Paid for Repairs in Armories and Drill-rooms, Oct. 20, 1869.	38,818 84
April 16.	Paid for Fitting up Armories and Drill-rooms, Oct. 2, 1869.	22,612 10
	Grand Total	$5,663,646 83

Editor's Note: The lists above are excerpted from a page of *The New-York Times*.

In October 1870, the *New-York Times* attacked "Slippery Dick" Connolly, the Comptroller (Chief Financial Officer) of the Ring, because he failed to issue his annual financial statement in September as the law required him to do. The *Times* accused him of manipulation and dishonesty, but as yet it had no proof.

Connolly responded by appointing his own six-man Committee of Investigation, headed by three prestigious millionaire businessmen—John Jacob Astor III, Moses Taylor and Marshall O. Roberts. Just before Election Day 1870, this committee issued its report, which found the city's finances sound and cleared Tweed and Connolly of any irregularities.

Eight months later, after the *Times* received proof of the fraud and published its first disclosure on July 8, 1871, Nast followed with a "Three Blind Mice! See How They Run!" cartoon in the July 22 issue, available on July 12, four days after the *Times* story. The *Times'* "Sharp Editorials" knife cut off the tails of the "White-Washing Committee," each of whose tails says "Prestige." The tail-less committee members shown left to right, are Astor, Taylor and Roberts.

A year later—after the Ring's Election Day defeat in November 1871—Marshall Roberts issued "An Apology to the Public (after the Play)"—as Nast put it in his December 2, 1871 cartoon. The curtain has come down on the actors with their feet stretching out, as Stage Manager Roberts bows to the audience, while holding his November 5, 1870 erroneous clearance report. The two sets of feet nearest to Roberts represent Astor and Taylor, while those on the far left probably are Connolly's.

THREE BLIND MICE! SEE HOW THEY RUN!
THE *Times* CUT OFF THEIR TAILS WITH A CARVING-KNIFE.

AN APOLOGY TO THE PUBLIC (after the Play).

Mr. MARSHALL O. ROBERTS. "The certificate was used as a cover and a shield by those who were robbing the city, and it has given me deep regret that the paper which I signed could have been thus used. For one, I take much blame upon myself for having so readily 'fallen into the trap,' and no one can treat the mistake with severer condemnation than I do, or more deeply regret its consequences."

Meanwhile, on the other disclosure front, Jimmy O'Brien took his transcript to at least one newspaper, Charles Dana's *Sun*, where it was rejected. He also reportedly flirted with the *Times*, possibly in June 1871 at a meeting in Saratoga with Publisher George Jones and New York State Democratic Party Chairman Samuel J. Tilden.

Learning about O'Rourke's disclosure to the *Times* may have forced O'Brien's hand. Somewhere around July 8, O'Brien appeared in George Jones' office and turned Copeland's transcript over to him unconditionally and without compensation. Jones then had Matthew O'Rourke and reporter John Foord work with Editor Louis Jennings to flesh out Copeland's ledgers.

On the eve of the most sensational disclosures, including evidence that $5,000,000 had passed through the hands of James H. Ingersoll to decorate and furnish the new courthouse, *Times* editor Louis J. Jennings fired a warning shot across Mayor Oakey Hall's bow, as if to let him know what would be coming. On Thursday, July 20, the lead editorial, entitled "Hall and His Friend," stated bluntly that the newspaper would prove, from Comptroller Connolly's own books, that the Tammany Ring, especially Connolly and Hall, were swindlers and thieves. Editor Jennings reminded readers that all the warrants (i.e., written authorizations of payments) had been signed by Connolly and Hall, "who must therefore be privy to the roguery which is going on." Ingersoll cashed the warrants and, according to the *Times*, distributed their respective shares to Tweed, Sweeny, Connolly, and Hall. "The last two as signers of the warrants are the chief thieves."

On Saturday, July 22, 1871, the new revelations were splashed across the front page of the *New-York Times* under a two-column quadruple heading: "The Secret Accounts / Proof of Undoubted Frauds Brought to Light / Warrants Signed by Hall and Connolly Under False Pre-tenses / The Account of Ingersoll & Co." On Monday, July 24, "The Secret Accounts" featured "The Account of Andrew J. Garvey."

Over the next few weeks, the *Times* published, in excruciating, eye-catching detail, the "Secret Accounts" of the Tammany Ring's vouchers for millions of dollars plundered from the New York Treasury over the preceding three years. The estimated sum stolen was set at $6 million, but it probably was between $30 and $200 million.

In reaction, Mayor Hall accused the *Times*, as its editor predicted, of being on a crusade of political and personal vengeance under the guise of public spiritedness. In fact, there was no hard evidence that Hall did receive any kickbacks, and, unlike Tweed and other Tammany associates, the mayor had continued to live quite modestly. Still, Hall and Connolly had signed warrants for suspiciously outrageous amounts made out to and endorsed over to "Ingersoll & Co."

Over the ensuing months, the mayor continued to stonewall, defending his honor against imputations of criminal behavior. In the meantime, coordination of an effective community-wide movement against the Tammany Ring had to wait until early September when influential citizens returned to the city from their vacation residences in the country.

In the intervening period, now that the specific facts and faces had been publicly revealed, Thomas Nast produced some of his most remarkable and enduring work, focusing popular opinion at least as vividly as the *Times* was able to do. Since Nast had sympathetic friends at the *Times*, he could well have had advance word of the forthcoming exposure.

By common consent, two of the most effective cartoons in the history of the medium, drawn on a single block of wood now preserved at the Library of Congress, commenced the final three months of Nast's crusade in *Harper's Weekly* to overthrow the Tweed regime: "Two Great Questions: 'Who Is Ingersoll's Co.?' [and] 'Who Stole the People's Money?'" They appeared immediately after the editorial pages in the August 19, 1871 issue, published on August 9.

In the top cartoon, Horace Greeley (right), editor of the *New-York Tribune*, has been studying the *Times'* detailed "Secret Accounts/Frauds of the Tammany Ring" as he confronts contractor James H. Ingersoll, the principal Tweed Ring bagman through whose hands much of the missing public money passed. The caricature insinuates the editor's embarrassment and irritation at having been scooped by his competitor. Tilting his glasses upward to command a sharper view, Greeley rephrases the question he addressed to Mayor Hall in a *Tribune* editorial of July 25: "Who is his [Ingersoll's] 'CO'?"—i.e., with whom does he work?

In response, Ingersoll introduces the editor to a gargantuan-sized Tweed, who bows courteously, and the Boss's band of furtive, apprehensive accomplices cowering beneath and behind him. Mayor Hall, who was struggling to evade the taint of criminality, peeps owlishly from beneath Tweed's broad-brimmed hat. Opposite Hall on the ground at the right is Nathaniel Sands, Tammany Republican and longtime secretary of the reformist Citizens' Association. Sands was a sort of double agent, also paid by Tweed as a tax commissioner and member of the board of education. He had been described previously in the *Times* (October 16, 1870) as "the Mr. Facing-Both-Ways of the day." On the left, Peter Sweeny grasps Tweed's coat, while Richard Connolly stands behind Sweeny.

In the bottom cartoon, "Who Stole the People's Money?," Tweed and his cohorts are positioned appropriately in a ring (circle), with each member denying blame by pointing an incriminating finger at the next man. The four leaders of the Tammany Ring are in front (left-right): Tweed, Sweeny, Connolly, and Hall. Tweed is pointing at Ingersoll, whose hatband reads "Chairs," in reference to the chairs purchased at inflated prices for the National Guard Armory. The unanimous refusal to take personal responsibility is emphasized by the nondescript figure behind Hall who is labeled "Tom, Dick & Harry."

Nast's inspiration for this cartoon came from a headline on the July 28 editorial page of Greeley's *Tribune*, which read: "Widening The Circle—Fixing The Responsibility." "Who Stole the People's Money?" became a classic visual metaphor for public figures "passing the buck," and is among the most reproduced, mimicked, and well known of all American editorial cartoons.

In early August 1871, the Tweed Ring had tried to bribe Nast—for an estimated amount up to $500,000—into taking a European vacation, but the artist resolutely refused. The contact probably was Jim Ingersoll, the focus of the top cartoon. Both Nast and Ingersoll were members of the New York National Guard's Seventh Regiment, Company G, and Ingersoll reportedly told the cartoonist, "Tommy, if you will take a trip to Europe for a year, you can have your expenses paid, and a new house will be built ready for your return, without your paying a cent for it."

One of the earliest signs of serious dissension in the inner circle of Tammany Hall came in the August 4 edition of the *Tribune*. An editorial explained that the Tammany Ring was reported to be identical with the Board of Apportionment—Hall, Connolly, Tweed, and Sweeny—and that they were in "absolute control" of city finances. It went on to imply, unmistakably, that from the moment of the *Times'* revelations, Peter Sweeny had declined to have anything to do with city financial matters and with requests from his Tammany associates and, instead, was riding out the storm of anti-Tammany public opinion at his summer home at Lake Mahopac (in Putnam County, just north of Westchester County, New York).

It was further hinted that State Senator Tweed, "the father of the Board," had absented himself from his governmental responsibilities, and was spending his time at his homes in New York City and Greenwich, Connecticut. Reportedly, the Boss was provoked by a two-percent cap on legislating further city taxes, and was also said to be unhappy with the state administration of Governor Hoffman, who had become especially unpopular after the Orange Riot in July. A *Tribune* editorial writer speculated that the reformers might take advantage of the apparent discord to entice one of the four Tammany principals to aid in the battle against the rest. (This remarkable prediction became solid fact a little more than five weeks later, following the discreet intervention of Samuel J. Tilden, chairman of the New York State Democratic Party.)

The *New-York Times* blasted away on suspected Tammany fault lines. On August 17, 1871, a lengthy editorial explained, "Why Connolly Was Kept In Office, and How It Was Done." The office of comptroller was described as "the great prize of the 'Ring.'" The editorial writer explained that although the "Tweed Charter" of April 1870, in order to silence opponents, had originally allowed **election** of a comptroller, Sweeny secretly removed the clause and saw to it that the mayor (Hall) had exclusive authority to **appoint** the comptroller for an iron-clad term of four years and eight months, lasting from late April 1870 to January 1, 1875. This was to insure that neither by accident nor design would any interloper be able to lay hands on Connolly's extraordinary and incriminating account books. The comptroller himself was perpetually terrified of discovery and retribution.

The President of the United States and His Cabinet, for 1872. (?)

133

The immediate inspiration for Nast's next major cartoon may have been planted by an earlier *New-York Times* editorial of August 5, 1871, entitled, "Mr. Connolly as Secretary of the Treasury." Despite its title, the editorial did not mention Connolly, but more broadly discussed Tweed's Independence Day oration in which he proposed, "to wrest if possible the National Government from those who now, in our opinion, are betraying it." *Times* editor Louis J. Jennings reacted in horror to the notion that the spiraling taxation and debt of the New York City government, in addition to its egregious corruption, might be transplanted to the federal government. Instead of the White House, he suggested the appropriate place for the Tammany Ring was the Big House. Nast probably knew about the *Times* editorial before it appeared in order to make a relatively short production deadline of 3-5 days.

After taking a brief vacation and drawing a couple of minor cartoons, Nast came back strong against the Ring in the August 26 issue of *Harper's Weekly*, available August 16, with "The President of the United States and His Cabinet, for 1872.(?)" The satirical bite of the scenario was based on Mayor Hall's reported buoyant claims that all of Tammany's troubles were going to "blow over" and that 1872 would see the Ring operating in Washington, D.C. The theme was grounded in the longstanding rumors that Tammany Hall planned to run Governor John T. Hoffman of New York as the Democratic presidential nominee against the incumbent Republican chief executive, Ulysses S. Grant.

Here, the gathering of the Tammany inner circle centers on a formal portrait of Boss Tweed, who casts as his shadow the image of his protégé, "President" Hoffman. Tweed's sardonic grin is explained by the plan for "Political Economy" in his hand, and the "spoils" that it promises. The shadow Hoffman grips a scroll labeled "Erie Bill," referring to a tangle of discreditable favors Tammany Hall pushed through the state legislature (with extensive bribery) in 1868-1869 for Jim Fisk's and Jay Gould's Erie Railroad. Overhead, the framed figure of George Washington, the nation's first president, has lowered his head and covered his eyes in shame. The image of Tweed and Hoffman is a parody of an earlier cartoon of Nast's, "Thrown Completely into the Shade" (March 18, 1871), showing Kaiser Wilhelm, recently crowned emperor of the newly united Germany, casting a shadow upon a painting of Napoleon I.

Beneath the central tableau, the threatened perils of a Hoffman presidency are reinforced by an emblem combining the head of the Tammany Tiger with the "Steal" Ring. On its sides stands an Irish-Catholic couple; the woman holds a liquor bottle atop her pike, as the man smokes a cigar and wears Indian feathers, reflecting his allegiance to the Tammany leaders known as "sachems"—i.e., Indian chiefs. In mimicry of the symbol of an American Eagle with an "E Pluribus Unum" banner in its beak, overhead is a vulture biting a banner reading "What Are You Going to Do About It?"

The Tammany presidential cabinet commences at the upper left with its oldest member, Comptroller Richard B. Connolly, who gestures toward the "U.S. Treasury" and makes the knowing assessment, "There's Money In It." Proceeding clockwise at the top is "The Secretary of State (and Church)" Peter B. Sweeny, known as "Brains," and Mayor Oakey Hall as Attorney General, posing jauntily with feather duster, broom, bucket, and shoeshine block in front of his notice: "All Kinds of Dirty Work Done Here, and Things Made as Clear as Mud." Next, is Secretary of War James Ingersoll, the Tammany operative through whom much of the money passed, including inflated payments for the National Guard armory referenced in the scene; following him is Andrew J. Garvey, a master craftsman who accepted extraordinary kickbacks for his skilled service, appearing as secretary of the interior. Completing the cabinet is Postmaster General Thomas Fields, an alderman, parks commissioner, and state legislator; and financier Jim Fisk as the Secretary of the Navy, based on his ownership of transatlantic steamship lines and a Hudson River ferry. In putting together this rogues' gallery, Nast created a kind of "class picture" of the Tammany Ring.

The President of the United States and His Cabinet, for 1872. (?)

135

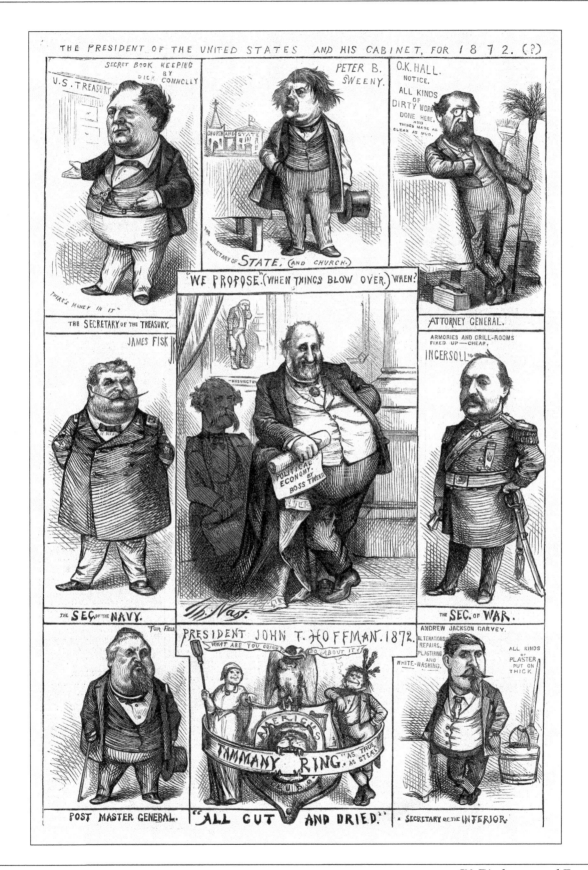

The proposed meeting of influential citizens was finally set in mid-August for the evening of Monday, September 4, 1871, at Cooper Union. Before and after the citizens' meeting at Cooper Union, tensions were heightened by serious consideration of the possible need for decisive vigilante action. The weekly *Nation* of August 31 remarked:

> "...although no one supposes the formation of a vigilance committee in New York would mean anything short of civil war, nevertheless we believe a good many sober and sensible men begin to recognize the possibility of its becoming expedient to exercise against the Ring the right of revolution, trying to inflict on its leading members the only penalty which has any terrors for them. We presume it is strictly correct to say that the one consequence of thieving which Hall, Tweed, and Connolly would now dread is a violent death. Public scorn, or even the penitentiary has little terror for them. This may sound like wild talk to some of our readers in the country, but we do not think it will to most New York observers. We do not know how the affair may end, but we do know that if [Judge] Barnard, Hall, Tweed, and Connolly close their careers in peace, and ease, and affluence, it will be a terrible blow to political and private morality."

On the morning of September 4, a page-one story in the *Times* gave a new partial accounting of questionable New York County expenditures totaling over $13,400,000, mostly for the notorious courthouse. An editorial promoted attendance at that night's meeting, called again for the "rule of four" to be swept away, and encouraged that "men of good character [be] ...placed at the head of the City government." The commentary included a threat that if the meeting were to be disturbed by Tammany thugs, then "the public will exact a swift and terrible vengeance."

The next day's *Times* reported on the citizens' meeting ("The People's Voice ... An Earnest Movement Made Against the Ring..." read the headline), which commenced with William Havemeyer, a former mayor, summarizing Tammany Ring abuses. He concluded his speech thunderously with the refrain Nast had popularized: "WHAT ARE YOU GOING TO DO ABOUT IT?" The next speaker, Judge James Emott, rephrased the question, to which an individual in the audience shouted, "Hang them," to "immense applause."

A few minutes later, lawyer and future ambassador to Great Britain, Joseph H. Choate, advanced dramatically to the front of the stage with a scroll of twelve strongly-worded resolutions, held it towards the audience and declared "This is what we are going to do about it!" The crowd responded enthusiastically for several minutes, and then Choate proceeded to read. He concluded by thanking the "public newspapers," particularly the *Times* for "its fearless and searching investigation and exposure of the public accounts and of the conduct of the present [city] officers," and then proposed that Havemeyer immediately appoint a "Committee of Seventy" to take the anti-Tammany Ring effort to the next level. These measures, endorsed by acclamation, were immediately announced. The Committee of Seventy subsequently played a leading role in the investigation and toppling of the Tweed Ring.

Nast's response to the *Nation's* editorial and the citizens' meeting, "The Only Thing They Respect or Fear," appeared on the cover of the October 21, 1871 issue of *Harper's Weekly*, but obviously was finished earlier. It depicts the Tammany Ring foursome reacting in different ways to the threatened possibility of death by gallows: Tweed bows in acceptance of his fate, Sweeny and Hall cringe in fear, while Connolly's figure is hidden, reflecting his diminished role since his prior removal as comptroller. The caption repeated the *Nation's* argument "that the one consequence of thieving which Hall, Tweed, and Connolly would now dread is a violent death." For the caption, Nast deleted the names in the original text since he featured Sweeny prominently but obscured Connolly.

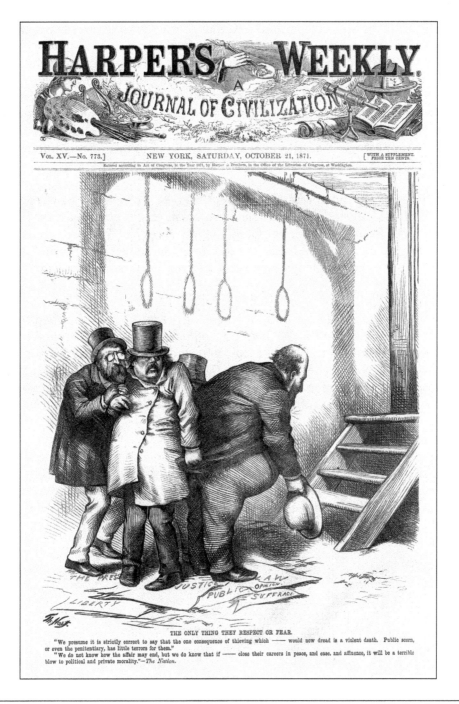

Given the fast-moving developments, Nast doubtless was handicapped and challenged by his relatively short lead-time; customarily, he had at least two weeks from conception to publication for the larger cartoons. One of his classics, "A Group of Vultures Waiting for the Storm to 'Blow Over'—'Let Us Prey,'" from the September 23, 1871 issue of *Harper's Weekly*, available Wednesday, September 13, must have been completed just prior to the long-anticipated anti-Tammany Ring protest meeting of September 4. By the time it appeared, on Wednesday, September 13, the Tammany Ring was in the midst of a crisis of dissolution, court-ordered paralysis, and Tilden's move to oust Connolly, all of which made Nast's satire particularly prescient and timely.

In the cartoon, a rapacious quartet of Tammany vultures hunkers down to ride out the storm of public disapproval, squatting upon the supine figure of "New York," whose fist is clenched in defiance. Bones in the foreground are labeled "New York City Treasury" and "Law," while the skulls are marked "Suffrage," "Justice," "Liberty," "Tax Payer," and "Rent Payer." Tweed, bleary and engorged, with his huge diamond stickpin stuck in his breast, as well as Connolly and Hall, all stare at the reader. Only Sweeny (left) looks up to see the giant boulder, dislodged by the luminous bolt of lightning, which threatens to destroy them. He raises a wing to protect himself or fly away. The other three appear unaware that the storm is not about to "blow over." A muzzle at Hall's claws, reading "For The Press," alludes to the mayor's attempts to silence or placate journalists. It is a striking vision of the bloodthirsty "gang of four," each with a cruel, dark beak at the tip of his nose.

The cartoonist repeated the phrase "blow over" from Mayor Hall's earlier contention about what would happen to the *Times'* revelations about Tammany Hall corruption. Nast may have picked up the storm and precipice motif from Charles S. Reinhart, a fellow *Harper's Weekly* artist. Reinhart's small back-page cartoon in the August 26 issue (published August 16), "Overtaken by a Storm," shows the Tammany foursome cowering on a mountain ledge as Justice pierces her sword through "Connolly's Monthly Statement."

However, the primary source for these malevolent predators was supplied by a dog-eared page still preserved in Nast's copy of the Rev. J. G. Woods's *Illustrated Natural History*, Vol. II (London, 1862). Nast possessed all three volumes of the work (1860-1863), and used it extensively throughout his career as source material for drawing birds, reptiles, and other fauna and flora. The *Illustrated Natural History* plate, entitled "Group of Vultures," was used by Nast to help establish the wild mountainous setting, the birds, the bones of a rib cage in the foreground, and even the position of a large vulture at the center between the two promontories.

The obvious pun that ends the caption was borrowed from Horace Greeley's offhand reference about carpetbaggers in a speech he delivered on June 12, 1871. Discussing the alleged venality of opportunistic Northerners causing mischief in the post-Civil War South, Greeley declared that the carpetbaggers' "motto is 'Let us pray.' But they always spell the pray with an 'e', and they always obey the apostolic injunction to pray unceasingly." Nast, ever susceptible to the temptation of an outrageous pun, set this one aside for use at the earliest available opportunity.

A GROUP OF VULTURES WAITING FOR THE STORM TO "BLOW OVER."—"LET US PREY."

Judge Barnard's Surprise Injunction

Thanks to Boss Tweed, Judge George G. Barnard sat on the New York Supreme Court (a lower state court), where he had long provided the Tammany Ring with beneficial service. While he may have had a competent legal mind, in his courtroom, Barnard made a mockery of decorum and justice. He sat with his feet on the bench, whittled pine sticks, drank from a brandy bottle, and cracked bawdy jokes, while ruling invariably in favor of the Tweed and Erie Ring interests. Nast drew Barnard as "The Clown in the Judicial Ring" in the issue of April 13, 1872.

THE CLOWN IN THE JUDICIAL RING
To what Base Usage the Bench is put.

One of his first acts as a Supreme Court judge had been to certify Tweed, who had no legal training, as a lawyer. Barnard and other Tammany judges aided the Tweed Ring by pardoning or releasing prisoners who worked for the Democratic political machine, by appointing court officers and commissioners amenable to its will, and by granting or removing, unfairly, injunctions that could severely damage corporations and/or individuals. Besides providing protective legal cover, the Tweed-controlled judges were instrumental in sustaining the Ring's political power by granting citizenship to large numbers of immigrants who padded the machine's voter rolls.

From September 7 through September 15, a series of surprising and consequential rulings by Judge Barnard, removed the legal barriers protecting the Tammany Ring. The Ring might have weathered the storm of public outrage in the autumn of 1871 had Judge Barnard not turned against his political mentor and poker-playing chum, Boss Tweed. On September 7, John A. Foley, an Irish (a factor in his selection to be the plaintiff) wealthy pen manufacturer and member of the Committee of Seventy, initiated a lawsuit against the city. Foley was seeking an injunction to keep city officials within the bounds of the two-percent tax levy and to prohibit the comptroller (then, Connolly) from issuing any bonds for additional funds—in essence, to stem the flow of money to and from the Tammany Ring. Since an individual (Foley) brought the lawsuit, it should have been dismissed.

The case fell within Judge Barnard's jurisdiction. Uncharacteristically, he listened attentively to the arguments, and then stunned nearly everyone by approving Foley's injunction. Over the next week, he issued orders that opened the books of the city treasury, set aside a grant to a city utility, and placed an injunction on city contracts. Afterward, various rumors attempted to explain the judge's actions, including the rumored scenario that Democratic State Chairman Tilden had promised him the gubernatorial nomination. Probably, Barnard simply calculated that it was time to jump ship.

Whatever the reason, his decisions opened the way for effective legal prosecution of the Tammany Ring. They did not, however, enhance his career. In August 1872, Judge Barnard was indicted, convicted and removed from office by the New York State Legislature.

As mentioned previously on page 95, the German vote could tip the balance in New York elections. A major step toward achieving that result occurred when a group of leading New York Germans met in late August at Utica with key members of the Democratic State Committee: Samuel J. Tilden, the chairman; Horatio Seymour, the former governor and 1868 Democratic presidential nominee; and Francis Kernan, a former congressman, future Democratic gubernatorial nominee (1872), and U.S. senator. According to the *New-York Times*, "The visitors were very outspoken and informed the members of the Committee that their people 'would not countenance or support Tweed and his fellows,' adding that unless a decisive stand was taken against Tammany by the State Committee, the German Democrats of New York would go with the rest of their countrymen in America over to the Republican party." On the evening of August 28, a crowded and excited meeting of the German Democratic Union General Committee demanded "an accurate exhibit of the Controller's accounts" and pleaded for the upcoming state convention to back reform in the city government. Similar protests from other German groups continued well into September.

Comptroller Connolly's financial stewardship had been under particular criticism by the influential German-language paper, the Democratic *New-Yorker Staats Zeitung*, which had long supported Tammany Hall. In late August 1871, its editor, Oswald Ottendorfer, published an announcement declaring that as long as the current directors were in place, his paper would no longer toe the Tammany line. Probably unbeknownst to Nast when he was working on the cartoon below, Ottendorfer would deliver one of the major addresses at the anti-Tammany Ring meeting at Cooper Union on September 4. The *Staats Zeitung* editor's strong message that evening—imploring those interested in "a permanent improvement in our city affairs" to put aside partisanship and work together to defeat Ring corruption—lent additional force to Nast's drawing.

On the last regular page of the September 23 *Harper's Weekly*, a Nast cartoon shows the Tammany Ring leaders pitched unceremoniously off the stern of the ship *Germania* by the city's German Democrats, "What the German Democrats Have Done About It." In this tempest on the high seas, the ship flies a large American flag with the Prussian eagle superimposed on its field of "blue" (where the state stars would be) in the upper corner. The artist's watery signature appears at the lower left, while the initials (J. N.) of his nine-year-old daughter, Julia, are concealed beneath the peak of the wave framed by lightning. Visible amidst the waves in the foreground are (clockwise from right) the top hat and spectacles of Hall, the unkempt hair of Sweeny, and the baldpate and hat of Tweed. Connolly, the last to go, is still tumbling terrified in midair.

WHAT THE GERMAN DEMOCRATS HAVE DONE ABOUT IT.

According to a biographer of Boss Tweed (Denis T. Lynch, 1927), in early September 1871, Tweed heeded Sweeny's advice to order James Ingersoll and his associates to destroy all their relevant account books and papers. A more public instance of such evidence tampering occurred on Sunday evening, September 10, three days after Barnard's injunction order and one day after the Committee of Seventy's request to examine city and county accounts. A forced entry into the offices of Comptroller Connolly was made by using a diamond to cut a hole in a glass door while the watchman was away getting something to eat. Thirteen bundles of incriminating payment vouchers were removed from an unharmed steel safe. Their charred remains reportedly were found later in a City Hall attic.

Tuesday afternoon, September 12, Boss Tweed agreed with a *Times* reporter's question that the theft of the payment-vouchers two days before had been "unfortunate," but made himself and his Ring colleagues into the victims: "It can't be looked upon in any other way as most unfortunate for all concerned. It takes away that upon which alone we could rely for our vindication. But I cannot say anything, Sir; my mouth is closed; you see my position." [The *New-York Times*, Wednesday, September 13, 1871.] Mayor Oakey Hall was not available to the press from September 14 through at least September 18, and Sweeny was almost impossible to locate.

Rumors continued to circulate of a divide between Hall and Sweeny on one side and Tweed and Connolly on the other. Matthew Breen, a Tammany insider, later claimed that at a meeting of the four, Hall and Sweeny urged Connolly to resign (a move the Boss feared), but the comptroller replied by reminding his cohorts that their fates were united: "they must sink or swim together." To the dismay of the *New York-Times*, Sweeny was not named, as were the other Tammany principals, in Judge Barnard's final injunction on September 15, even though he had been listed in the temporary injunction of the previous week. This gave rise to speculation that Barnard was cooperating with Sweeny to force Connolly out of office. The next day, September 16, the *Times* reacted to a report that Governor Hoffman was hoping to redeem Sweeny:

"The people demand the overthrow of the whole gang, and the uprooting of the entire system of tyranny and corruption which they have fastened upon the public. They will not be content with the lopping off of two or three of the lower limbs, while the "Brains" of the conspiracy [Sweeny] is left to plot new frauds and organize new "Rings." All or none—let us spare not one of this gang, or we shall have to do all this work over again at no distant day."

On Tuesday morning, September 12, the *Times'* tongue-in-cheek editorial entitled "Heartless Robbery," written within hours after the discovery of the burglary in the comptroller's office, supplied Nast the idea for his cartoon "Too Thin," which appeared eight days later (September 20) on the cover of the postdated September 30 issue of *Harper's Weekly*.

"If the people will not allow their rulers enough money to furnish their offices properly [with safes], [then] they must expect to lose valuable documents. When Hall and Connolly heard that these vouchers had been stolen, they were almost heart-broken... Imagine then, [Connolly's] grief and consternation when he found out that they had been stolen from under his very nose. We should have thought that everybody would have sympathized with him. But instead of that, people burst into a loud laugh when the story got wind, and went about asking each other with a broad grin, 'Have you heard of this robbery in the Controller's office?' Even the City Hall officials, instead of showing any proper feeling, went about saying, in the slang of the hour, that it was 'too thin.'"

Are their hearts made of stone? … [A few paragraphs later, the *Times* predicted yet] another mysterious robbery, and the Controller and the Mayor will stand with their hands on their hearts, and tears pouring down their cheeks, assuring the public that they know nothing about it."

Stealing the vouchers didn't achieve anything except more bad publicity for the Ring. Exact copies of the vouchers were kept at the National Broadway Bank, as Connolly informed Tilden. At the request of acting Comptroller Andrew Green, Tilden and two assistants began a careful examination of the Tammany Ring's accounts, which took about three weeks to complete.

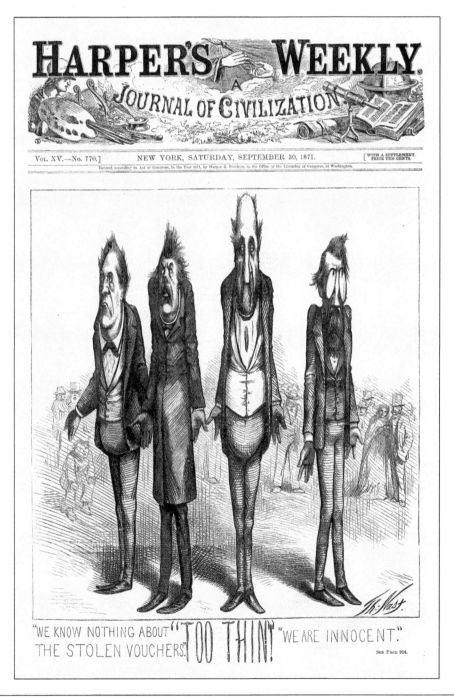

The day after the theft was made public, Mayor Oakey Hall wrote to Comptroller Richard Connolly, his colleague and ally, requesting his resignation. Understandably, Connolly declined to serve as the lone fall guy for all the transgressions of the Tammany Ring. In a panic, he appealed for assistance on September 14 to Samuel J. Tilden, the state chairman of the Democratic Party, using former Mayor William F. Havemeyer as an intermediary.

Since early August, Tilden had been carefully planning the orchestration of a covert plan to secure a Democratic solution to what he clearly felt to be a Democratic Party problem. He deliberately played no part in the mass meeting at Cooper Union on September 4. On Monday, September 11, Tilden sent a letter to 26,000 "citizens" (presumably, registered New York Democrats) with an eye towards the upcoming party convention in Rochester on October 4-5. The message was swiftly leaked to the press:

"The league between corrupt Republicans and corrupt Democrats which was formed during Republican ascendancy was too strong for honest men in 1870. The charter of that year had the votes of nearly all Republicans. I denounced it in a public speech. Whenever the gangrene of corruption has reached the Democratic Party, we must take a knife and cut it out by the roots."

Tilden believed that Sweeny and Hall had parted company with Connolly and Tweed in hopes of establishing themselves as a new "reform" element. Prior to his meeting with Connolly on Friday morning, September 15, the *Times* carried an interview in which Tilden denied that he had any relationship to, or sympathy with, any such selective rebirth of the Ring, and doubted that the forced resignation of the comptroller would satisfy the people: "The medicine is [not] powerful enough for the disease." The following week, Tilden gave an interview to the *Brooklyn Eagle* (September 21):

"I told Mr. Connolly when he first sought an interview with me on last Friday… that he might as well make up his mind that, as a political power, he and all others connected with the transactions which had excited the public indignation, **had ceased to exist**. My opinion is that the fall must carry down the organization which these men control. In other words, the Democratic party of this city and county must be reorganized by an Edict of the Democratic party of the State."

When Connolly turned to him for help on September 15, 1871, Tilden would not commit himself to defending the comptroller from later prosecution; however, the party chairman reviewed the law and determined that Connolly was allowed to appoint his own successor. On Saturday, September 16, on the advice of Tilden and Havemeyer, Connolly named Andrew H. Green as his deputy comptroller. A Democrat of impeccable integrity, as well as Tilden's close friend and former law partner, Green became acting comptroller when Connolly took a leave of absence later that same day. With Green in place, the reformers could protect the records on which criminal and civil lawsuits would be based, as well as publicize, and thereby restrain, expenditures in all city government departments.

As the *Tribune* had prophesied on August 4, one of the Tammany Four had broken with the Ring and turned to the reformers. With Connolly's withdrawal, Nast would gradually ease the former comptroller away from the center of action in his political cartoons.

After Green replaced Connolly, Tilden's alignment with the anti-Tweed Ring movement became increasingly open. The secretive Tilden did not officially join the non-partisan Committee of Seventy until a year after its formation, despite later assumptions to the contrary. However, that fall, he accepted their reform-ticket nomination to the state assembly, while claiming that his goal was to fight Tammany Ring influence in the state government.

"The Wearing of the Green" was the cartoonist's first reference to Andrew Green, some six weeks after his installation. It was one of six Nast cartoons in the issue of November 11, available six days before the election.

Sweeny (obscuring the virtually invisible Connolly), Hall and Tweed glower in angry frustration before a placard extracted from Green's October 10 letter to "The Heads of Bureaus/Department of Finance," instructing them not to retain workers who do not work (sinecures), or are incompetent. The St. Patrick's Day reference in the cartoon's title reminds readers of Tammany's large (and despised) Irish-Catholic constituency, as well as being a pun on the acting comptroller's name.

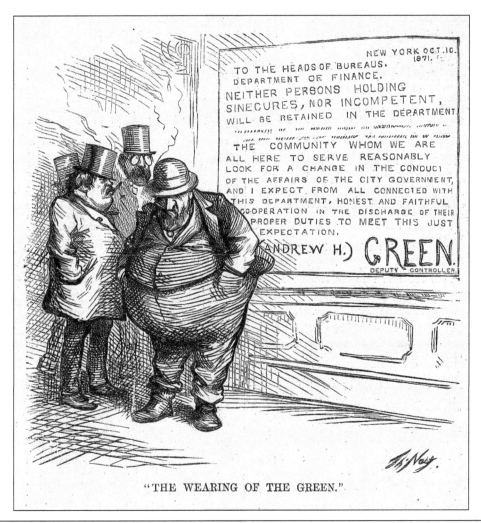

"THE WEARING OF THE GREEN."

Nast's next major satire was "Stop Thief!" in the October 7, 1871 issue of *Harper's Weekly*, published September 27, and perhaps begun as early as the day following the break-in and theft of fraudulent payment vouchers at the comptroller's office on September 10. On September 20, in the wake of Connolly's withdrawal as comptroller, the *New-York Times* editorialized sarcastically about "The Innocence of A. Oakey Hall":

"Stop thief!" cries Hall; "Stop thief!" cries Tweed; "Stop Thief!" cries Sweeny; "Stop thief!" cries the [pro-Tammany] *World*, and all the rest of the crew which for years past have lived without work on the public Treasury. ..."We must make him [Connolly] 'the scapegoat'; send him into the wilderness as a sin-offering, and amid the clamor of gongs and tumultuous voices, make the credulous public rejoice with us, that Connolly is the guilty one and that the guilty one has fled."

In this instance, the striking metaphorical parallel and the timing between Louis Jennings's *Times* editorial and Nast's irrepressibly hysterical image appearing seven days later strongly suggests that Jennings knew the cartoonist was already working on a related idea, rather than the other way round. It is conceivable that this pictorial comment on the disintegration of the Tammany Ring was first intended for the September 30 issue (available September 20) to coordinate with the *Times* "Stop Thief" editorial of September 20. Nast had five illustrations (four were cartoons) in that number and may have needed additional time for so ambitious a composition as "Stop Thief!"

Nast frequently incorporated into his cartoons allusions to the work of Charles Dickens, the British novelist who was popular with American readers. The relevant setting for the cartoonist's "Stop Thief!" is Chapter Ten of Dickens's novel *Oliver Twist* (1838), in which the young title character realizes he has fallen in with Fagin's band of pickpockets and, directly thereafter, is mistaken for one. Oliver begins running away from the scene of the crime, only to have the victim yell after him, "Stop thief!" The real pickpockets "no sooner heard the cry, than, guessing exactly how the matter stood, they issued forth with great promptitude; and, shouting 'Stop thief!' too, joined in the pursuit like good citizens." Oliver, terrified and exhausted, was soon brought down, "covered with mud and dust," and hauled before a police magistrate.

In "Stop Thief!" the American caricaturist marks the moment when the Tammany Ring turns from arrogance and stealth to panic and perspiration. In the immediate foreground, a "formal" farewell is paid to the defecting "Slippery Dick" Connolly who has stumbled or been pushed into the muck of the gutter. His fellow Tammany Ring associates—Hall, Sweeny, and Tweed (left-right)—follow close behind, the last preceded by an apprehensive little Scottish Terrier, perhaps in recognition of the Boss's ancestral homeland. The next phalanx of fleeing Tammany cronies includes (left to right): "Jubilee Jim" Fisk, financier; Tom "Torpedo" Fields, state assemblyman and commissioner of public parks; Thomas A. Ledwith, police magistrate; James H. Ingersoll (hat in hand; balding with moustache), chair manufacturer, carpet vendor, and Tammany bagman; Andrew J. Garvey (in shadow, with goatee and moustache), "Prince of Plasterers"; Hank Smith (behind Tweed), Tammany Republican and president of the Board of Police Commissioners; and, Nathaniel Sands (the stout man running beside Tweed), tax assessor, Board of Education member, secretary of the reformist Citizens Association, and double agent and odd-job man for the Tammany Ring.

Sands had been behind the call for a mass meeting, tentatively planned for August 8 or 10, to uncover the "real thieves," with the intention of undermining the effects of the scheduled Anti-Tammany convocation at Cooper Union on September 4. Sands' meeting never took place. With Tweed and Sands kicking up dust at the head of Nast's crowd scene, this picture sweeps in more than one direction, aptly conveying the confusing, conflicting, and alarming situation for the Tammany Ring from early August through mid-September 1871.

"STOP THIEF!"

"They no sooner heard the cry, than, guessing how the matter stood, they issued forth with great promptitude; and, shouting 'Stop Thief!' too, joined in the pursuit like *Good Citizens*."—"OLIVER TWIST."

However, on the last regular page of the October 7, 1871 issue of *Harper's Weekly*, a small Nast cartoon, "That's What's the Matter," presents a very different image of Tweed from that in "Stop Thief!" The Boss, evidently still master of the situation, stands defiantly arrogant, with one beefy elbow resting beside a glass ballot box and the other on his hip. Daring honest citizens to cast their votes, Tweed blows smoke from his cheroot and grumps, "As long as I count the Votes, what are you going to do about it? say?"

"THAT'S WHAT'S THE MATTER."

Boss Tweed. "As long as I count the Votes, what are you going to do about it? say?"

The Greenwich Scenario

As the fall 1871 election approached, Nast attempted to rile the city's working class against the Tammany Ring. In several cartoons, he contrasted the opulent lifestyle of members of the Ring with the privations suffered by urban working-class families because of the high cost of living resulting from the Ring's "tax, borrow (through bonds), assess—then spend and pocket" policies.

The first such cartoon, entitled "The Tammany Lords and Their Constituents" by Harper's (and "The Rich Growing Richer, The Poor Growing Poorer" by Nast), appeared in the September 2 issue of *Harper's Weekly* (available August 23), where it was coordinated for maximum effect with a two-page spread of illustrations and an accompanying feature article on the "Summer Palaces of the Ring." (See pages 123-125.)

In the upper picture, Connolly, spatially detached from the other three, reclines on a "Bed of Roses," his back against a sculptured "Golden Calf." He joins his three comrades on the right (Hall, Tweed, and Sweeny, left-right) in lifting their glasses as they toast their constituents, "May they live long, so that we may prosper." In the background are a four-team carriage attended by servants, yachts, an elaborate fountain, and a reasonably accurate depiction of Boss Tweed's ostentatious mansion in Greenwich, Connecticut.

Greenwich was 80 minutes away from New York by train. Tweed bought 80 acres of property in his wife's name (Mary Jane Tweed) in 1865 for $18,000, and built a fancy home called Linwood.

He also established the Americus Club in Greenwich on a separate property two miles away on Long Island Sound. In 1871, the membership included a dozen of the characters portrayed in Thomas Nast's cartoons: Police Commissioner Hank Smith (Vice President); bagmen Andrew Garvey, James Ingersoll and Elbert Woodward; whistle-blower Jimmy O'Brien; Auditor James Watson; Erie Ring chiefs Jim Fisk and Jay Gould; Sheriff Matthew Brennan; contractor John Keysor; and cronies Edward Shandley and Tom Fields.

Significantly not included because they generally didn't socialize—were the other three Ring principals—Oakey Hall, Peter Sweeny and Richard Connolly. That didn't stop Thomas Nast from drawing them in his cartoon, which combined Linwood in the background with the seaside atmosphere of the Americus Club in the foreground..

Not shown because it wasn't commonly known then and is not known by most Nast or Tweed scholars now, is a house on 24 acres of land which Tweed bought on June 9, 1870 for Lydia G. McMullen, the wife of William McMullen. According to "Other Days in Greenwich," a book written in 1913 by Greenwich resident Frederick A. Hubbard, the transaction closed in the office of Tweed's attorney and Tweed was present. Tweed introduced Mrs. McMullen as his niece, and it was generally understood that Tweed helped support the couple. The house was fixed up under the supervision of plasterer Andrew Garvey with the bills charged to New York City.

It is probable that Lydia McMullen had a romantic relationship with Tweed, with her husband's knowledge. According to the station agent, Tweed would get off the late evening train from New York between the station stops in Greenwich and Cos Cob (the next stop), and spend the night at the McMullen house on multiple occasions. This part of his life was not reported by most of his biographers, but it may have played a role in his escape. (See page 246.)

The Tammany Lords and Their Constituents

In the scene below, a landlord passes the financial burden of high "Assessments and Taxes" onto his poor tenants, and blames the despairing husband for voting the Tammany ticket. (The wife is apparently modeled after Nast's wife, Sarah.) Here, in the squalid room beyond, her beleaguered spouse is surrounded by unpaid bills, an empty market basket under the table, and an infant's casket on top. The little girl in the lower right lies on a "Bed of Thorns" in contrast to Connolly's bed of roses above.

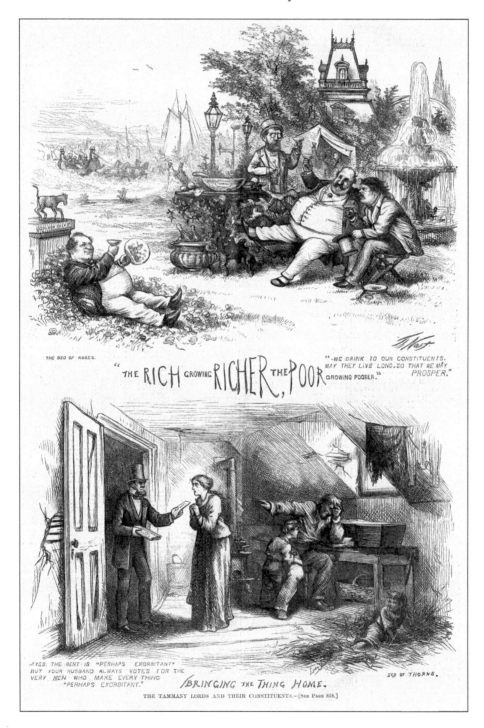

The Tammany Lords and Their Constituents

This cartoon was the earliest of at least five by Nast that were adapted in the autumn of 1871 as campaign broadsheets with plainly-worded messages to catch the attention of working-class voters who might not be regular readers of *Harper's Weekly*. Probably distributed between October 30 and November 4, just before Election Day on November 7, it read:

"Poor Men of New-York, read and consider!

"The debt of the City of New York is ONE HUNDRED MILLIONS OF DOLLARS. It has been incurred by the waste, extravagance and fraud of your Rulers. It must be paid to the last cent by taxation.

Who pays the taxes? Is it the rich landowner? Is it the butcher? Is it the baker? Do you not know that the land owner raises his rent as the taxes increase? That in like manner, the merchant raises the price of his goods? The butcher the price of his meat? The baker the price of his bread? Remember when you pay your rent—Remember when you buy your clothes—Remember when your children take their poor and scanty meal—that on every dollar of your hard-earned wages, you pay a certain and relentless toll to the men who have robbed you!! Do you want this burden doubled? Do you want higher rents, dearer clothes, dearer meat, dearer bread? Do you want to pay for more fine Fifth Avenue houses for these thieves who have stolen your city's money? More blazing diamonds for their shirt frills? More silks and satins for their women? More cheese and dainties for their bellies? This is no overdrawn picture. Is it not true that these thieves are rolling in wealth and luxury while you are fighting off starvation by the sweat of your brows? Remember, as long as their rule shall last, "The rich shall grow richer, and the poor shall grow poorer!" Whom, then shall we keep in power—the thieves and corruptionists, or the honest reformers? VOTE THE REFORM TICKET!"

Lest anybody miss the point, the proclamation was followed by a poem, "The 'BOSS'!":

The "Boss" he was a greedy man,
The "Boss" he was a thief;
He went into the poor man's house,
And stole his piece of beef.

The poor man went to his house,
The "Boss" he "wasn't home"
The "Boss" went to the poor man's house,
And stole his marrow bone.

Then rally at the polls, boys,
On Tuesday of next week,
And with your honest votes, boys,
We'll make those rascals squeak.

VOTE THE REFORM TICKET!

A week after the November 7, 1871 election resulted in resounding defeat for Tammany candidates, Nast received a letter from Elbert Ellery Anderson, a reform-minded Wall Street lawyer, accompanied by another cartoon broadside ("Too Thin"):

"My dear sir,
I write a line to you to acknowledge my conviction of the great service your cartoons rendered during the late election—I enclose your copy of the print as I got it up with the illustrative reading matter annexed to it. I caused fifty thousand of these to be scattered all over the poorer quarters of the city just before election day and I have no doubt your very clever pictures were in some degree instrumental in producing the result which was obtained.
Yours very truly,"

Wholesale and Retail (Theft)

Nast's contribution to the September 16, 1871 issue of *Harper's Weekly* was the memorable "Wholesale and Retail." Like "The Tammany Lords and Their Constituents" which appeared two weeks earlier, "Wholesale and Retail" attempted to undermine working-class allegiance to Tammany Hall by both contrasting and linking the ill-gotten wealth of the Tweed Ring with the poverty of their constituents. In it, Nast assesses the relative social status of grand larceny committed by the Ring as opposed to petty theft attempted by the penniless and famished. The issue was available September 6, so the cartoon was completed before the September 4 meeting of influential citizens at Cooper Union.

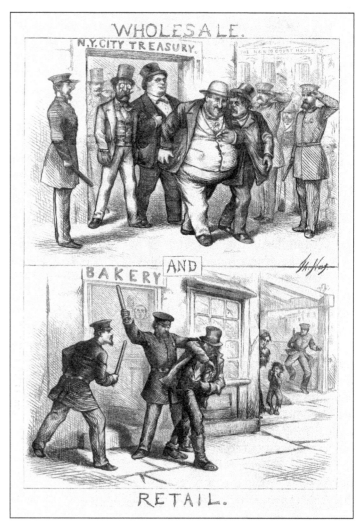

In the upper scene, the four potentates of Tammany Hall exit majestically from the "N.Y. City Treasury," their pockets bulging. To greet them an honor guard of New York's finest, billy clubs down, comes smartly to attention and salutes. Here, for the next to the last time, Nast's Tammany quartet is shown together on a comparatively equal basis. Mayor Hall clings to the arm of Controller Connolly (with whom he would soon be in conflict), while Tweed consults with the conspiratorial Sweeny. In the background (upper right), "The New (?) Court House" in City Hall Park is still under construction 13 years after the initial appropriation of a quarter-million dollars by the state legislature in 1858. Questions about cost overruns first arose in 1863.

In the bottom scene of "Wholesale and Retail," police accost with raised billy clubs a poor man who has stolen a loaf of bread to feed his hungry family. The image is borrowed directly from a panel in Nast's first cartoon for Harper's Weekly, drawn when the artist was only 18, for the March 19, 1859 issue as a criticism of police corruption. (See page 27, sketch 5.) Redrawn over a dozen years later as an anti-Tammany illustration, the composition was vastly strengthened and clarified to make the central point. The thief wears ragged clothing, including one shoe and a boot from which his bare toes protrude. The mother with their emaciated baby and terror-stricken son, cower around the corner.

Wholesale and Retail (Theft)

"Wholesale and Retail" joined the "Tammany Lords and Their Constituents" among the five anti-Tweed Ring satires reprinted as inexpensive campaign broadsides before the election on November 7, 1871. The following descriptive paragraphs were added to the broadside:

MEN OF NEW-YORK!

"On the 5th day of May, 1871, your Mayor, your Comptroller, your "Boss," and your "Brains" passed a resolution to pay all claims against the city which had been declared valid by the old Board of Supervisors.

"Within three months after the passage of this resolution, by means of fraudulent vouchers and of forged endorsements, SIX MILLIONS of Dollars were ROBBED from your City Treasury, and divided up among these men and their followers. No wonder their classic features beam with content; their bellies are full and their pockets are stuffed. Genial benevolence shines through their goggles.

"See one of your poorer classes, whose wife, with scanty garment, vainly seeks to shelter herself from the piercing cold; whose child, with piteous cry, weeps for a crust of bread to stay the pangs of hunger. In a moment of despair, the father's hand seizes from the baker's well-stocked window, a bit of bread for his hungry baby. Oh, men with wives and children, how fearful is his sin! See how the vigilant guardians of your city's honor strike the thief down with their clubs. Away with the felon to jail.

"Look at the other picture. Your big-bellied thief robs from your city treasury a Million of Dollars. He lives in his palace; he drives his carriage; he sports his diamonds; the bones he throws to his dogs are better food than your children get in many a weary week. Is this just? And yet the police take off their hats to him!

"Men of New-York! you have the affidavit of one of the purest men in this city—SAMUEL J. TILDEN; You have the written statement of the first lawyer of the country—CHARLES O'CONOR—that your 'Boss' took, in three months, as his share of the 'stealings,' One Million of Dollars, Think of it! It is more money than most of you would earn in one thousand years, and this man robbed it from you in three months!

"In the classic language of the day, the 'Boss' ought to let up. But he won't! Let us induce him to retire. VOTE THE REFORM TICKET."

On September 9, the *Evening Post* of Hartford, Connecticut, commented upon Wholesale and Retail" and Nast's other anti-Tweed Ring cartoons:

"They tell to every eye the whole story. They hang in every shop window; they are dropped in your lap in cars where you cannot help seeing them; they go to thousands and thousands of families and homes. ... (Nast) puts on paper the thought of the public, its honest sober sense; and no one need stop to read it; it is caught at a glance, and the effect is carried longer than that of any labored argument or long recital. And good men, honest men every where will thank him for it."

"The Ring Inviting Riot"

From the time of Judge Barnard's preliminary injunction on September 7, which restricted city expenditures, financially struggling city workers became increasingly anxious to receive their due wages, which were already in arrears. According to the *New-York Times* a week later, an estimated 2300 men had not been paid for six weeks. On 13 September, three days after the comptroller's office had been ransacked and fraudulent payment-vouchers stolen, disgruntled laborers forced their way into the same office to demand their money. The deputy comptroller assured them that all would be made well as soon as Comptroller Connolly arrived to sign the payroll vouchers. Connolly arrived after lunchtime, but was unwilling to act in view of the court's injunction. Instead, it was announced that funds would be made available the next morning after a special arrangement had been struck between the mayor's office and Broadway Bank, which held the city accounts.

This seemed to satisfy the workers, most of who apparently were employed at laying water mains for the new Croton aqueduct, but they nevertheless complained that that were being ill-treated in comparison with those in the public parks department (headed by Sweeny) or those on "sinecure lists," who had been paid promptly. The aqueduct workers told a *Times* reporter that they were compelled to come downtown to collect payment and "lose days in obtaining the money which they should have had handed to them every Saturday night." They added that were expected to "walk the whole length of the City from their homes to their work, ready to steal an apple, although as a rule [they were] honest, or a turnip or an onion from an up town garden, which ordinarily they would not think of entering but for hunger." At the same time, Tweed, in his nearby office of Public Works, was the very soul of discretion. He spoke sage words to the effect that "Brevity was the soul of wit and, at least in my case, the safest course." He declined to complicate matters by saying something to the reporter that might prove "entirely erroneous."

After that initial, seemingly spontaneous instance of worker protest, such sentiments were orchestrated increasingly to serve the purposes of the Tammany Ring. A news story in the *New-York Times* of September 28, "The Ring Inviting Riot," reported that a "highly-inflammatory article" in a Tammany Hall organ (apparently, the *Star* of September 27) had created "intense indignation" in the city by "inciting the unpaid workers to riot and bloodshed...." The *Times* charged that Tweed, Sweeny, and Mayor Hall were maneuvering workers to embarrass Acting Comptroller Andrew Green by besieging his office with "loud cries for money." The *Star* blamed the *Times* for the injunction that halted wage payments, and the Tammany newspaper suggested a mass meeting of the 5000 city workers in the Parks Department. The *Times* insisted that the "intelligent laborer" was not fooled by the manipulations of the Tammany Ring and its organ. Page one of the next day's *Times* (September 29), quoted the Boss disclaiming any foreknowledge of the *Star* article and denying that it was intended to "incite a riot."

The anticipated insurrectional conclave of enraged park laborers, scheduled and advertised for Saturday night, September 30, at Eighth Avenue and 59th Street, turned out to be a complete fizzle. Three separate police contingents of 100 men, sent to guard the appointed meeting place, as well as the homes of George Jones, publisher of the *Times*, and John Foley, who initiated the lawsuit that provoked Barnard's injunction, "had a dull time of it," according to the *Times* report of October 1.

The City Treasury. Empty (and) Full.

Nast responded to the situation in a cartoon, "The City Treasury: Empty [and] Full," in the October 14, 1871 issue of *Harper's Weekly*, published on October 4. Unless he received extra time for this plate, the artist's deadline for completing the drawing would have been September 25—after the aqueduct workers barged into the comptroller's office, but before news of Tammany's ill-fated attempt to organize a mass meeting of workers. The cartoon shows the New York City Treasury as a huge safe, barren of cash—"Empty to the Workmen," with a layer of "debts" on its floor. A young girl and her laborer father stare in disbelief at the empty safe, while the wife of a worker sobs into her handkerchief.

Concealed behind the safe are "The Four Masters That Emptied It"—Tweed, Sweeny, Hall, and Connolly, who feast in smug, sybaritic ostentation. Unlike his surviving compatriots, Connolly, who had withdrawn as comptroller, sits stiffly in the shadow with his back to the gaping safe, his smile forced, and his toast subdued. On the wall behind the foursome are pictures of (clockwise from left): the Americus Clubhouse in Greenwich, Connecticut (an exclusive club which the Tammany leadership owned and operated); Tweed's townhouse at 511 Fifth Avenue, with its elaborate garden and huge fountain; the Boss's country estate at Greenwich; and the lavish wedding of his daughter, Mary Amelia, on May 31, 1871, at Trinity Chapel on West 25th Street in New York City.

Yet again, the cartoonist thunders home the point of the need for political participation against the Tammany Ring with (at the top) the taunt turned slogan, "What Are You Going to Do About It?" Utilizing this composition's rich versus poor theme, it was also offered as a campaign broadside. On October 6, a *Times* editorial instructed, "Any one who wishes to see at a glance the truth about the condition of the City Treasury, and the reasons the laborers cannot be paid, may do so by looking at Nast's cartoon in the current number of *Harper's Weekly*."

EMPTY. "WHAT ARE YOU GOING TO DO ABOUT IT?" FULL.

EMPTY TO THE WORKMEN. THE FOUR MASTERS THAT EMPTIED IT.

THE CITY TREASURY.

As Nast's "The City Treasury" satire appeared, New York Democrats were gathering at Rochester to hold their state nominating convention on October 4-5, in advance of the election on November 7, 1871. Encouraged by the success of his strategy to replace Connolly as comptroller with reformer Andrew Green, party chairman Samuel Tilden's plan was to isolate Tammany Hall at Rochester, and to replace the incumbent state attorney general, Marshall Champlain, with Tilden's ally, Charles O'Conor. Expressing his customary legalistic sensitivity, Tilden hoped to "do everything that can be done without compromising the party." He wanted Tammany Hall shut out of the state convention, the uniting of other Democratic factions, and a reform coalition established in New York City. The chairman warned, "If that course is not pursued, [then] I will resign" as party chairman. However, despite the fact that he was not able to oust Tammany Hall, Tilden did not resign.

Instead of developing along the lines which Tilden planned, the Democratic State Convention ended as a triumphant victory for Tweed at a time when rumors of the imminent arrest of Tammany Ring figures were sweeping the city. As Tilden later conceded, he had severely underestimated the power of Tweed's patronage, his money, and the general susceptibility of upstate delegates. The persuasive abilities of the horde of imported New York thugs transported across the state for free by the Erie Railroad (controlled by Jay Gould and Jim Fisk, with Tweed as a director) was a key factor in keeping Democrats on Tweed's side.

Prior to the convention, Tweed's mood was bolstered by his unanimous re-election on September 24 as chairman of Tammany's general committee. The Boss dismissed Tilden and his key advisors, Horatio Seymour and Francis Kernan, as "three troublesome old fools." At the convention, Tilden was deftly outmaneuvered by Tweed on the question of which rival New York City delegation was to be seated, when the latter moved "the previous question" with no debate allowed, proposing that neither group be allowed. Ultimately, Boss Tweed emerged with a set of nominees he found acceptable, and contentedly saw O'Conor denied nomination for attorney general by a sizeable margin.

Eleven days later, though, Governor Hoffman appointed O'Conor as special assistant attorney general in New York City, allowing him to direct civil suits against the members of the Tammany Ring. **O'Connor would become the single legal opponent whom Tweed feared the most—and for good reason.**

On October 6, the *Tribune* headline on its story about the State Democratic Convention proclaimed, "Tweed Victorious Throughout." The Boss's renewed spirit of confident intransigence was revealed in his argument that "the present outcry against the Ring would be forgotten long before the campaign of '72 and ,without his forces in New-York, the Democracy had no prospect of carrying the State." If the Tilden forces continued their campaign against Tammany, the Boss threatened to "array his 140,000 constituents on the Republican side, and sweep the very shadow of Democracy from the State." Tweed brazenly charged his opponents with being obstructionists who were doing "all they could to smash up the party because they could not run it."

Nast's reaction, "The 'Brains' That Achieved the Tammany Victory at the Rochester Convention," appeared in the October 21, 1871 issue of *Harper's Weekly* (published October 11), and was an immediate classic. Along with "Who Stole the People's Money?" it became one of the most frequently imitated of the artist's cartoons.

This backhanded salute to the apparent ease with which Tweed had routed the forces of reform introduced a sinister porcine figure with the moneybag head and the dollar-sign face. The concept probably had its roots in Tweed's sensitivity to the fact that Peter Sweeny was regularly designated as the brains of the Tammany Ring, and to the cartoonist's assurance that the readers would be aware of this.

In "The Brains," the pictorial impact is achieved masterfully, with the greatest simplicity. There are no labels, if one discounts the oversized "signature" diamond shirt-stud. The Boss stands defiantly in a sort of force field of crosshatched shadow behind him, with his facial features and moral character both represented by the ruthless, squinty, large-nosed dollar sign. Tweed's hands are thrust deep into his pockets as if he is ever ready to draw out more monetary ammunition. The image, which appeared on the last regular page of the issue, is roughly four and three-eighths inches square.

THE "BRAINS"

THAT ACHIEVED THE TAMMANY VICTORY AT THE ROCHESTER DEMOCRATIC CONVENTION.

Whatever political capital Samuel J. Tilden, the state party chairman, had lost in open combat with Tweed at the Democratic State Convention, he recouped with interest by his adept management of the appointment of Charles O'Conor as a state prosecutor in New York City, with the begrudging compliance of the Boss's longtime protégé, Governor John Hoffman, and of the state attorney general, Marshall Champlain. This matter was discussed between Champlain and Tilden at a private meeting in the latter's Gramercy Park home in Manhattan on Sunday morning, October 15, 1871. Tilden later told the *New-York Times* (published October 20) that Champlain had agreed to "bring any suits in relation to the frauds which might be recommended by Mr. O'Conor or myself."

On Tuesday, October 17, an exploratory meeting took place in Hoffman's executive chamber at Albany between the governor, the state attorney general, and a committee of seven men sent by the reformist Committee of Seventy to urge the governor to place New York City under martial law to avert the danger of riot or revolution. (Although not nominally a member of the committee, Tilden was clearly supportive of its objectives.)

Governor Hoffman remained "opposed to the exercise of military power, except in time of war and when absolutely necessary to preserve the peace in time of disorders at home, to put down riots and disturbances." If such an occasion were to arise, he promised to use the state militia "with just as much force and energy as I can command."

More importantly, Governor Hoffman agreed to instruct State Attorney General Champlain "to take any suggestion you [the Committee of Seventy] make to him, to take into his counsel the man that is acknowledged to be the leader of the bar in New York—Mr. Charles O'Conor." On Thursday, October 19, Tilden hosted a meeting with Champlain and O'Conor, at which it must have been agreed that O'Conor would immediately take charge of a Bureau of Municipal Corruption, to be set up in the building at 59 Wall Street housing his law office. O'Conor named two Democrats and two Republicans to his prosecutorial staff.

As stated previously, over the preceding three weeks, at the request of Acting Comptroller Andrew Green, Tilden and two assistants had begun a careful examination of Tammany Ring accounts in the National Broadway Bank; these were known on Connolly's authority to contain exact copies of the stolen vouchers. Headlines over the *New-York Times* report [October 18] on page one announced: "Criminal Proceedings To Be Taken Against Tweed First" . . . "Incontrovertible Evidence of His Malfeasance."

"The investigation into the City's account with the Broadway Bank has ... decidedly implicated Mr. William M. Tweed and his associates in the frauds that have sapped the strength of the City. The long demanded evidence against him and them has been found and it is stated that the first attack will soon be made upon Tweed. ...[T]hose books disclose all that can be desired to convict Tweed, not only of complicity in the frauds but [of] engineering the machinery [with] which the money of our citizens has been drawn from the Treasury to enrich the Ring."

A *Times* editorial of Monday, October 23, leaked the precise amount of public funds deposited by Tweed into his personal account at Broadway Bank between May and September 1870. The first reported sum of $932,838.50 opened the path to Tweed's arrest and eventual conviction (November 1873). The next day, Samuel Tilden signed an affidavit concerning his findings, his first formal act on behalf of the Committee of Seventy. As filed, it was accompanied by a list of 190 county vouchers and the indication that at least $6,300,000 had been fraudulently taken from the public treasury.

Five years later, Charles Wingate, a newspaper correspondent, reformer, and sanitary engineer, explained an invaluable breakthrough in the investigation in the *North American Review* of October 1876:

"The accounts of Tweed, Connolly, Sweeny, [James] Watson [the county auditor], and [Elbert] Woodward [clerk to the Board of Supervisors] in various banks showed that on every warrant in favor of certain persons, the first named received about 24 per cent, the second 20 per cent, the third ten percent, and the last two five percent each. The proportions, however, were not absolutely exact; the variation it is true was not great, being less than 2 per cent, but still it existed. The perfect accuracy of Mr. Tilden's conclusions was demonstrated at last when, long subsequently, the Ring contractor, Ingersoll, having turned state's evidence, explained this variation. It seems that, not content with raising each bill so that the original charge was reduced to 35 per cent of the whole, these absolutely insatiable thieves had also caused the warrants to be antedated, in order that interest might be charged from such date to the time of payment. In this interest, Tweed, for some reason, did not share, nor did it appear on the face of the bills, being computed subsequent to their approval and included in the warrant. Its presence, therefore, caused the greatest difficulty in the investigation to Mr. Tilden, and only when it was accounted for was the accuracy of his results absolutely verified. The success of this investigation was the most important link in the whole chain of evidence against the Ring. It made it complete."

Yet, despite his crucial eleventh-hour role in bringing down the Tweed Ring, so intense was Tilden's obsession with keeping knowledge of his connection with the Committee of Seventy as secret as possible, he told a large public rally five days before the November 7, 1871 election:

"And on this occasion, in this great crisis in the affairs of our city, knowing nothing about the action of your committee [of Seventy] except what I have heard here, caring nothing [for] who unites with me or with whom I unite in this grand and great object, I stand before you to advocate a union of all honest men against a combination of plunderers."

Nevertheless, Tilden used his anti-Tammany Ring credentials as the foundation to build a career in elective office, which rapidly elevated him to the state legislature (1872), the New York governorship (1874), and the Democratic presidential nomination (1876), before losing the bitterly disputed Electoral College vote in 1877 to Republican Rutherford B. Hayes and retiring as the grand old man of the party.

Tilden's affidavit was published in the *Times* of October 26, by which time the document had been instrumental in allowing State Prosecutor Charles O'Conor and State Attorney General Marshall Champlain to obtain a judicial warrant for the arrest of Tweed. The Boss was arrested the next day, Friday, October 27, just after 1:30 P.M. at his office in the Public Works Department, and immediately released on bail in the amount of $1,000,000.

Inside the issue of November 18, published on November 8, the day after the election, is Nast's full-page view of "The Arrest of 'Boss' Tweed—Another Good Joke." Sheriff Matthew Brennan gently touches Tweed's shoulder as the law officer makes light of his official duty. The artist tapped the account of the arrest by the Tribune, which reported the jocularity of the scene and the fact that Tweed was immediately allowed to post bail. In Nast's rendition, the Boss, amused, turns toward Brennan, while Sweeny smirks and points, and Mayor Hall leans forward to share the joke.

In the shadow (right), Connolly appears apprehensive, perhaps in anticipation of his own arrest (November 25). On the floor, Tweed's spittoon has been in service, and his old "Big Six" fire hat rests atop the desk. The wastebasket, a surrogate ballot box, is custodian of the people's business, as in other cartoons drawn in the campaign. Looming above, the large figure of Justice readies to strike retribution, with her scales clamped under her arm, as she pulls her sword from its scabbard.

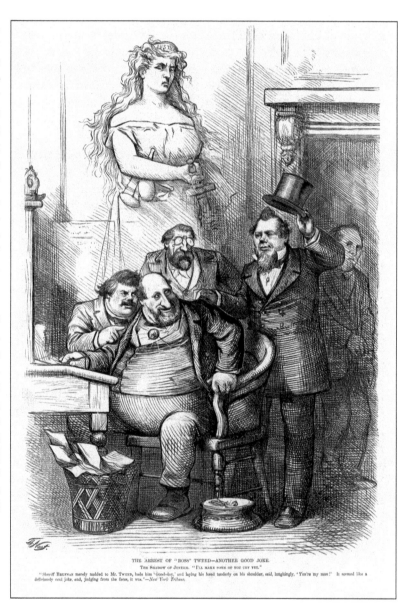

THE ARREST OF "BOSS" TWEED—ANOTHER GOOD JOKE.
THE SHADOW OF JUSTICE. "I'LL MAKE SOME OF YOU CRY YET."
"Sheriff BRENNAN merely nodded to Mr. TWEED, bade him 'Good-day,' and laying his hand tenderly on his shoulder, said, laughingly, 'You're my man!' It seemed like a deliciously cool joke, and, judging from the faces, it was."—*New York Tribune.*

In the few days before the election, the *New-York Times* worked to combat any apathy among reform voters by referring to Tammany's "invincibility" and to "creeping hopelessness" of the anti-Ring movement. It urged, "[that] every man, then, resolve to vote against the thieves ..."

In similar fashion Nast's cartoon on the last regular page of the November 4, 1871 *Harper's Weekly* offered another strong admonition to anti-Ring voters. The issue was actually available on October 25, two days before Tweed's arrest.

In "The Boss Still Has the Reins," Tweed sits in the driver's seat of the "Tammany" carriage driving past the new courthouse, his face set in determination as he whips the horses forward. But the two horses react in seeming rebellion, with the maverick "Democrat" kicking up dust and the spirited "Republican" rearing its head—a clear message to voters of their potential power to upend the Tammany Ring. Sweeny sits beside the Boss, while Mayor Hall wearing livery (servant's costume), sits behind him with his arms crossed. Next to Hall, Connolly has shriveled into shadowy indefiniteness.

One result of the increased attention and press comment accorded Nast's anti-Tweed Ring series was the increased circulation figure of 275,000 copies announced by *Harper's Weekly* over the editorial masthead of the issue dated November 4, 1871. This was almost triple its normal circulation of 100,000, and was firm proof of how Nast had captured the public's interest.

THE BOSS STILL HAS THE REINS.

For the climactic, pre-election *Harper's Weekly* issue of November 11, published November 1, Nast amazingly supplied six cartoons, occupying almost four and a half pages, including the centerpiece double-page spread, "The Tammany Tiger Loose," two full-page cartoons, and three smaller ones, for the most spectacular one-week performance of his professional career.

The largest tableau, "The Tammany Tiger Loose," was conceived as a reciprocal composition to the artist's "Amphitheatrum Johnsonianum," drawn four-and-a-half years before (*Harper's Weekly*, March 30, 1867) to criticize President Andrew Johnson's lack of response to anti-black riots in New Orleans and Memphis during Reconstruction. In "The Tammany Tiger Loose," the viewer's vantage point has shifted from the imperial box in the earlier cartoon to the floor of the arena. Thus transplanted, the onlooker is menaced directly by the fiercely mesmerizing eyes and snarling jaws of the beast. Wearing an "Americus" collar, the Tammany Tiger is in the act of mauling Columbia, identified by her fallen crown labeled "The Republic," having already shredded the "Law," shattered the glass ballot box, and slain Justice and Commerce (represented by the Roman god, Mercury).

The cartoonist would have been aware of a major painting on a coliseum theme by the French master of historical realism, Jean-Leon Gérôme: "Hail Caesar, We Who Are About to Die Salute You." Completed in 1859, Gérôme's painting again generated acclaim when it was exhibited at the Paris World's Fair in 1867, the same year Nast drew his coliseum-based "Amphitheatrum Johnsonianum." There is no known preliminary sketch for any part of "The Tammany Tiger Loose," suggesting that the cartoon evolved directly from a print of Gérôme's "Hail Caesar."

In Nast's drawing, as in Gérôme's painting, the vast audience is shown sweeping away to the viewer's left, while the witness is placed on the ground of the amphitheater itself. Details include the scattered corpses, the gigantic awning for protection from the sun, and the similar positioning of Gérôme's corpulent Caesar, recast by Nast as Imperator Tweed gripping his "Iron Rod" of inflexible control. The Boss is flanked on the left by Sweeny (evidently an avid partisan of the famished tiger) and on the right by a sheepish Mayor Hall. Governor Hoffman, having distanced himself from his former associates, is hiding in the shadow behind Sweeny. Richard Connolly, the departing comptroller, downgraded or banished from Nast's cartoons for six weeks, glances apprehensively over Tweed's shoulder to complete the original quartet of rascals.

Also identifiable are (left-right): Hank Smith, the police commissioner; Nathaniel Sands, Tammany Republican and duplicitous secretary of the reformist Citizen's Association; Tom Fields, (to the right of Connolly), Tammany Republican and state assembly candidate, barred from taking his seat after being arrested on November 9 for election fraud; Edward J. Shandley, (to the right of Hall), police magistrate and Tammany candidate for county registrar who lost in a landslide to Republican Franz Sigel; Andrew Garvey (with goatee), the Ring's master plasterer and kickback frontman; James Ingersoll, chair-maker and key Tammany bagman; financier Jim Fisk (with pointed moustache); behind Fisk, his business partner, Jay Gould, seated beside David Dudley Field, Tammany's powerhouse lawyer; Thomas Ledwith, (in front of Field and to the right of Fisk), another police magistrate and a candidate for the state supreme court who lost in the election.

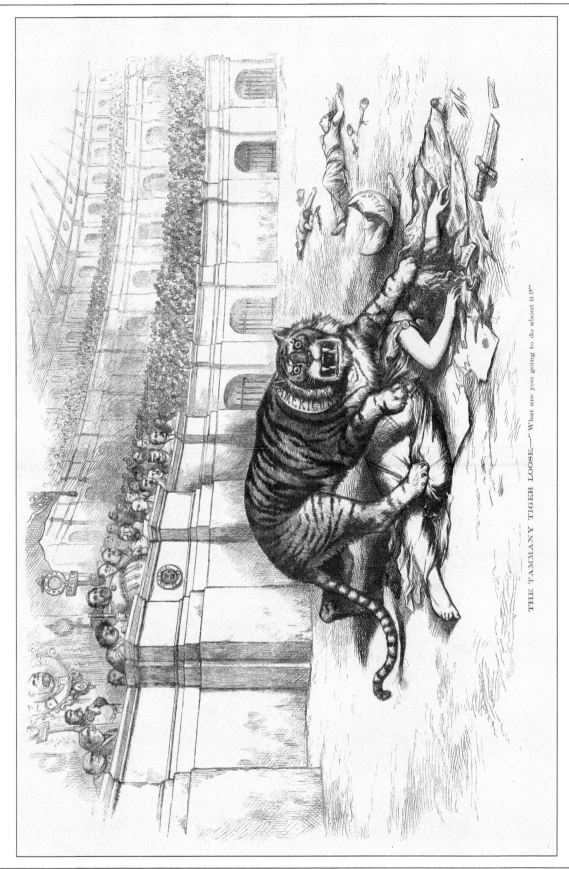

THE TAMMANY TIGER LOOSE.—"What are you going to do about it?"

The development of "The Tammany Tiger Loose" was highly complex. Since 1866, Nast had used the encircled head of a tiger (often mistaken for a bulldog) as a Tammany totem, but in late August or September 1871, he may have been thinking ahead to a more powerful way of jolting voters' anti-Tammany sentiments.

Years later, Nast explained that the genesis of the Tammany Tiger emblem, the riveting visual focus of this cartoon, began with a memory from his boyhood. The symbol of the Big Six volunteer fire company to which Tweed formerly belonged (1839-1850) was the head of a tiger in a ring, and it was later adopted as the mascot of Tammany's social club, Americus. The artist used the emblem repeatedly in anti-Tammany cartoons, allowing it to break out the Ring to its full, threatening embodiment for the first time in "The Tammany Tiger Loose."

Nast first used the subtitle, "Well, What are you going to do about it?" in June 1871, associating it with Boss Tweed (see pages 100-101), but here, five months later, he flings the taunt into the face of the voting public. This stunning pictorial challenge to the authority of Boss Tweed and Tammany Ring corruption and misgovernance was available to work on the imagination of voters for six full days before the decisive election.

For guidance in drawing his tiger, Nast leaned heavily on a page from the Rev. J. G. Woods's *Illustrated Natural History* (Vol. I, 1860, London). The "Male Tiger" print became so battered by frequent reference over the years that Nast was eventually forced to trim and mount it on a piece of light card-paper for safekeeping. He derived the furious concentric spirals of the tiger's eyes from Woods's engraving. A second tiger plate in *Illustrated Natural History*, showing open jaws and teeth, was obviously helpful, as well.

The impact of "The Tammany Tiger Loose" on the public and press was immediate. Nast later recalled that on a train ride home in early November 1871, he saw a man looking at the cartoon in great agitation and then clenching his fist to strike the tiger in the head, exclaiming, "We are going to kill you," in apparent response to the subtitle: "What Are You Going to Do About It?" As Nast told the reporter, "with a twinkle in his eye": "I knew that I, too, had made a hit." [*Kansas City Times*, February 7, 1892.]

The day after the cartoon's publication, Thursday, November 2, the *New-York Times* was ecstatic:

"The new number of *Harper's Weekly* … is a tremendous battering ram against the Ring. Some of the finest pictures ever produced by Nast adorn this number. A splendid drawing represents the Tammany Tiger rending the Republic to pieces in the arena, while Caesar Tweed and his followers look on from the gallery. This is probably the most impressive political picture ever produced in this country. Put it into hands of wavering voters, and let them mark the truths that it conveys, and after that it will be strange if they think it consistent with their duty to stay away from the polls next Tuesday. …Let everybody read *Harper's* this week."

Three pages after "The Tammany Tiger Loose," readers saw Nast's call for vigilance against voting fraud, "Going Through the Form of Universal Suffrage." In the caption, Boss Tweed reminds voters that while they have the right to cast ballots, Tammany Hall controls the counting process. Below it in bolder print, another caption quotes the *New-York Times* confident admonition to vote "and leave the rest to take its course."

On the right of the picture, Sweeny (with his increased corpulence), Tweed, and Hall smoke contemptuously as they supervise the casting of ballots into a wastebasket. Behind Tweed, the shadowy figure in profile seems intended to be Connolly.

The class and ethnic mix of American citizens is represented by a white working man (carpenter) and then a patrician, followed by voters of Irish, German, and African heritage. Four New York City policemen are there to keep a sharp eye out for any voting irregularities, but seem satisfied with the Tammany scheme. Plastered on the wall are posters proclaiming lucrative rewards for counting out anti-Tammany tickets, and boasting of Tammany's possession of "the law in our hands." The doorway over the receptacle might be marked "The C[ount]" and clearly announces: "What Are You Going to Do About It?"

Art historian Albert Boime believes that the composition, pose, gesture, informality of bearing, and even the wastebasket of Nast's "Universal Suffrage" influenced Edgar Degas's famous painting of his uncle's "Cotton Office at New Orleans," begun a year later in that city. (See www.The World of Thomas Nast: Van Gogh and Degas.)

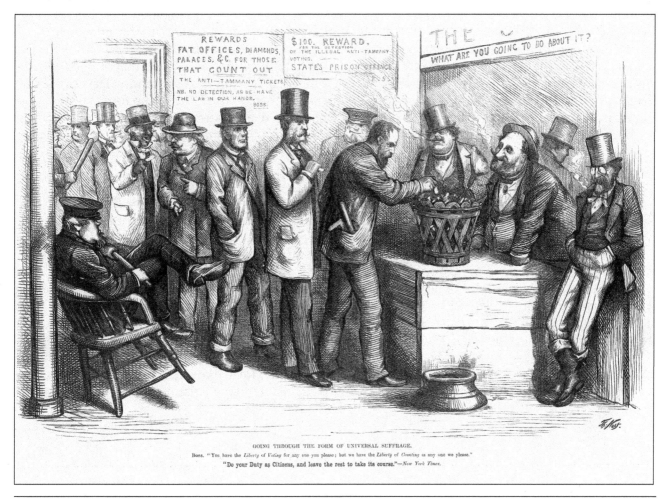

GOING THROUGH THE FORM OF UNIVERSAL SUFFRAGE.

Boss. "You have the *Liberty of Voting* for any one you please; but we have the *Liberty of Counting* in any one we please."

"Do your Duty as Citizens, and leave the rest to take its course."—*New York Times.*

Nast's warning was timely and necessary. On Saturday evening, November 4, 1871, Boss Tweed faced a large and supportive audience for the final time before the Tuesday election. Despite having been arrested and released on bail the previous week, he identified the enthusiastic ovation greeting him as "in great degree an expression of popular opinion," as opposed to the sentiments of the press, which "have already indicted, tried, convicted, and sentenced me." Tweed characterized his reelection campaign as an occasion for him to "appeal to a higher tribunal and have no fear of the result." Throughout the speech, the Boss presented himself as the victim of unprincipled opponents, flattered his constituents, and promised to continue to serve their interests. In his concluding remarks, he confidently asserted, "Rest assured that all the ante-election charges that have been made against me will dissolve as dew before the rising sun when they are subjected to the calm, dispassionate, impartial investigation of the courts of law."

That same Saturday, the *New-York Times* began a drum roll to Election Day with a sharply worded editorial entitled "Are We to Lose Our Last Rights?" It criticized Police Superintendent John Kelso, a Tammany loyalist, for requiring "under all circumstances" that Mayor Hall's voting inspectors were to be protected "in the undisputed possession of the ballot-boxes." To the *Times*, that placed the police force solidly behind the Tammany Ring and against any protest the reformers might lodge, allowing Hall's inspectors "to do as they please." The editorialist argued that such a move went beyond anything the city's citizens would countenance, and would "bring down a storm" upon the Ring: "If the people will submit to being robbed, they will not submit to a flagrant violation of the fundamental principles of liberty…"

The following day, November 5, a lengthy page–one story in the *Times* warned of an "Infamous Plot" by the "Ring Thieves to Stuff the Ballot-Boxes." The newspaper explained an elaborate plan for switching genuine boxes with fake ones, virtually under the noses of the voters. In the latter, Tammany ballots would, of course, predominate, with some Reform ballots altered by Tammany workers for the semblance of regularity. "If not stopped, and it now rests with the public to perform that important duty, the Tammany Ring will carry every election district in the city on Tuesday next by fraud." The Democratic *Herald* reported the same "alleged conspiracy," and revealed that James O'Brien, the former sheriff and Tammany whistleblower, "is said to be the individual who smoked out the fraud." Two days later, reporting on the events of Monday, "The Day Before The Battle," the *Times* noticed that the revelation of the massive scheme of vote fraud planned by Tammany Hall had sent its members into a panic as they tried to ferret out the traitors and respond to the damage.

> "There were hurryings to and fro, between the offices of 'Boss' Tweed and the City Hall, Court-house, and Bureau of Elections. Letters and packages were transmitted constantly, and a stream of men poured in and out of the doors, and scattered to the various car lines, bearing dispatches to every ward and district in the City."

On Monday, November 6, it was announced that four of the city's state militia companies would be ordered to their armories ready for service on Election Day. On Tuesday morning, Election Day, the *Times* alerted voters that the Committee of Seventy had made "the most complete arrangements for watching the polling places." The newspaper warned ominously, "New plans were made by the Tammany chiefs on Sunday and fully promulgated yesterday," which consist of "personal intimidation, mock fighting, arbitrary arrests by the Police, and distribution of false ballots." Readers were urged to acquire the real reform ballot before entering the polls in order to guard against receiving a phony one.

The newspaper explained that the Tammany men had made "the most thorough canvass" and used "rum, promises, and dollars" to ensure that their constituents "vote early and vote often…." Liquor dealers were visited to "test their fealty to the Tammany ticket," and the doubtful were threatened with prosecution for liquor-law violations. The journalist calculated, "Probably in no previous campaign has there been such persistent effort made to organize the laborers for the purposes of the Ring."

Another article in the Election Day *Times* reported that Peter Sweeny and his brother-in-law, John J. Bradley, the city chamberlain (treasurer), had brazenly met at police headquarters with Police Commissioner Hank Smith, presumably in an effort to secure police cooperation in facilitating voting for Bradley in his state senatorial race against James O'Brien.

On the last page of the regular November 11 issue was "The Lion's Share," in which Tweed the lion, Sweeny the cat, and Hall the ass all look bloated and irritated from having "had their share," which "now . . . seems to disagree with them." Around the corner in the background is undoubtedly Connolly's supine carcass with its legs up, "dead" and gone for purposes of the Ring.

THE LION'S SHARE.

They have all had their share, and it now seems to disagree with them.

Calling the Ring to Account

On the first page of the November 11 issue's supplement, is "Next!" On the right stands the demanding presence of Jackson S. Schultz, an attorney who was a founding and executive board member of the reformist Committee of Seventy. On October 6, Schultz issued a statement that John H. Keyser, a plumbing contractor with the city, had admitted guilt and was turning over $650,000 in trust to the Committee of Seventy while awaiting the investigation. Keyser's mansion in South Norwalk, Connecticut (see page 125), was one of the "Summer Palaces of the Ring" featured in the September 2, 1871 issue of *Harper's Weekly*, which provided the basis for the rich versus poor contrast in Nast's "The Tammany Lords and Their Constituents" cartoon of the same number. (See page 150.)

Keyser, however, initially maintained his innocence, arguing that his name on the payment vouchers had been forged; later he admitted to inflating his bills by a third. The plumbing contractor turned his books over to the Committee of Seventy, and, granted immunity, became a state witness against the Tammany Ring. He claimed that, despite questions about his $2 million in billings to the city, he was owed money. At the end of October, Schultz brought a lawsuit on behalf of Keyser against Tweed for $42,000 in unpaid goods and services. That legal action, however, occurred after Nast's cartoon not only had been completed, but also had almost certainly been readied for printing. Therefore, the artist concentrates on Keyser's return of tainted funds to the city, and urges the contractor's former Tammany Ring associates to act likewise in turning their money over to the Committee of Seventy. In reaction, Boss Tweed exposes his empty pockets and Mayor Hall digs deeply into his, apparently finding nothing, as (left-right) James Ingersoll, Andrew Garvey, Peter Sweeny, and Richard Connolly (largely concealed) eye Schultz uneasily.

The wording on the sign on the front of the desk says: "Mr. John H. Keyser's (The Poor But Honest Plumber) $650,000 Returned (On Trust)".

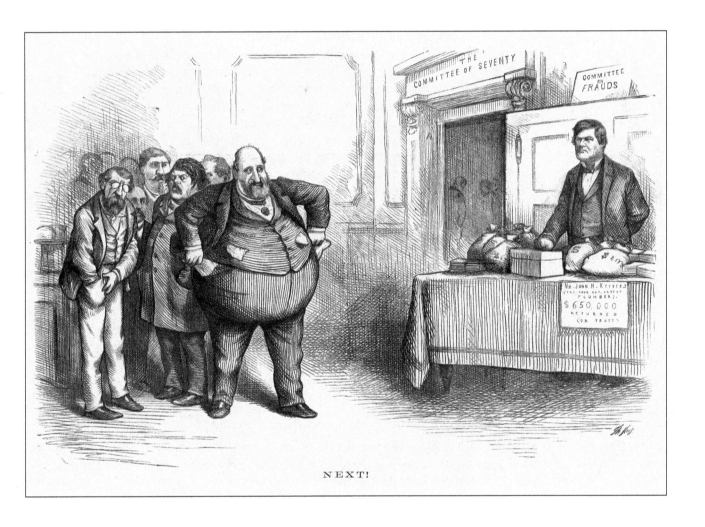

One early indication of a political upset in the making came Monday night—Election Eve—from organized betting on the likely result. At Johnson's Pool Rooms at Broadway and 28th Street, bids on the election "sold lively, but it was noticeable that the Tammany candidates uniformly sold lower than previously." Another telling development was the closing of Tammany Hall headquarters on election night—to the dismay of Tammany loyalists who had, as usual, gathered outside the building to hear election results announced and to cheer the Tammany winners. The *New-York Times* reported that election night, unlike previous years, was quiet with "few arrests even for such trivial matters as disorderly conduct." The Tammany leaders and loyalists met at police head-quarters where they received the bad news. The *Times* of November 8 described the scene from the night before:

> "At night, when the returns began coming in, and the story of the heavy vote for the people's ticket was poured into the ears of the Tammanyites gathered in the rooms and corridors, dismay overcame the crowd. By nine o'clock, the majority had heard more than enough, and slunk away to their holes, while those who remained were as demure as though in attendance upon a funeral. On the other hand, the friends of Reform were jubilant in the extreme. As the heavy vote for [reform candidates] . . . and honesty came in . . ., strangers grasped each other's hands with the fervor of friendship . . . . There was universal surprise as the returns came in; the news was too good to be true, although announced from the mouth of the Tammany Superintendent of Police [James Kelso] . . . But it was a joy that was too deep for outward show, and as a consequence, Head-quarters has not been so quiet for years at the close of an election as it was last night. Tammany hugged its grief in silence, and its foes were too grateful to be noisily exuberant over its downfall."

When the results were tabulated, the reformers had elected all 15 aldermen, 13 of 21 assistant aldermen, and 14 of 20 state assemblymen (including Samuel J. Tilden). The only major defeat for the reformers, and redeeming grace for Tammany Hall, was the reelection of Boss Tweed to the state senate.

The heady spirit of righteous enthusiasm from the night before bubbled over onto page one of the 5. A.M. special edition of the *Times* for Wednesday, November 8. Celebrating the victory for reform and defeat for Tammany Hall, the newspaper led with euphoric headlines: "New-York Redeemed," "Great Uprising of the People for Reform," "A Glorious Republican Victory Secured," "The State Ticket Elected by 12,000 Majority," "The Legislature Two-Thirds Republican," "All of the New-York Reform County Ticket Elected," and "Tammany's Hordes Broken Up Everywhere."

The *Herald* of November 10 published an interview with Tweed, who had retained his state senate seat, although by a diminished margin. The Boss's presence belied rumors that he had fled abroad, and he denied that he had or would resign any of his positions.

Editorials in the *New-York Times* on Thursday morning, November 9, 1871, signaled the beginning of what would be a long-running debate over who most merited the laurels for overthrowing the Tweed Ring. The *Times* praised several men active in the political world: James O'Brien, former sheriff, whistleblower, and newly elected state senator; the Committee of Seventy; and Reform Democrats led by: Samuel J. Tilden, the state party chairman and newly elected state legislator; William Havemeyer, former New York City mayor; Charles O'Conor, the state prosecutor against the Ring; and Andrew Green, the new city comptroller.

On Wednesday, November 15, in the lead editorial of the post-dated November 25 issue of Harper's Weekly, George William Curtis called the election defeat of the Tammany slate "a triumph of a free and fearless press." On the final page of the issue's supplement appeared an unsigned cartoon, possibly by Charles S. Reinhart, show-casing "The Power of the Press." In it, Thomas Nast sits calmly sketching atop a modern, high-speed printing press (the accurate detail of which may have been copied from an advertisement), while the machine crushes the Tweed Ring quartet underneath it.

THE POWER OF THE PRESS.

In particular, Curtis reminded readers not to forget, "that its glory is largely due to the courage, the fidelity, and the ability of one great journal, the *New-York Times*. The next day, the *Times* of November 16, perhaps to atone for a glaring omission in their previous week's commentary and in gratitude for Curtis's salute, ran a brief editorial paragraph attesting, "Our victory . . . would hardly have been complete without its pictorial record by Nast, who has followed the thieves so sharply all through the fight."

The cover drawing of "What Are You Laughing At? To the Victor Belong the Spoils" would have been completed over the weekend following the election in order to make the deadline for publication on the upcoming Wednesday, November 15 for the November 25, 1871 issue. The catchphrase, "To the victor belong the spoils [of the enemy]," which is used here ironically, was coined in 1832 by U.S. Senator William L. Marcy of New York to justify political patronage. (Tweed's middle name has often been erroneously identified as "Marcy," rather than the correct "Magear"—his mother's maiden name.)

The sketch provides a sequel of sorts to "The Tammany Tiger Loose" by continuing the analogy of the Tweed Ring with the decadence and decline of Ancient Rome. More specifically, though, the cartoon is a parody of the popular painting "Marius Amid the Ruins of Carthage" (1807) by John Vanderlyn, an American painter of the neo-classical school.

The cartoonist probably knew the Vanderlyn painting from reproductions. Gaius Marius (157-86 B.C.) was a distinguished Roman general and an ambitious politician of plebeian origin, who served as a tribune, praetor, and seven times as consul. He lost a power struggle with his rival, Sulla, and was forced to flee to northern Africa. When the local governor sent Marius orders to leave, he is supposed to have replied "Go tell [the governor] that you have seen the exile Marius sitting on the ruins of Carthage" (Today, Tunis, the capital of Tunisia.)

In Nast's vision, Boss Tweed sits disabled, his legs sprawled apart, and surrounded by the fallen rubble of Tammany Hall; "TAM" is chiseled on the rock below Tweed's left foot in the right foreground. Tweed stares, dazed and wild-eyed, straight at the viewer, seemingly gazing into the depths of his own bleak future. The Boss's left hand dangled limply over the side of the empty safe of the "New York Treasury," the gaping depths of which are concealed from view by the warrior's shield. Tweed wears his giant diamond shirt-stud and, below it, a medallion of a sad-faced Tammany Tiger. The Boss's brow is marked with what seems to be an ironic dollar-sign headband (or crown of thorns?), while the dome of his head sports devil-horned hair (as it does in other Nast cartoons).

On the left of the cartoon is a placard on a fragment of truncated column reading, "The Tammany Boys Whipped Out Of Their Boots," and to the right is a larger sign with newspaper headlines announcing Tammany's election debacle. The "spoils of victory" litter the foreground: a whiskey bottle, a cigarette pack, cards, boots, shoes, and shabby, silk top hats—emblematic of Tweed's now-defeated, mid-echelon bureaucrats and hangers-on, familiarly known as the "Shiny Hat Brigade." Labels identify Tammany Ring cronies defeated in races for the state senate—Henry Woltman, Henry Genet, and John J. Bradley (the first two were incumbents); the state supreme court—Thomas A. Ledwith; and New York County registrar—Edward J. Shandley. Peter Sweeny's resignation as city parks commissioner is represented by the abandoned moneybag satchel (lower right) reading "Tammany Brains."

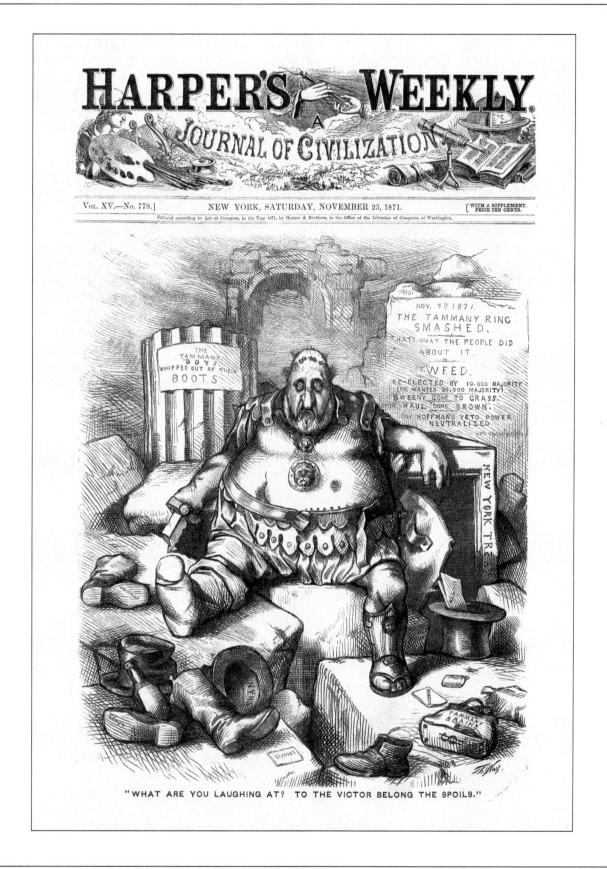

Three pages after "To the Victor Belong the Spoils," the same motif of the destruction of Ancient Rome was expanded into a scene of wanton devastation at Tammany Hall: "Something That Did Blow Over—November 7, 1871." Mayor Oakey Hall was credited with coining the phrase boasting that the Ring's problems would soon "blow over," which Nast ridiculed once again in the title of this cartoon.

At the center, Tweed is consoled by a "Shiny Hat" lackey and an Irish-Catholic constituent, who minister to the Boss with fan and alcohol bottle, respectively. Behind the trio, as in the "Marius" parody, is a Roman arch. The billowing smoke (or dust) prodded contemporary viewers to remember engravings of the recent Great Fire in Chicago (October 7-9, 1871). In the upper-left, Mayor Hall clings precariously to an uncertain pillar of bricks. In the events that followed, Hall turned out to be the lone political survivor of the Tammany Ring, ultimately managing to complete his mayoral term ending on January 1, 1873.

Richard Connolly, the former comptroller who would be arrested on November 25, the issue date of this cartoon, appears (lower-left) crushed beneath the empty treasury safe. Just to the right lies Judge Edward Shandley, defeated Tammany candidate for county registrar. Pinned at the right-center is Mike Norton, the unsuccessful Tammany candidate for the state senate; beneath him, the arm of John Bradley, defeated in his state senatorial race and soon to resign as city chamberlain, gropes futilely for the leg of his fleeing brother-in-law, Peter Sweeny, who absconds with the "Brains" moneybag. Under the pillar on which Sweeny steps lies Thomas Ledwith, a police magistrate running for a seat on the state supreme court*. On the far right, Tom Fields is in agony under a fallen beam. He had won his state senatorial race against Horatio Seymour, the former governor and presidential nominee, but was charged with vote fraud and forced to resign his seat to escape prosecution**. Other failed Tammany candidates for the state senate, Henry Genet and Henry Woltman, are partly obscured by the rubble in the background.

* For a more graphic cartoon of Ledwith, see page 214.
** For a more graphic cartoon of Fields, see page 223.

SOMETHING THAT DID BLOW OVER—NOVEMBER 7, 1871.

The following number of *Harper's Weekly*, dated December 2, 1871, and published November 22, contained a vigorous image of Lady New York with a "US" decoration on her classical gown, gesturing toward a giant ballot box globe, which is flattening Tweed, Hall, and Sweeny. She instructs the world— "To Whom It May Concern"—to follow her example of purifying political corruption through ballots not bullets (as the poster pasted up by Uncle Sam proclaims). Crowds of world leaders stream from the "US PUBLIC SCHOOL," now an instrument of global education, which closely resembles the architecture of the White House in Washington.

In the front rows behind the ballot box are (left-right): Pope Pius IX; an Irishman; King Victor Emmanuel II of Italy, who elbows the Pope; a Chinese man; Alfonso XII of Spain, who later returned from exile to reign briefly as king (1874-1885); Emperor Franz-Josef of Austria, with the Double-Eagle emblem on his hat; Otto Von Bismarck, the German chancellor, with the Prussian Eagle atop his helmet; Emperor Wilhelm I of Germany, with the spiked helmet, bending over the ballot box in profile; and John Bull, the personification of Great Britain. Barely visible in the shadow under Lady New York's outstretched arm is the profile of Napoleon III, the deposed French emperor, who wears the military cocked hat of his uncle, Napoleon I, whom he sought to emulate.

At the upper right, Uncle Sam, on a ladder, is scrubbing City Hall which is emblazoned with "The Ballot is Mightier than the Bullet," "Victory for the Republic" and "Down with Corruption." At the bottom of City Hall, a man and a woman are scrubbing too; the woman has on the bonnet of Mrs. Grundy, a favorite Nast fictional character.

Behind that couple, and facing the wall of the City Hall, a short young man or boy is jumping excitedly in celebration with his arms waving wildly. That, almost certainly, is Thomas Nast's representation of himself giving vent to his feelings of exultation.

Jailing the Tammany Tiger

The issue ends with a small, two-column Nast cartoon visually suggesting "What the People Must Do About It," in answer to Tweed's (erroneously) alleged taunt, "Well, What are you going to do about it?" Hall, Tweed, Sweeny, and Connolly appear as glum and anxious Tammany tigers, which have been chained in a cage.

WHAT THE PEOPLE MUST DO ABOUT IT.

TO WHOM IT MAY CONCERN.

NEW-YORK. "NOW YOU SEE WHAT I DID ABOUT IT. GO AND DO LIKEWISE."

From the outset of the legal and judicial process against the Tweed Ring, Nast was impatient with what he interpreted as a tortuous and slow pace on the path to conviction and punishment. In his bleak, smirking celebration of justice-delayed, "The Dead Beat," in the December 23, 1871 issue (available December 13), the Ring alumni settle down to an elegant soiree of champagne, fruit, and tobacco.

The abundance of cigar smoke conjures up a vision of Dick Turpin and Jack Sheppard, the infamous and legendary eighteenth-century English desperadoes, hanging from their respective gallows. Turpin's ghost addresses Sheppard's: "There's no use talking. To them belongs the palm [prize]. They have completely outdone us." In the left background of this spectral image appears a triad of dire omens: vultures circling in the smoky fog near the setting sun.

Nast's punning title literally describes a cheat or swindler, while the cartoonist's figurative intent was "The Dead, Beaten." Host Tweed sits, dreamily blowing smoke rings, with one leg resting informally on an ottoman—elevated as in two other recent images (perhaps to suggest gout resulting from overindulgence). The wicker wastebasket, having become an important symbol, is overflowing with "Arrests," "Bail," "Law," and a discarded newspaper proclaiming "The Will Of The People – Nov. 7th."

Most significant among those present is ex-Comptroller Richard Connolly (left) deliberately blowing smoke in Mayor Oakey Hall's face. Three months earlier, Hall tried unsuccessfully to force Connolly to resign, so he could put his own man in this critical position. (Civil War General George McClellan was his choice, but cautious George turned him down.) Connolly did as Samuel Tilden and William Havemeyer advised him, and appointed Andrew Green as deputy while he effectively took a leave of absence. Connolly did resign on or about November 18 and, much to his surprise, was arrested on the 25th, more than two weeks before this cartoon was published.

Other confident and satiated Ring members at the party include (left-right): Judges George Barnard and Thomas Ledwith, in front of whom sits Assemblyman Tom Fields; the balding Hank Smith, president of the Police Commissioners; financier Jim Fisk with his trademark moustache, and behind Fisk, his business partner, Jay Gould; beside Gould is his lawyer and Tweed's, David Dudley Field. Peter Sweeny, with furrowed brow, sits at the table beside Tweed; Judge Edward Shandley is in the background above the Boss's head; Tammany Republican Nathaniel Sands, recently ousted from the reformist Citizens' Association, is behind Tweed's chair; and, on the far right, stands Thomas G. Shearman, Field's law partner and fellow counsel for Fisk's and Gould's Erie Railroad, and co-founder of present law firm Shearman and Sterling.

THE DEAD BEAT.

The Ghost of Dick Turpin to Jack Sheppard. "There's no use talking. To them belongs the Palm. They have completely outdone us."

In the wake of the election, the ejection of the Ring members and their associates from their positions of power, and the judicial efforts to punish them, Thomas Nast continued his efforts to caricature what happened.

He necessarily did it chronologically. However, it is more meaningful for today's readers to follow each of the principal Ring characters—or a group of Ring associates—through their post-election travails and travels individually, without having to relate to the intermittent cartoons that pertained to other Ring-related people and topics.

For all the Ring members except Boss Tweed, their exits from the political and judicial scene—and therefore from Nast's cartoons—were essentially over by the end of 1872, the year following the election. Only two of the bad guys—Boss Tweed and Bagman Andrew Garvey—ever went to jail. Several fled to Europe, and all but Richard Connolly ultimately returned. The city of New York recovered damages and other payments totaling less than $2 million out of the $13 million mostly fraudulent dollars spent on the new court house.

Here are their wind-up stories as portrayed by Nast, the *New-York Times* and other relevant sources.

Boss Tweed's post-Ring travails encompassed three trials, two separate sojourns in prison, one escape and a year on the lam and, finally, death in jail—over a span of almost six and a half years. He will be featured in the next two chapters, beginning on page 225.

Richard Connolly was the first of the four Ring leaders to break with the others, although it happened gradually over the last four months of 1871. Thomas Nast dealt with that by depicting him as a lesser player, or in shadow, as his phase-out progressed.

Irish-born Connolly was 62 in 1871, about 15 to 18 years older than his principal confederates. He was a big man, whose height was exaggerated by the stovepipe hat he usually had on. He was clean-shaven, wore gold-rimmed spectacles, and had an obvious belly, although not on the scale of Tweed's.

"Slippery Dick" was considered to be relatively ignorant compared to Peter Sweeny or Oakey Hall. However, he was a good bookkeeper, and developed a multiple-entry accounting system which enabled the Ring's fraudulent payments to be readily concealed. Personally, he was considered to be cold, crafty, cowardly and dishonest—obsequious to his superiors and arrogant to most others.

Nast obviously understood Connolly well.   In "Wholesale and Retail" published on September 6 (issue date September 16), Connolly is shown confidently striding out of the New York City Treasury—right behind Boss Tweed—with his pocket full. The dark coloring of his suit and hat make him stand out from the other three Ring members. This cartoon almost certainly was drawn before the vouchers were stolen on the night of September 10 from Connolly's offices.

Two weeks later, after the vouchers were stolen, in "Too Thin" published on September 20 (issue date September 30), Connolly's face (far left) has "guilty" written all over it.

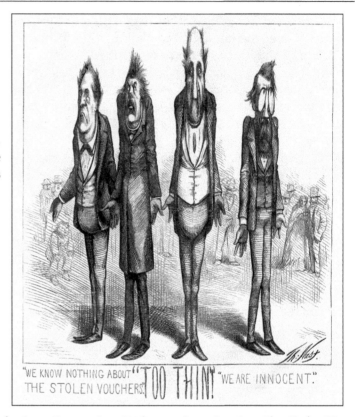

"WE KNOW NOTHING ABOUT THE STOLEN VOUCHERS. "TOO THIN!" "WE ARE INNOCENT."

A week after that, in "Stop Thief!, published on September 27 (issue date October 7), all the Ring members and associates are running wildly away from the New York Treasury, but only Connolly has fallen, losing his stovepipe hat in the process. His fall reflects his replacement by Andrew Green, who now possesses the power of Acting Comptroller while Connolly is on leave prior to his resignation on or about November 18.

"STOP THIEF!"

"They no sooner heard the cry, than, guessing how the matter stood, they issued forth with great promptitude; and, shouting 'Stop Thief!' too, joined in the pursuit like *Good Citizens*."—"OLIVER TWIST."

In the following issue published on October 4 (issue date October 14), showing the four masters who emptied the New York Treasury, Nast hides about a third of Connolly's face and body behind the door to the Treasury safe. Connolly is beginning to fade from view.

In the Ring's next weekly appearance on October 11 (issue date October 21), Connolly has disappeared from view as the four face the gallows in "The Only Thing they Respect or Fear;" only part of his stovepipe hat is visible. Nast probably intended to reflect Connolly's cowardice, as well as his effective abdication from the Comptroller's office.

Three weeks later, in the last pre-election issue which appeared on November 4 (issue date November 11) and contained six Nast cartoons, Connolly is out of the picture both figuratively and literally. In "The Lion's Share," his three Ring confederates have indigestion, but Connolly as some kind of domestic animal is dead—on his back with his legs up in the shadow.

THE LION'S SHARE.

They have all had their share, and it now seems to disagree with them.

A week or so after the November 11 issue date showing him figuratively dead in "The Lion's Share" cartoon, Connolly, who was on a leave of absence, formally resigned; a week after that, on November 25, he was arrested by Sheriff Matthew Brennan. Bail was set at $1 million which he reportedly was set to meet. When prosecutor Charles O'Conor came to Connolly's house to collect, he raised the bail to $1.5 million at the last minute. Connolly's wife Mary controlled the family's money and told her husband to go to prison; she wasn't paying the extra $500,000. In Nast's cartoon published on January 3, 1872 (issue date January 13),—"The Last of the Four"—Connolly is shown in jail.

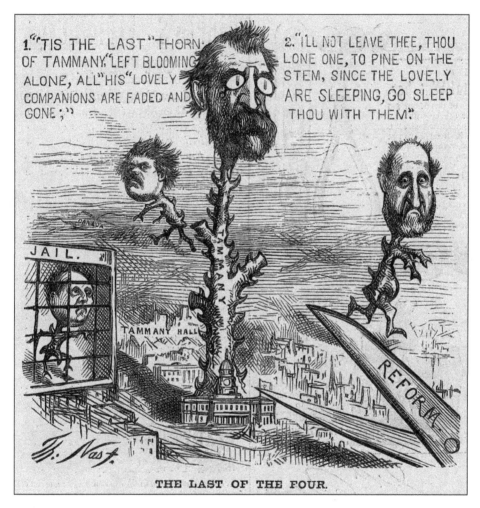

1."'TIS THE LAST "THORN OF TAMMANY,"LEFT BLOOMING ALONE, ALL "HIS" LOVELY COMPANIONS ARE FADED AND GONE;"

2."I'LL NOT LEAVE THEE, THOU LONE ONE, TO PINE ON THE STEM, SINCE THE LOVELY ARE SLEEPING, GO SLEEP THOU WITH THEM."

THE LAST OF THE FOUR.

However, on December 31, four days before publication, Connolly's bail was reduced to a reported $500,000, which he paid and promptly fled to Europe via Canada. During the next eight-plus years, he spent the remainder of his $6 million in Egypt, Switzerland and France. He never returned home, in contrast to fellow Ring exiles Peter Sweeny, Andrew Garvey, James Ingersoll and Elbert Woodward. He died of Bright's Disease in a hotel in Marseille, France in 1880.

After the election, the *Herald* reported that Peter Sweeny had secretly resigned as Commissioner of Public Parks on November 1; the announcement wasn't made until November 8, the day after the election, and became effective Friday, November 10. The Democratic *Herald* treated the development as high tragedy: "The old Roman saying . . . may—in sympathy only, not in reality—be applied to the fall of Tammany. That saying was 'When the Coliseum falls, Rome falls: and when Rome falls, then the world.' Tammany has been the political Coliseum of the world of democracy in our midst since the foundation of our political institutions and though subject to many reverses in its day, it was reserved for the election of yesterday to really overthrow its power and influence." The newspaper designated Sweeny, "the noblest Roman who ever ruled."

In the *Harper's Weekly* issue of November 25, 1871 (available November 15, eight days after the election), Thomas Nast took one minor, one middling and one super shot at Peter Sweeny. On the cover, in "To the Victor Belong the Spoils," Sweeny's resignation as Commissioner of Public Parks is represented by the abandoned moneybag satchel reading "Tammany Brains." Three pages later in "Something That Did Blow Over," Sweeny is a prominent figure, fleeing the scene carrying the "Brains" moneybag in one hand and holding his hat with the other.

On the facing page is "The Political Suicide of Peter 'Brains' Sweeny." As the first of the Ring to depart, Sweeny received a six-panel solo send-off from Nast.

The first panel shows Sweeny moving away from the polls, outside of which a sign proclaims "Down with the Ring—The Battle Cry of Freedom." Sweeny always read the political tea leaves well, and "The Reasons Which Have Prompted This Action—These Reasons Are Of An Overwhelming Character" anticipated his defeat. In panel two, he writes: "I have withdrawn wholly from public life."

In the third panel, as Sweeny gets the public boot, with the sole marked "the prison," he brandishes his tendered resignation and falls dead over Richard Connolly's already lifeless body.

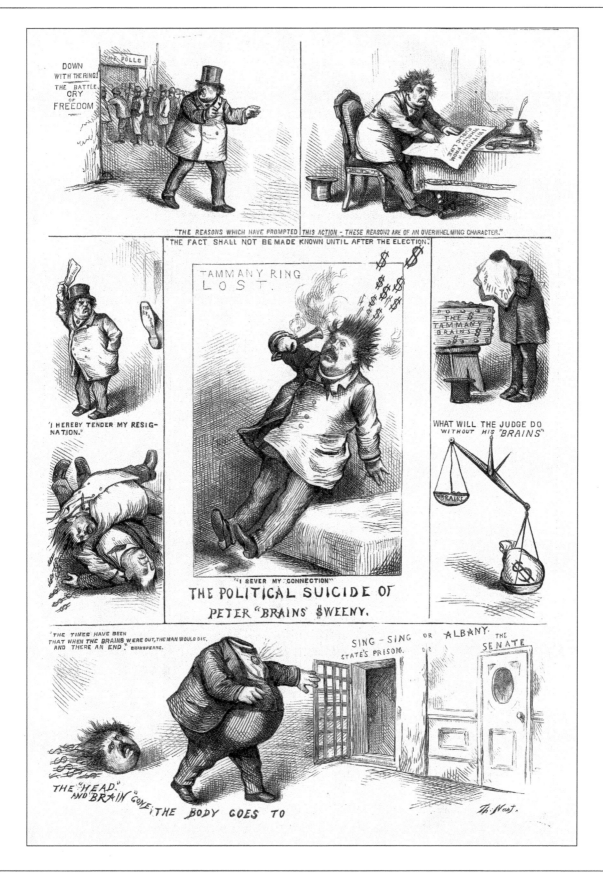

The center panel states "Tammany Ring Lost" as Sweeny blows his brains out and Nast puns with "I sever my connection." The cartoonist emphasizes Sweeny's massive straight hair—his identifying feature—blowing straight back along with a shower of dollars. The cartoon's title is below.

In the center-right panel, Judge Henry Hilton, Sweeny's colleague on the City Park Commission, grieves at the loss of his Tammany "Brains," which previously had balanced Tammany's cash on the scales.

The climactic scene in the bottom panel builds on Nast's sensitivity to the widespread belief that Sweeny had always been the Ring mastermind. With Sweeny's head and brain on the floor, the headless body of Boss Tweed appears to be moving towards the open door of Sing-Sing, the state's prison on the Hudson River (in today's Ossining), rather than to the state senate in Albany (to which he has been reelected) whose door is closed to him.

The Shakespearean quotes are from MacBeth (Act III, Scene IV) when the guilt-ridden MacBeth speaks of the ghostly reappearance of the murdered Banquo. "The times have been that when the brains were out, the man would die, and there an end" is the controlling quotation at the left top of the panel. "The 'head' and 'brain' gone, the body goes to" …is the punning phrase (too) that leads the headless Tweed to Sing-Sing or Albany.

Sweeny did not like the public arena. He was an introvert who disliked publicity and especially courtrooms; in 1858, when he was District Attorney, he had to resign because he became tongue-tied in front of a jury.

He didn't want to face what he knew was coming, so he fled to Canada in December for alleged health reasons. The *Times* asked on December 22: "Who goes to Canada in the dead of winter when he is sick?"

Nast's final cartoon in which Sweeny played a direct role was "The Last of the Four," published in the January 15, 1872 issue of *Harper's Weekly*. Sweeny is shown heading north towards Canada.

THE LAST OF THE FOUR.

From Canada, he eventually joined his brother James in Paris. James, who always had fronted for Peter as the recipient of Peter's share of the Ring's proceeds, died in France. Ultimately, Peter Sweeny returned to New York in December 1876, and settled the claims against him for $400,000 in June 1877—all paid from James' estate—leaving him with the $6 million he took through the Ring. Retired in disgrace from public life, he divided his time between Paris and New York. He died in Lake Mahopac, NY at age 86 in 1911.

Sweeny's payment was the only recovery New York City obtained from any of the four principal Ring participants, exclusive of the jumped bail payment (reportedly $500,000) from Richard Connolly when he fled to Europe in January 1872.

Oakey Hall was Tweed's hand-picked mayor, whose education, legal background, social status and outgoing nature made him an ideal front for the Ring. Mayor Hall, along with Comptroller Richard Connolly, approved all the Ring's fraudulent payment vouchers, and became primary targets after the *New-York Times* disclosures in July 1871.

Hall's name, position and appearance made him an ideal caricature for Thomas Nast. Hall's own personal trademark was the depth and variety of his elegant wardrobe, including a green suit for St. Patrick's Day. Along with his beard and long wavy hair, Nast's trademark for Hall was his pince-nez glasses and their black string which framed owlish eyes. The cartoonist accentuated Hall's spectacles to the extent that they alone could represent him.

H'ALL THAT'S LEFT.

After the first *Times* disclosure on July 8, 1871 until Hall mysteriously left for Europe in 1877, Nast featured Hall in 16 cartoons, all but one published before his mayoral term ended on January 1, 1873.

The New Horse Plague

Since June 1871, horses in New York City had been succumbing to a type of influenza, which incapacitated most equine victims for a week or two, and killed some of them. The "horse plague" was a serious problem for the city because nineteenth-century urban transportation was so reliant on the animal.

After the July 8 *New-York Times* disclosure—in the back of the Orange Riot issue of *Harper's Weekly* (July 29)—a small Nast cartoon shows "Mare" Hall as such an ailing horse, languishing in Tweed's luxurious stable as the Boss and Sweeny look on sadly. The caption prognosticates that the mayor's chance for recovery is doubtful, a fate also awaiting the rest of the Tammany Ring.

THE NEW HORSE PLAGUE.

Tweed's Mayor [mare] has it so badly that recovery is doubtful. Alas! they know how it is themselves.

Behind

After the theft of the vouchers on September 10, 1871, Hall and his three co-conspirators proclaimed their innocence in Nast's "Too Thin" cartoon in the issue of September 30, available September 20. In that same issue, Nast's "Which Nobody Can Deny" portrays "Honest Democrats" as a large boot kicking Mayor Oakey Hall unceremoniously in the seat of his pants. According to the caption, the *Leader*, a Tammany-owned newspaper edited by Hall, had recently made the optimistic assertion that "the Democratic Party was behind him [the mayor]."

By late September, Mayor Hall was taking action to halt newsstand sales of the illustrated monthly *Wild Oats* because of a cover drawing of the Tammany Ring foursome as the "Sing Sing Chorus" in prison stripes and ball-and-chains. He threatened to take a similar action against Harper's Weekly, but did not. (However, Tammany's friends did manage to delay publication of Nast's 83-page controversial book with 72 illustrations, *Miss Columbia's Public School or Will It Blow Over?*, until after the November election.) During this period, Hall continued to evade the press, and rumors circulated that the mayor had suffered an emotional breakdown.

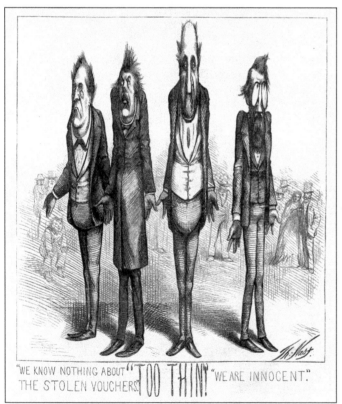

"WE KNOW NOTHING ABOUT THE STOLEN VOUCHERS." "TOO THIN!" "WE ARE INNOCENT."

"WHICH NOBODY CAN DENY."
"The Democratic Party is behind him" (Mayor HALL).—*N. Y. Leader* (His Paper).

The Legal Battle Begins

On October 3, 1871, a judicial warrant was issued against Mayor Oakey Hall "for various offenses and malfeasance in his office amounting to misdemeanor." A grand jury was selected, and then heard the case in theoretical secrecy on October 19-25. Witnesses included the new deputy controller Andrew Green, whistle-blowers William Copeland and James O'Brien, *New-York Times* publisher George Jones, and Samuel Tilden. None of them could testify to first-hand knowledge of willful or unlawful acts on Hall's part.

Hall admitted signing vouchers for the inflated expenditures, but denied knowledge that the amounts were incorrect; he blamed Tweed and Connolly. After much testimony, the jury dismissed the charges against the mayor, but reprimanded him for being "careless and negligent in the discharge of his duties."

On October 11, eight days before Mayor Hall's grand jury commenced hearing evidence, Nast's "Portraits of the Mayor's Grand Jury" appeared in the postdated October 21 issue of *Harper's Weekly*. Playing upon the unfounded rumor that an uncle and cousin of the mayor had been selected as members of the grand jury, it showed 12 miniature portraits of Oakey Hall.

PORTRAITS OF THE MAYOR'S GRAND JURY.

Round One: Cleared But . . . .

Again turning to his crystal ball, a Nast cartoon in the October 28 *Harper's Weekly*, probably completed at least ten days before the grand jury panel was seated, and published on October 18, correctly predicted the eventual outcome: a failure to indict Hall. "Our Mare Still Lives" is a reprise of three cartoons published in July and August in which Mayor Hall was depicted by Nast as a casualty of the "horse plague" epidemic, which had been disrupting city transportation since June 1871. Here, the city's chief executive, too weak to stand in Tweed's lavish stable, is supported by the sort of sling used to treat the animals who had some prospect for recovery. (This cartoon also includes a set of initials [J. N.] of Nast's young daughter, Julia, in the lower-left corner.)

"OUR MARE STILL LIVES."

Mayor "Haul"

Nast published six cartoons in the issue of November 11, (available November 1, six days before the election) headed by "The Tammany Tiger Loose." The least important of these featured Mayor HAUL, the first time Nast referred to his ill-gotten gain and/or evidence of Tammany wrongdoing.

The cartoon featured Grand Duke Alexis of Russia, third son of Emperor Alexander II, who would begin a three-month tour of the United States in New York City on November 21. Mayor Hall was being pressed to withhold formal courtesies (he did not) as an expression of official disapproval of reported acts of tsarist oppression. Here, the mayor stands, with arms crossed (as in "The Boss Still Has the Reins"), and bluntly informs Alexis of his (fictional) decision not to meet the young Russian nobleman. In response, the grand duke doffs his cap in polite appreciation, above the title taken from Shakespeare's *Hamlet*: "For This Relief, Much Thanks!" Behind Hall, Tweed looks on with stern approval.

"FOR THIS RELIEF, MUCH THANKS!"—Shakspeare.

MAYOR HAUL. "I will not receive you in an Official Capacity."
GRAND DUKE ALEXIS. *"You do me Honor."*

Nast vs. Greeley (and Hall)

Thomas Nast never forgave Horace Greeley, editor of the *Tribune*, for giving Oakey Hall the benefit of the doubt on the question of the mayor's guilt or innocence in regard to Tweed Ring corruption. On November 23, 1871, the *New-York Times* stated, "Mr. Greeley is at this moment engaged in the desperate effort to prove that Mayor Hall has nothing whatever to do with the great frauds which we have exposed." Greeley probably considered Hall as more of a dupe than a crook. The maverick *Tribune* editor further angered the cartoonist by preparing to challenge President Ulysses S. Grant, Nast's hero, in the 1872 election.

Six days later, the post-dated December 9 issue of *Harper's Weekly* was published with Nast's pictorial slam against Greeley and Hall, "H. G. Diogenes Has Found the Honest Man." Diogenes was an Ancient Greek philosopher of the Cynic school who supposedly searched with a lantern for an honest man, as does Greeley in this cartoon. Mayor Hall, who had been cleared but reprimanded five weeks earlier by a grand jury, stands on the steps of the "Hall of Honesty"—a dual reference to City Hall and the mayor's name—stripped down to his stocking feet with turned-out empty pockets. In front of Hall is what may be intended as a threadbare wallet and, sticking out behind it, a whitewash brush.

H. G. DIOGENES HAS FOUND THE HONEST MAN.
H. G. D. "Whoever says you ain't is 'a vulgar braggart and liar, chattering slander with as little sense of responsibility as a magpie.'"

The papers in Greeley's pocket poke fun at his penchant for vitriolic attacks on those who disagreed with him, his pretentiousness, and his recent authorship of a book on scientific agriculture, *What I Know About Farming* (1871). Greeley knew Boss Tweed, having previously served with him and Tammany Republican Nathaniel Sands on the Tobacco Manufacturing Association's board of directors.

An Awful Dose

In the same December 9 issue, Nast pictorially noted the resignation (effective on or about November 18) of Comptroller "Slippery Dick" Connolly, and of Mayor Hall's extremely reluctant appointment of the reform-minded deputy (and acting) comptroller, Andrew H. Green, in his place. The *New-York Times* of November 21 had commented, "Mayor Hall and all his tribe would rather see [Green] at the bottom of the sea playing with mermaids than [as] Comptroller of New York City."

Nast's "An Awful Dose" is a bottle of "Green Bitters" on the table in Hall's sickroom. The patient, "Tammany Haul," limp and wasted, pleadingly inquires of "Doctor New York" whether the "horrid 'Green' stuff" will allow him to recover. The physician intones, "Nothing will save you, you're so far gone."

On November 26, three days before this scene appeared in print, a *Times* editorial headline chortled "Now for Hall!" It argued, "Every reason that could be alleged for the arrest of ex-Comptroller Connolly may be urged with double force in favor of the arrest of Mayor Hall."

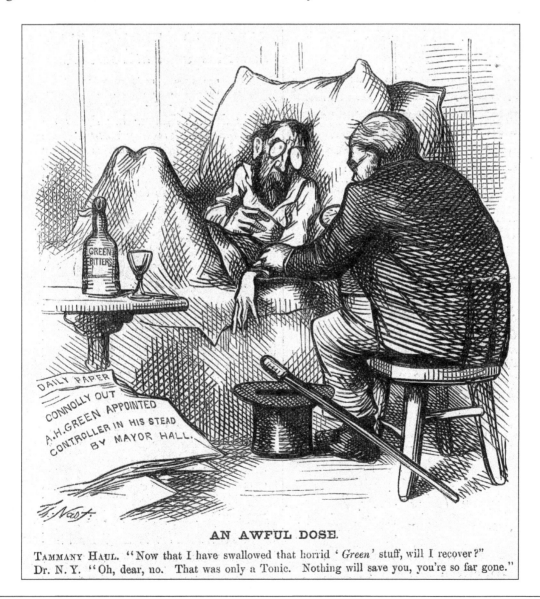

AN AWFUL DOSE.

TAMMANY HAUL. "Now that I have swallowed that horrid '*Green*' stuff, will I recover?"
Dr. N. Y. "Oh, dear, no. That was only a Tonic. Nothing will save you, you're so far gone."

Honest Haul

Nast sustained the same refrain from "An Awful Dose" in "Honest Haul As Richard III" in the December 30, 1871 issue of *Harper's Weekly* (published December 20). Shakespeare's twisted paragon of evil minces forward to claim credit for Andrew Green's "Programme of Reform," and for his own exemplary behavior since the November 7 election.

The soliloquy is taken from Act I, Scene III, in which King Richard admits to using the Bible selectively to "clothe my naked villainy … And seem a saint when most I play the devil." Nast's figure of Richard III is loosely modeled on three of John Gilbert's illustrations (c. 1859). A century after this cartoon appeared, at least one cartoonist turned to these lines from Shakespeare to portray President Richard Nixon during the Watergate scandal, but without realizing Nast's previous application.

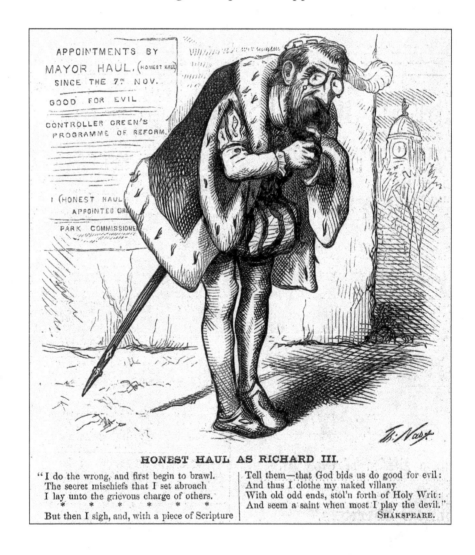

HONEST HAUL AS RICHARD III.

"I do the wrong, and first begin to brawl.   Tell them—that God bids us do good for evil:
The secret mischiefs that I set abroach   And thus I clothe my naked villany
I lay unto the grievous charge of others.   With old odd ends, stol'n forth of Holy Writ:
  *   *   *   *   *   *   And seem a saint when most I play the devil."
But then I sigh, and, with a piece of Scripture   SHAKSPEARE.

Hall's position as editor came to an end this week; his paper, the *Leader*, was published for the last time on December 29.

Jester Hall

The following week Nast again showed Hall as a Shakespearean character: Touchstone the Jester from "As You Like It," reading "Where Ignorance is Bliss, 'tis Folly to be Wise."

"Tammany (O.K.) Hall Jester" claims "I am in Blissful Ignorance of Every Thing that has happened since I have been Mayor of New York." Looking worried, he is reading his jester's role in the play, sitting cross-legged on the floor, and raising his finger to make the point. Meanwhile, the head of a second jester, lying on the floor behind Hall's left knee, peeks out with an expression of disbelief and incredulity on his face at Hall's statement.

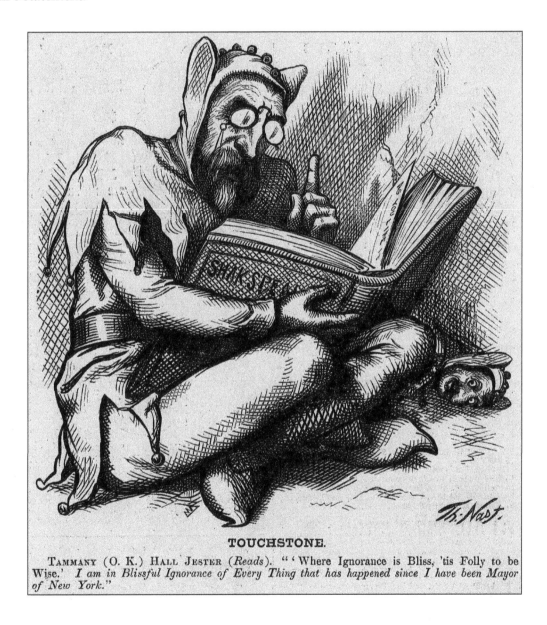

TOUCHSTONE.

TAMMANY (O. K.) HALL JESTER (*Reads*). "'Where Ignorance is Bliss, 'tis Folly to be Wise.' *I am in Blissful Ignorance of Every Thing that has happened since I have been Mayor of New York.*"

Hall: The Last of the Four

While Nast waited for something substantive to happen in the Tweed Ring prosecution, he developed a number of modest alternative scenarios. In the January 13, 1872 issue of *Harper's Weekly* (in print January 3), Nast's "The Last of the Four" took note of the determined survival of Mayor Oakey Hall by firmly planting him on the roof of City Hall as a pruned Tammany rosebush.

The ruins of Tammany Hall lie in the background, while Richard Connolly looks out from jail, Peter Sweeny exits north to Canada, and Tweed runs toward the right side of the picture, worriedly eyeing the huge "Reform" shears approaching City Hall (before which flies a microscopic Irish flag).

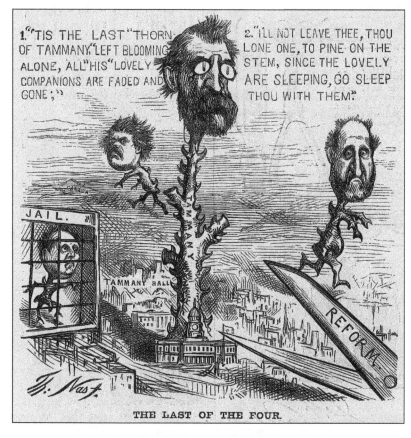

THE LAST OF THE FOUR.

This image is one of the few times when one of Nast's Tweed Ring cartoons was overtaken by events. Connolly, who had been jailed in November, finally managed to secure reduced bail (reportedly $500,000) and gain his release on January 1, 1872. As this cartoon was published, he was preparing to cross the Atlantic for permanent exile in Egypt, Switzerland, and France. Sweeny's trip to Canada in mid-winter for alleged health reasons fooled no one.

"The Last of the Four" is based on the popular poem and song by Thomas Moore, "The Last Rose of Summer," from his *Irish Melodies* (1835). Nast's selection of Moore probably was prompted by the poet-lyricist's Irish origins. The cartoonist tartly adjusted the lush, romantic sentiment of the original.

Hall's Final Year as Mayor: The Start

Oakey Hall was under terrible pressure from all sides in the fall of 1871 and winter of 1872. A second grand jury was convened in November, and the public expected an indictment against Hall. The new strategy was to charge him with a misdemeanor: neglect of duty for failing to audit a specific account.

His social life was also going downhill. Some of the elite clubs he belonged to no longer wanted him as a member. Former friends and associates began to ostracize him.

In his annual New Year's address, Hall asked for understanding. This prompted Nast to draw him with a sandwich board: "You Know How It Is Yourself" signed by "Mayor Haul." The cartoon appeared on January 10, in the post-dated January 20, 1872 issue of *Harper's Weekly*.

THE MESSAGE MAYOR HALL OUGHT TO HAVE SENT.

Back in the Courtroom

Rumors had it that Hall would be indicted and tried again. Thomas Nast responded with a cartoon in the February 3, 1872 issue of *Harper's Weekly*: "Haul 'Turned Up' . . . Here We Are Again." Hall appears as a Jack-in-the-Box.

HAUL "TURNED UP."
"Here we are again."

On February 10, 1872, Mayor Oakey Hall was indicted by a second grand jury on five misdemeanor charges. Specifically, it focused on a $41,563 warrant payable to Andrew J. Garvey for labor and materials for the new courthouse, and signed by Hall and Connolly. Four similar misdemeanor claims—two for fraudulent bills submitted by Garvey and two by James Ingersoll— also were included.

The trial began on February 19. Most of the same witnesses testified as they did at the first trial. It did not go well for the prosecution until the unveiling of a surprise witness, Andrew Garvey, the "Prince of Plasterers." Hall and most others had believed reports that Garvey and his wife were in Europe. In fact, the former contractor and bagman had actually returned and been hiding incognito in New York City, having agreed to turn state's evidence in return for immunity from prosecution. Like a ghost arisen from the grave, his unexpected entrance stunned the courtroom, especially the defendant and his lawyers, a reaction recorded by Thomas Nast in a back-page cartoon of the March 23, 1872 issue of *Harper's Weekly* (in print March 13).

A prosecutor is dressed as a traditional figure of a sorcerer, trickster, or master of transformations, originating in classic Italian *Commedia dell'Arte* and traditional British pantomime. The character was customarily clad in loud, diamond-patterned tights and tunic, and carried a signature wand to work his wizardry. The pantomime art of George Fox was a staple of the Bowery Theater, a favorite haunt of young Nast, whose childhood home was nearby.

Here, the prosecutor-sorcerer has waved his wand to conjure up "the Demon Garvey." Mayor Hall, whose outturned pockets replicate his appearance in "H. G. Diogenes Has Found the Honest Man" (See page 194), is shaken, his knees buckling, as Tweed and Sweeny flee in terror behind him. In the background is a small image of Justice on her throne.

THE SUDDEN APPEARANCE OF THE DEMON GARVEY.

Garvey admitted on the witness stand to submitting false claims to the city's Board of Audit, of which Hall was one of four members, along with Tweed, Sweeny and Connolly. However, no direct evidence of the mayor's knowledge of the fraud was presented. On March 12, the day before the cartoon was published, Matthias Clark, the foreman of the jury, died, and a mistrial was declared three days later. Mayor Hall had escaped the sword of justice for a second time.

*   *   *

In late October 1872, Hall was tried again. This time, the case went to the jury which became deadlocked: seven Republicans for conviction and five Democrats for acquittal. Hall still survived.

Thomas Nast spent from June through November of 1872 portraying Horace Greeley in the same vein as he drew the Tweed Ring the previous two years. Greeley was running against Nast's hero, President Ulysses S. Grant, on a Liberal Republican-Tammany Hall-Southern Democrat (former Confederates) fusion ticket, and Nast was merciless.

Greeley lost the election the week after Hall's trial ended, and died on November 29. Hall led the funeral procession, as Mayor, ahead of President Grant, three governors, George Jones of the *Times* and George William Curtis, editor of *Harper's Weekly*.

Nast did attend Hall's trial on at least one day. Whether preoccupied with Greeley or because he did not think it cartoon-worthy, he ignored the trial and the result.

Mayor Hall's Exit

While Thomas Nast ignored the Mayor's legal exoneration, he celebrated the end of his term with two zinger cartoons in the Harper's Weekly issue of January 4, 1873, available the day after Christmas.

Nast again presented "Mare" Hall as a victim of the "horse plague" which still was afflicting the equine population of New York. This time the dead mare/mayor is dumped unceremoniously off a refuse cart into the East River.

* * *

William Havemeyer, the new mayor, had served in that role previously under the Tammany banner. A wealthy sugar merchant, a leader of the Committee of Seventy and a close friend of Samuel Tilden, Havemeyer played a key role in the September negotiations which led Richard Connolly to take a leave of absence and transfer his authority as Comptroller to Andrew Green as Acting Controller.

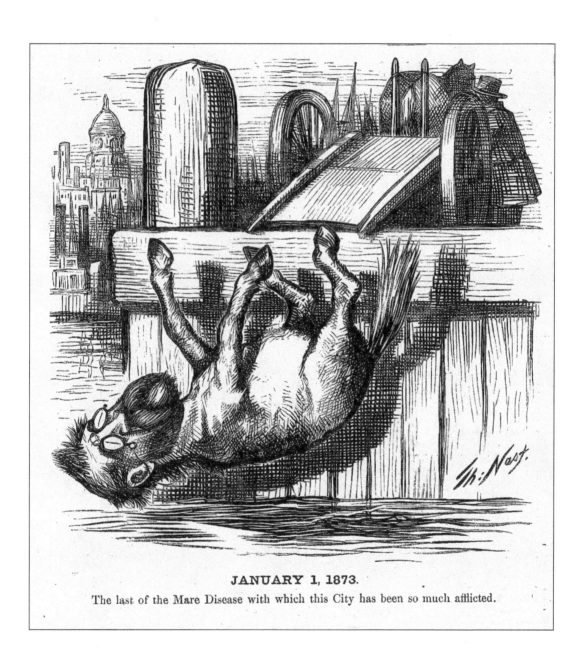

JANUARY 1, 1873.

The last of the Mare Disease with which this City has been so much afflicted.

The Finger of Scorn

Thomas Nast saved his best for last in portraying the end of Oakey Hall's mayoralty. Maybe the law couldn't get him but the scorn of society could and did.

Nast probably anticipated that Hall would never be convicted. However, he knew that Hall was being shunned by many of his former friends and associates, and was not particularly welcome in his upper-crust clubs. Moreover, his wife, Katherine Louise Barnes Hall, a leading socialite who had never mixed with her husband's political cronies or their wives, was really upset by his loss of respectability. Ultimately, their marriage broke up.

Nast's full-page cartoon in the January 4, 1873 issue, available the day after Christmas 1872, conveyed the thought bluntly. Titled "The Finger of Scorn Shall Follow Them if Law (Sometimes Called Justice) Can Not," it showed Hall as a blind man being led away from City Hall by his seeing-eye dog. In this case, it is a bulldog (substituting for a tiger) wearing an Americus (Tammany social club) collar. Hall is wearing a signboard which says "Pity the Poor but Honest Blind Gentle Man Who Saw Nothing of the Tammany Ring's Stealings." From behind City Hall, a huge hand with a pointed "Finger of Scorn" points directly at Hall's head.

One of two signs on City Hall says "Herculean Job to Clean this Mare's **STABLE**". Hercules is in front of the sign pushing a large broom sweeping away: "fraudulent signatures, sinecures, municipal corruption, rings, election fraud, Tammany officials, Tammany newspaper advertisements, Tammany Board, Tammany police, Hall's bargains, Mayor Hall's excuses and Hall's last appointments."

The other sign on City Hall reads: 1873 "I wish the citizens a Happy New Year and real **REFORM**."

Behind Hall, former Governor John T. Hoffman, now out of office as well, with his initialed trunk near him, is walking towards a sign proclaiming "Steamers to all parts of the world." Other Ring members walking away from City Hall and towards the water include: Boss Tweed using a cane and leaning on the arm of his attorney, David Dudley Field; Tom Fields (to Tweed's lower right); Peter Sweeny (to Tweed's upper right); and Richard Connolly (to the right of Hall's signboard).

THE FINGER OF SCORN
SHALL FOLLOW THEM, IF LAW (SOMETIMES CALLED JUSTICE) CAN NOT.

Finally . . . Acquital

Almost a year after he left office, Hall faced a third trial; it began on December 22, 1873, and ended on Christmas Eve. A key issue for the jury was whether Hall could be convicted on simple neglect of duty or whether it had to be *willful*. The judge ruled that *willful* applied, and told the jury that if a verdict wasn't reached by 10:30 pm, they would be locked up for the night. Understandably, Hall was acquitted.

Hall finally was innocent in the eyes of the law. Nast and *Harper's Weekly* did not comment on the outcome. The Times was unhappy and editorialized that "the prosecution was rather lamely conducted."

*　　*　　*

H'all That's Left

Nast probably never expected to draw a specific cartoon about Oakey Hall again, but he did so in the *Harper's Weekly* issue of April 21, 1877—four-plus years after "The Finger of Scorn." In the interim, Hall had an unsuccessful theatrical venture as playwright and actor, and had resumed his practice of law. He was not accepted in "polite society," his marriage was on the rocks, and he reportedly was having affairs with actresses and other women.

In late March 1877, Hall disappeared. Rumors of his whereabouts included murder and suicide. It eventually turned out that he had sailed for England under an assumed name, and was living in London with a woman who had preceded him from New York.

Nast once again captured the essence of the situation with "H'all That's Left," a picture of the former Mayor's pince-nez glasses hanging on a peg. That was enough to identify his former frequent target.

Hall returned to New York for good in 1892. He died six years later on October 7, 1898, with more debts than assets to show for his colorful life. Peter Sweeny and Jimmy O'Brien attended his funeral.

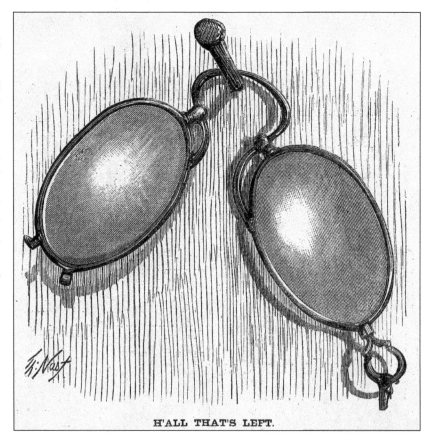

H'ALL THAT'S LEFT.

John Hoffman was Tweed's hand-picked Mayor of New-York for the four years (1865-1868) before Oakey Hall took over that position. A career Tammany politician, he established a solid reputation with both Republicans and Democrats for his performance as a judge in the trials of the Civil War draft rioters.

His stature, and his apparent Germanic heritage— actually his father was of Finnish ancestry—to attract the German vote, made him a "respectable screen" for the Ring, as Nast portrayed him. His height and his handlebar mustache were Nast's keys for caricature.

A RESPECTABLE SCREEN COVERS A MULTITUDE OF THIEVES.

Potential Presidential Candidate

In 1869, Hoffman began the first of two terms as governor of New York, with Tweed's active support. In 1871, when his name was actively floated—again with Tweed's backing—as a Democratic candidate to run against Nast's hero, President Ulysses S. Grant in 1872, Nast went out of his way to ridicule the prospect.

Political Orphan

In mid-1871, however, Hoffman began to distance himself from the Ring with his veto of the Code Amendment. (See page 106). After the Ring's Election Day debacle, Nast showed Hoffman only as a secondary character until the *Harper's Weekly* issue of January 20, 1872, when he was featured in one of four cartoons on a single page. (Two featured Tweed and one featured Hall.)

As an "Orphan Boy," Hoffman, hat in hand, tearfully mourns the death of his 1872 presidential hopes as Tammany's touted candidate. Now a political orphan, he slouches outside the White House, which is nearly obscured by a thicket of trees and the equestrian statue of Andrew Jackson (symbolizing patronage, or the "spoils system"). Hoffman's lament is a tortured variation on "The Orphan Boy's Tale" (1802), the most popular composition by Amelia Opie, a British poet and writer, known for her cloying mixture of sentimentality, pathos, and domestic tragedy.

LITTLE JOHNNY T. HOFFMAN (THE ORPHAN BOY).

"STAY" (*some party*), "stay, for mercy's sake,
    And hear a helpless orphan's tale:
Ah, sure my looks must pity wake!
    'Tis want" (*to go to the White House*) "that makes my cheek so pale.
Yet I was once a mother's" (SWEENY) "pride,
    And my brave father's" (TWEED) "hope and joy;
But in the" (*Tammany*) "proud" (?) "fight" they "died—
    And I am now an orphan boy."

                Not quite "AMELIA OPIE."

Hoffman's Betrayal of Tweed

A week after portraying Governor Hoffman as an orphan boy, Nast showed Hoffman killing his proverbial father, Boss Tweed. Once again, Nast used an extremely well known Shakespearean reference.

On Christmas night, December 25, 1871, a new production of Shakespeare's "Julius Caesar" opened at the Booth Theatre at Sixth Avenue and 23rd Street, with Edwin Booth in the role of Brutus. Shortly thereafter, Nast parodied Jean-Léon Gérôme's celebrated 1867 painting, "Death of Caesar," for the January 27, 1872 issue of *Harper's Weekly* (published January 17), to depict Governor John Hoffman's repudiation of Boss Tweed. While defending the "Tweed" charter in his annual message to the New York State Legislature, Governor Hoffman blamed the individuals who governed New York City—the unnamed Tweed Ring—for the corrupt abuses perpetrated against the city.

Hoffman strongly denounced the practice of vote fraud: "The crime is, under our form of [democratic] government, one of the worst, in its nature and in its effects, and should be punished accordingly. It is a practice which, if persisted in, is more likely to overturn our government than any open war that can be levied against it."

In a remark clearly aimed at Tweed, who had been reelected as a state senator, the governor firmly stated his view that anyone obtaining office by bribery should be barred from holding it. This position was affirmed subsequently by the state senate. Consequently, the Boss never resumed his seat and formally resigned it on March 27, 1872.

Gérôme's painting shows Caesar lying dead and alone as the conspirators exit the chamber. In "Et Tu, Brute?—Then Fall, Caesar," it was central to Nast's purpose that Brutus/Hoffman, the great friend and disciple of Caesar/Tweed, be shown in the act of delivering a final thrust as he shields his eyes from the face of his former mentor.

In the left background, the conspiratorial group of born-again reformers stampeding into the passageway includes a figure (perhaps intended as Tweed's ultimate Tammany successor, John Kelly) wielding a "Tammany" sword; editor Manton Marble holding aloft his *World* dagger; and (probably) the face of James Gordon Bennett Jr., editor of the *Herald*. The text on the arch under which they flee refers to the "New Departure" movement, a group of primarily Northern Democrats, such as Samuel J. Tilden, who accepted the Civil War settlement and Reconstruction amendments; they now emphasized economic issues, in contrast to many Southern Democrats who still embraced the "Lost Cause." Nast, characteristically skeptical, adds on the arch's left pillar, above the thundering herd of virtuous senators: "Beware of Honest Men."

Hoffman's repudiation of Tweed in January 1872 was in tune with his decision not to be a presidential candidate later that year. The national leadership of the Democratic Party was undoubtedly relieved, even as Hoffman served out the remaining year of his term.

In January 1873, tarnished by his association with the Ring, Hoffman retired from politics and returned to the practice of law. After suffering from heart disease for several years, he died of a heart attack on March 24, 1888, while on a trip to Germany.

"ET TU, BRUTE?—THEN FALL, CÆSAR."

"Though the Charter was not all it should have been, it was the best that could then be obtained, and it promised relief from great and long-continued wrong, under which the people of the City had been suffering, and from a system of government the abuses under which are now coming to light. The misconduct recently exposed was not a consequence from any of its provisions.

"The responsibility for the wrong-doing which has very justly aroused public indignation does not rest so much upon the Charter as upon individuals who held office in the City before the Charter was passed, and took office also under it.

"The complaints with regard to the late election in New York and Brooklyn, made through the Press, are chiefly of false counting of ballots and false returns by inspectors of election. The general suspicion of the existence of such an evil is almost as injurious as the practice itself: our people, if led to believe that it is carried on extensively, will neglect to vote, and will lose their habit of submitting quietly to the result of an election. The crime is, under our form of government, one of the worst in its nature and in its effects, and should be punished accordingly. It is a practice which, if persisted in, is more likely to overturn our Government than any open war that can be levied against it. Effectual laws against bribery of the electors, and to take away an office obtained by bribery, thorough protection of the right of challenge on election day, severe penalties against miscounting of votes and against illegal voting, ought to suffice for the protection of the ballot, and will suffice if citizens, juries, and public officers will do their duty."—GOVERNOR HOFFMAN'S MESSAGE, 1872.

XII: Aftermath: What Happened to the Bad Guys

Hoffman's Charter Veto

However, when Hoffman later vetoed a new reform charter for New York City in April, Nast again linked the governor with the Tammany Ring in the cover illustration of the May 18, 1872 issue of *Harper's Weekly* (in print May 8). In "What Are You Going to Do About It?" Hoffman sternly rejects the "People's Charter" drafted by the reformist Committee of Seventy as unconstitutional, to the obvious irritation of Lady New York and the shameless delight of Tweed, who holds the 1870 charter stamped "constitutional." In a "ring" behind the Boss stand (left-right): Hall, Connolly, and Sweeny.

A full-page Nast design for the December 16, 1871 *Harper's Weekly* (in print December 6) tackled the unfinished business of cleansing the government, undertaken by Uncle Sam and Columbia, in "Let the Good Work (House-Cleaning) Go On." Columbia instructs Uncle Sam to continue "cleaning the ballot-box," while she gives a good scrubbing to the dirty judicial bench, smudged with graffiti such as "Judge Buyme," "Judge Fraud," and "Judge Bribe."

Tammany judges aided the Tweed Ring by pardoning or releasing prisoners who worked for the Democratic political machine, and by appointing court officers and commissioners amenable to its will. Besides providing protective legal cover, the Tammany judges were instrumental in sustaining the Ring's political power by granting citizenship to large numbers of immigrants who padded the machine's voter rolls. In the election year of 1866, for example, Judge Albert Cardozo naturalized up to 800 people a day, Judge John McCunn swore-in over 2000 on one day alone, and Judge George Barnard worked most of October from 6 p.m. to midnight rapidly initialing unread naturalization papers creating over 10,000 new citizens.

In this cartoon, other problems are highlighted by the framed pictures (left-right): the "Ludlow St. Jail," the "Coroners Offices," the "Police Department," the "Sheriff's Office," the "Erie Rail Road Ring," the "School Board," and the "Public School" itself. In tribute to the domestic virtues of sanitation, the washboard by the stove is labeled "Board Of Health." (The tiny initials "J N" above the central panel of the woodstove in the fireplace probably indicate that Julia Nast, age nine, was "helping" her father when this drawing was executed.

LET THE GOOD WORK (HOUSE-CLEANING) GO ON.
Miss Columbia. "UNCLE SAM, YOU KEEP ON CLEANING THE BALLOT-BOX, WHILE I GIVE THIS A SCRUBBING—GOODNESS KNOWS, IT NEEDS IT!"

Judge Thomas Ledwith

One of the first clean-up items on the agenda of the *Times, Harper's Weekly* and Thomas Nast was to get rid of the corrupt judges. On November 16, 1871, a Times editorial focused on the New York City Bar Association's plan to remove the worst offenders from the judiciary. In the December 2 issue of *Harper's Weekly*, (published November 22, two weeks after the election), editor George William Curtis wrote: "The revolution which has overthrown Tammany will not have done its immediate work until it has purified the bench."

Nast already was on the attack with a cartoon published on November 8, the day after the election (in the issue of November 18) with the horrendous Biblical title of "A Dog Returneth to His Vomit." It showed Judge Thomas Ledwith as a dog slinking back to his Tammany lair. Completed before the election, the cartoonist had safely and correctly assumed that Ledwith would be beaten soundly by Judge George C. Barrett, the Reform nominee. (See pages 174-175.)

"A DOG RETURNETH TO HIS VOMIT."
(Prov., xxvi., 11; 2 Pet., ii., 22.)
As Solomon and the Apostle Peter compare Sinners who continually relapse into their sins.

Judge Albert Cardozo

In the January 27, 1872 issue of *Harper's Weekly*, available January 15, Nast took two more shots at the Ring's crooked judges. One cartoon, "The Corrupt Judiciary on the Bench," shows the figure of Justice as she dumps the five-man bench, with all five going backwards head-over-heels. Her command: "Now then, all together!"

It should be noted that all these judges served on the New York State Supreme Court, which really was a first-round court and was out-ranked by the State Court of Appeals. In 1876, as a result of that court's overturn of Tweed's sentence, Nast launched a powerful campaign against the Court of Appeals as well. (See pages 239-243.)

CORRUPT JUDICIARY ON THE BENCH.

Justice. "Now then, all together!"

"DEEDS TO BE PUT ON RECORD."

Bill [*disposing of his Stealings*]. "Rich, my son, take this Gift from me; run to Judge Cardozo; he will accept this as Bail, you as my Bondsman."

[*A la Boss Tweed, only on a small scale.*]

The other cartoon, "Deeds to Be Put on Record" shows Bill, a common thief, disposing of his stealings from a safe, as a policeman leans over to collar him. Bill hands the money to a disreputable accomplice saying: "Rich, my son, take this Gift from me; run to Judge Cardozo; he will accept this gift as Bail, you as my Bondsman." In parentheses below: (A la Boss Tweed, only on a small scale.)

Justice Albert Cardozo resigned in July 1872 after a long hearing. However, he continued to practice law. His son Benjamin was appointed to the United States Supreme Court by President Franklin D. Roosevelt in 1932.

Judges George Barnard and John McCunn

Justice John McCunn was removed from the bench by the State Senate, and died three days later. Tweed prosecutor Charles O'Conor came to his funeral because McCunn had begun his legal career in O'Conor's law office

Justice George G. Barnard was impeached by the State Senate in March 1872 and re-moved as a judge five months later. He was a close friend of Tweed's and always did the Boss's bidding . . . until he saw the handwriting on the wall in September 1871 and issued an injunction which stopped the Ring financially in its tracks. Nast found Barnard a tempting target and portrayed him more than 10 times while attacking the Ring. The Clown in the Judicial Ring from the April 13, 1872 issue, available April 3, was inspired by a *Tribune* commentary of March 25.

"M'CUNN manufactures Citizens at the rate of 8 a Minute, or 480 an Hour."—*N. Y. Tribune.*

THE CLOWN IN THE JUDICIAL RING
TO WHAT BASE USAGE THE BENCH IS PUT.

"The court-room of Judge BARNARD has been a place of amusement, where lawyers and others go to hear something 'good,' especially if a case is on the calendar in which the Judge is supposed to be strongly interested. Every day his indecent sarcasms and vulgar jests keep his court-room crowded with laughing spectators. Many of these 'funny things' have been reported in evidence before the Judiciary Committee now in session, by men whose presence in court has afforded opportunities of hearing them."—*N. Y. Tribune*, March 25th, 1872.

A *Harper's Weekly* cartoon just prior to the 1868 election (which is not by Thomas Nast) shows Judge John McCunn's naturalization mill manufacturing "Citizens at the rate of 480 an Hour" for the benefit of Democratic presidential candidate Horatio Seymour (at lower left).

Andrew J. Garvey

Andrew Garvey fled to Europe in the fall of 1871 after the Ring scandal was exposed and his name, role and detailed $3 million or so of fraudulent payments were featured in the press. He returned in early 1872, and appeared as a surprise witness at Oakey Hall's second trial in February—to the consternation of the defense—in return for immunity from prosecution. After the foreman of the jury died, a mistrial was declared.

THE DEMON GARVEY.

Garvey also was the star witness at Boss Tweed's first trial in January 1873, which ended with a hung jury. He was not recalled at Tweed's second trial in November 1873, because his previous vacillation under cross-examination made him an uncertain witness at best. He did testify in 1877 in the Board of Alderman's investigation into Tweed's imprisonment. He lived comfortably but obscurely in New York and England for another twenty years. At his death in 1897, his estate was estimated at $200,000.

James H. Ingersoll

James Ingersoll (far right in lower cartoon) reportedly had as much as $5 million in fraudulent payments pass through his hands, although a good portion of it was redistributed to other Ring members. He was tried and convicted on two counts of forgery in 1872; the forgeries occurred when he endorsed city treasury checks made out to other contractors and then deposited them to his own account.

Ingersoll was sentenced to five years in prison but served only sixteen months; Governor Samuel J. Tilden pardoned him in return for this agreement to testify against other Ring members. After his release in April 1875, he failed in a couple of businesses and died in the early twentieth century as a poor man.

James Ingersoll and Boss Tweed were the only Ring members to serve extensive time in jail.

Elbert Woodward

Elbert Woodward fled to Canada after the Ring broke up. Ultimately, he was arrested in Chicago in 1876 and brought to New York City to face charges. He avoided jail by striking a deal to pay $150,000 in restitution, make a full confession, and testify against Tweed if required.

Although not central to the Tweed Ring per se, James Fisk, Jr. was a close business associate of Boss Tweed. In 1870, Fisk and his partner Jay Gould made Tweed a key player in their Erie Ring by giving him stock, cash and a seat on the Erie Railroad board. Tweed controlled Judge George Barnard, who subsequently issued favorable injunctions for the Erie management in its battle for control with Cornelius Vanderbilt. In conjunction with bribes originating from Fisk and Gould, Tweed also steered legislation favorable to the Erie, and unfair to its competitors and customers, through the state legislature.

Jim Fisk was eleven years younger than Tweed but, of all his friends and acquaintances, Tweed probably enjoyed the affable and boisterous Fisk more than anyone else as a man with whom he could truly relax and be comfortable; both were outgoing back-slappers. Fisk built the Grand Opera House which contained the offices of the Erie Railroad; set up his mistress, Helen Josephine "Josie" Mansfield, a few houses away, and enjoyed her along with plenty of other female companionship (his wife lived in Boston and rarely saw him); and was the personification of "wine, women and song."

For Thomas Nast, Fisk was a cartoonist's dream. Portly, always nattily dressed, and with a unique waxed mustache that extended out several inches from his face, Nast drew him leading John Hoffman's caravan to Washington and as the potential Secretary of the Navy in "President" Hoffman's cabinet.

Ice and Coal

In the May 13, 1871 issue of *Harper's Weekly*—six months prior to the election—a twelve-verse illustrated ballad called "Ice and Coal" sharply contrasted the life of "The Monopolists' Ring" with that of the poor masses. Two excerpts make the point.

Silver glitters and crystal shines
Among delicate cakes and rarest wines
Ice in the goblets, ice on the grapes
Ice tinted and flavored in pudding glace
Ice in vases of classic shapes,
Ice crusting the coolers with flasks of frappe
As plentiful, sparkling and flashing in short,
As the aldermen's diamonds the party all sport.
The Monopolists' Ring, if none else can, are able—
Each as cruel and cold as the Ice-King of fable—
To enjoy their own plunder around their own table;
And, gloating over the market report,
Cry, "Come, hand up the Moët, and pass the toast round,
"Here's to ice in September a shilling a pound!"

Meanwhile in the far-off city the hand
Of an angel smites with a flaming brand,
Where the languor of thousands wearily drags
Past the blistering bricks, o'er the scorching flags.
Out of noisome dens in alley and slum,
Stricken and faint, the multitudes come;
From the ten-storied tenement's simmering hive
Crawl a myriad children, half alive;
Round the filthy docks, where the scum seethes warm,
Lapping the rotten piles, they swarm;
On the broiling roofs, in the dusty square,
They gasp for a breath of the dewless air;
Putrid and stagnant it hangs, where decay
Foul fever breeds, and day by day
A hundred sudden sun-strokes slay.

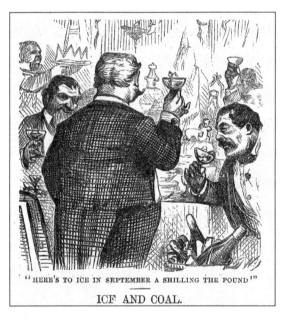

"HERE'S TO ICE IN SEPTEMBER A SHILLING THE POUND!"

ICE AND COAL.

The lead illustration for this ballad gave Nast an opportunity to portray the elegant Jim Fisk with his back to the audience, raising a toast: "Here's to Ice in September a Shilling the Pound."

The Erie Ring: Jim Fisk and Jay Gould

Jim Fisk's Murder

On the afternoon of Saturday, January 6, 1872, Jim Fisk was shot twice at close range as he ascended a staircase in the Grand Central Hotel on Broadway. Gravely wounded, Fisk was visited at the scene by Tweed, who was out on bail; David Dudley Field, their mutual attorney; and many others. Although deeply affected, Tweed reportedly asked if his dying friend had any private papers on him he wished to turn over, but he did not. At 10:45 the following morning, Fisk died in a room on the second floor of the hotel. His killer was Edward S. (Ned) Stokes, the new companion of Fisk's former mistress, Josie Mansfield; both men were married to other women.

The violent act was a stunning conclusion to a long, sordid squabble fought out in the courts and newspapers over Fisk's dishonest business transactions and his revealing trove of love letters to Josie, blackmail, extortion, and the smoldering flames of amorous frustration. Fisk's love letters to Josie had been placed for "safe-keeping" in the hands of Peter Sweeny, but the Tammany Ring was deeply troubled by her rumored knowledge of Erie Railroad matters, and by possible future testimony about criminal behavior that might implicate them. Nast would have read an open letter from Mansfield to Fisk published by major dailies on or after October 31, 1871, which planted the warning that she could and would do him great damage: "Unfortunately for yourself, I know too well the many crimes you have perpetrated..." In a pre-election interview, Nast observed, "One woman holds in her hands the key to unlock the diabolical secrets of Tammany."

The *Harper's Weekly* issue of January 27, 1872 (available January 17), contained a long article about the murder, its immediate legal aftermath, and the circumstances of the business and court dealings between Fisk and Stokes that led Stokes to kill him, as well as a picture of Stokes.

In addition, a Nast cartoon "Gone to a Higher Tribunal" shows "Mr. David Dudley Field (Erie Ring Counsel)" in front of Fisk's bed or coffin, with his body on top covered by a sheet. Two portraits of Fisk in his fancy uniforms hang on the wall. Field is gesturing as if to say "It's out of my hands now."

Mr. David Dudley Field (Erie Ring Counsel) "GONE TO A HIGHER TRIBUNAL."

The first trial of Ned Stokes ended with a hung jury, but a second concluded with his conviction on the charge of murder in the first degree and a sentence of death by hanging. However, a few months later, the Court of Appeals unanimously overturned the verdict on points of law and ordered a new trial, at which the assailant was convicted of third-degree manslaughter. Judge Noah David then sentenced Stokes to four years in state prison, the maximum length of time allowed by the lenient verdict.

"Dead Men Tell No Tales"

In "Dead Men Tell No Tales," in the February 24, 1872 issue of *Harper's Weekly* (published February 14), Nast depicted the mixed emotions which Fisk's comrades probably faced upon his abrupt death. The phrase "Dead men tell no tales" had been used in English literature as a proverb or aphorism back to at least the mid-sixteenth century.

Four morose, long-time companions stand at Fisk's graveside in Brattleboro, Vermont (left-right): George Barnard, the Tammany judge who had treated Erie owners Fisk and Gould favorably in his courtroom; David Dudley Field, counsel for both the Erie Railroad and Boss Tweed; Jay Gould, the famed financier and Fisk's business partner; and Boss Tweed, who sat on the Erie Railroad's board of directors and was Fisk's close friend. Tweed leans on Fisk's tombstone, holding a handkerchief under his eyes.

Gould announces, "All the sins of Erie lie buried here," but Justice points knowingly to her eye and replies, "I am not quite so blind." The tip of her sword rests suggestively on the contour of Fisk's snow-covered grave. Two papers stick out of Gould's pocket—"Stolen Stocks" and "New Erie Schemes."

Judge Barnard stands behind the others, looking away from them all and furtively at the backs of Field and Gould, who block his view of the grave. Five months earlier, Barnard had issued his unexpected injunction against the Ring, which stopped Tweed and his associates from any further expenditures, and there was no love lost between them now.

Underneath the cartoon was a short article with the same title: "Dead Men Tell No Tales." It discussed the pending repeal of the Erie Classification bill, also called the Confiscation bill, which was an attempt by the Erie Railroad Board—Fisk, Gould and Tweed—"conspirators" to unjustly confiscate 60,000 shares belonging to English shareholders through legislative action. An enabling bill had passed in 1869, with the help of legislative bribes by Gould and Tweed. It was repealed in March 1872 as *Harper's Weekly* urged.

The Tammany Turncoat Republicans

Nathaniel Sands

Nathaniel Sands was a respected Republican who had led the Taxpayers Association in its battle against the Ring in its early days. Boss Tweed gave him an on-the-books $10,000 a year job as Tax Assessor, while paying him $75,000 a year under the table as commissions for helping Comptroller "Slippery Dick" Connolly arrange city loans. He also served with Tweed and Horace Greeley on a Tobacco Company (or Association?) board, and helped support the Ring's corrupt efforts in textbook publishing by proposing the resolution to ban Harper's textbooks from the public schools.

Sands held a prestigious position as Secretary of the Citizens' Association, of which former mayor and leading industrialist Peter Cooper was president. When his $75,000 in commissions was exposed in late 1871, Nast showed Cooper kicking him out of the Citizens' Association. (Left)

Nast portrayed Sands as the fawning Uriah Heep character in Charles Dickens' "David Copperfield" in this November 25, 1871 cartoon which appeared eight days after the election. A year later, in attacking presidential candidate Horace Greeley, Nast linked Greeley to his reputed tobacco partnership with Tweed and Sands. (Right)

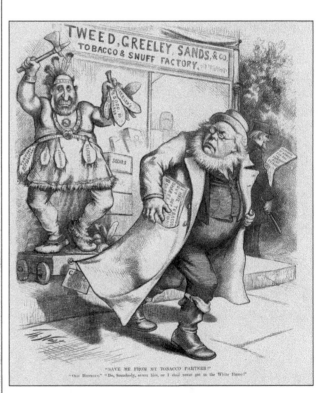

HEEP — OF SANDS.

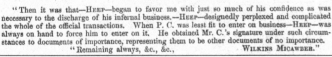

"Then it was that—HEEP—began to favor me with just so much of his confidence as was necessary to the discharge of his infernal business.—HEEP—designedly perplexed and complicated the whole of the official transactions. When P. C. was least fit to enter on business—HEEP—was always on hand to force him to enter on it. He obtained Mr. C.'s signature under such circumstances to documents of importance, representing them to be other documents of no importance.
"Remaining always, &c., &c.,   WILKINS MICAWBER."

"SAVE ME FROM MY TOBACCO PARTNER!"
"OUR HONESTY." "Do, Somebody, arrest him, or I shall never get to the White House!"

Tom Fields

Tom Fields was a ward leader, city alderman and parks commissioner, who assumed a larger role in Nast's cartoons than the one he actually played. Nast evidently liked to draw his overweight figure, and used him frequently as a leading Ring associate.

In the November 1871 election, Fields won reelection to his seat in the New York State Senate, which Nast portrayed in a March 30, 1872 cartoon. However, Fields was denied the seat because of fraudulent voting.

He was tried and convicted of bribery in October 1872, but the conviction later was overturned by a higher court. In the meantime, Fields fled to Canada where he spent the rest of his life. Nast showed Fields jumping bail — pursued by the police — in the *Harper's Weekly* issue of November 30, 1872.

NEW FIELDS OF OPERATION.
The next Tammany "Reform" Movement at Albany.

A FIELDS OF ACTION.
"He that runs away will live to *steal* another day."

Hank Smith

Hank Smith was president of the New York City Police Commission, in which role he was able to provide immunity to Ring-connected criminals and enforce the will of the Ring leaders and their associates. Smith enabled the Ring to effectively control the police force, as an adjunct to its control of the courts.

In addition to his police position, Smith also was president of the Bowling Green Savings Bank, which went bankrupt in February 1872. An investigation turned up all sorts of fraud involving loans, missing city bonds and crooked bookkeeping. In particular he had misused a widows and orphans fund, as well as money collected for victims of the 1871 Chicago fire. He was indicted, but fled the country to escape trial. He did return before his death two years after his 1872 indictment.

Although Hank Smith was a Republican, he was close to Tweed personally, and served as vice president of the Americus Club. Thomas Nast showed his corpulent figure in several cartoons with other Ring members. However, in the issue of March 16, 1872, Smith rated his own cartoon.

He is shown in full police uniform with a "Tammany Power" belt as "The Guardian Angel of The Poor People's Money," leaning against a pole outside the "suspended" Bowling-Green Savings Bank.

To the right of the pole, "Police Commissioner Hank Smith" appearson a bank window, while on the left, "Pres. Hank Smith" and a list of his crimes is written on another bank window.

Nast's line under the title reads: "Does It 'Take a Thief to Catch a Thief?'"

THE GUARDIAN ANGEL OF THE POOR PEOPLE'S MONEY.
Does it "Take a Thief to Catch a Thief?"

Tweed's first arrest: "Another Good Joke" took place on October 26, 1871. (See page 160.)

On Friday evening, December 15, 1871, Boss Tweed was again arrested by Sheriff Matthew Brennan and taken the following morning before Judge Gunning Bedford of the Court of General Sessions. Having been indicted by a grand jury on 120 counts of grand larceny, forgery, false pretenses, conspiracy, and other felonies and misdemeanors, the Boss was denied bail and ordered committed to the city prison, known as "The Tombs," to await trial. Tweed's counsel immediately obtained a writ of habeas corpus, allowing the prisoner to be brought swiftly before Judge George Barnard, his former protégé, who was sitting in the Supreme Court chamber of Tweed's new courthouse.

Judge Barnard agreed to review the lower court's refusal to allow bail. With Tweed facing his own life-sized portrait hanging behind the judge, Prosecutor Charles O'Conor protested the granting of bail, concluding with a withering quotation from Shakespeare's "King Lear" (Act IV, Scene VI) about the easy access to "due process" for the wealthy, not available to the poor:

"Plate sin with gold . . . And the strong lance of justice hurtless breaks
Arm it in rags, a pigmy's straw does pierce it."

Unmoved, Judge Barnard reversed Judge Bedford's decision, granting Tweed bail of $5,000.

An article in the January 6, 1872 *Harper's Weekly* (published December 27, 1871) cast a jaundiced eye on the privileged treatment Tweed had received, including his being allowed to wait in the district attorney's office while the writ of habeas corpus was being prepared.

"In the ordinary course of things Mr. Tweed would have been immediately transferred from the presence of Judge Bedford to the Tombs, without enjoying the hospitalities of the District Attorney's office; but there is a vast difference between the treatment of a common criminal and one who has the District Attorney for a friend, his own son as Assistant District Attorney, and a firm ally in the Sheriff."

Below the *Weekly* article, a small Nast cartoon was described as faithfully reflecting "the sentiment of the thinking public on the arrest and bailing out of this man." Entitled "Stone Walls Do Not a Prison Make," it shows a colossal figure of Boss Tweed being pushed by Lilliputian-sized police into a gaping hole on one side of the "City Jail," while he emerges out the opposite side, wearing a satisfied smirk and being pulled free by similarly diminutive friends. The caption underneath reads: "'No prison is big enough to hold the Boss.' In on one side and out at the other."

"STONE WALLS DO NOT A PRISON MAKE."—*Old Song.*
"No Prison is big enough to hold the Boss." In on one side, and out at the other.

In the same January 6, 1872 issue, another Nast caricature, "Can the Law Reach Him? —The Dwarf and the Giant Thief," again depicts a monumental figure of Boss Tweed, this time towering over the not so long arm of the law. Tweed watches in benign fascination as a policeman, who has easily nabbed an ordinary escaped convict by the neck, tries vainly to direct the Tammany giant toward the "States Prison."

Boss Tweed's resignation as Commissioner of Public Works was accepted by Mayor Hall on December 28, 1871, the same day the Boss withdrew as a director of the Erie Railroad. The next day, he gave an interview to several reporters in which he denied that he would flee the jurisdiction (his trial would not begin until January 8, 1873), and affirmed his intention of taking his seat in the state senate. Nast addressed that subject two weeks later. (See page 228.)

CAN THE LAW REACH HIM?—THE DWARF AND THE GIANT THIEF.

The January 20, 1872 issue of *Harper's Weekly* (published January 10), contained a quartet of two-column images by Nast on one page, dealing with the fates of Tweed, Hall and Hoffman. The cartoon on the left comments on Tweed's resignation as head of the Department of Public Works, and prophesies his future home: the state prison at Sing-Sing. The brooding Boss appears as Emperor Napoleon III sitting on the ruins of his crushing defeat at Sedan in September 1870 during the Franco-Prussian War. Resting on a rock pile, near the pick and shovel of hard labor, he still seems to be favoring his right leg (left side for viewers). Wilhelmshöhe was the royal resort near Kassel in central Germany to which the French emperor was temporarily exiled after his abdication. The cartoonist completes the cartoon's theme by placing Tweed under Prussian guard at Sing-Sing on the Hudson River, often referred to as "the American Rhine." "Die Wacht Am Rhine" ("The Watch on the Rhine") was a favorite song of German soldiers during the Franco-Prussian War.

The image on the right —"Can the Body Cast Off Its Shadow?"—presents the exit of Tweed as grand sachem of the Tammany Society, and wonders whether the city's chief Democratic organization can reform itself. Tweed had been forced to resign his leadership position on December 30, 1871, when he was temporarily replaced by reformer Augustus Schell (who was ultimately succeeded by John Kelly after a struggle with John Morrissey. (See page 21.) Dressed as an Indian chief ("sachem"), the dark shadow of "Stealing is the Best Policy" is impossible for the "honest" body of Tweed to shake off.

AFTER SEDAN—WILHELMSHÖHE.

CAN THE BODY CAST OFF ITS SHADOW?
The Tammany Society has expelled TWEED as Sachem. — *Daily Papers.*

In the same January 20, 1872 issue of *Harper's Weekly*, Nast's "The First Step at Albany" has Tweed apparently up to his incorrigible old ways, this time with regard to his own state senate seat. He is attempting to repeat his successful maneuver of the previous spring, when he saved the Ring's 1871 legislative program from stalemate by buying the vote of a bribable Republican member of the assembly, Orange S. Winans. (See pages 98-99.)

At the closed door of the State Senate, to which he had been reelected in November, Tweed stands with paste-bucket, brush, and satchel of money bulging to mimic the swollen curve of his paunch. The advertisement he has just pasted up calls for "Eleven Winans." In lieu of a caption, the excerpt from the *World* explains that if 11 of the 32 state senators (27 of whom were Republicans) would back the former Tammany Boss, he will be allowed to take his seat in that chamber. The *Times* noted, "If anybody supposed that Mr. Thomas Nast and *Harper's Weekly* were done with Mr. Tweed and his friends, …[then] the latest number of the *Weekly* will undeceive them." Tweed never did take his seat and formally resigned it on March 27, eleven weeks after this cartoon appeared.

THE FIRST STEP AT ALBANY.

"If TWEED can get Eleven of the thirty-two Senators to take this indulgent view, he will have a safe tenure of his seat for the present. From what we have been able to learn of the Republican Senators, we do not deem this impossible. It seems to be the opinion of competent judges acquainted with the members that this is likely to be one of the most corrupt Legislatures in the history of the State. Now TWEED is nobody's fool; there are few better judges of men; and if he secures his seat for half the session, he will perhaps engage enough corrupt Republicans in his interest to make it impossible to oust him. If the Legislature had been Democratic, we should have had reform. But being Republican, it may yield to TWEED, as so many Legislatures have done before. It is merely a question whether his remaining resources will permit him to bribe high enough. If his pecuniary means do not fall short, he will doubtless retain his seat in this Republican Senate."—*New York World*, December 30, 1871.

After months of maneuvering in the case against Tweed, the prosecution was ready to commence on January 7, 1873, when the Boss's lawyers moved again for delay, claiming lack of time to review all the pertinent materials. Judge Noah Davis denied the motion, adding the observation, "Considering the brevity of human life, this rate of preparation would postpone the trial to the next generation." Tweed's counsel then moved for dismissal on various grounds, with David Dudley Field complaining about the large number of counts (220) against his client. To which Judge Davis replied, "More counts than in a German principality; nevertheless, your motion is denied." After rejecting other defense arguments, Judge Davis ordered the trial to begin the next morning. During the proceeding, Tweed seemed relaxed and confident, even laughing and nodding at the judge's pun about German counts.

Under terms of a Tammany-backed law (1870), a Commissioner of Jurors was the sole arbiter of the jury pool, and the position was filled in 1873 by a Tammany appointee. It was widely presumed that Tweed's jury would be bribed or otherwise improperly influenced; that probably happened, although it was never proved or confirmed. After three days of questioning by counsel, the jury was selected, and on January 13, 1873, a stormy trial of 15-days duration began, with Andrew Garvey and Samuel J. Tilden as star witnesses for the prosecution.

Judge Davis placed matters in the hands of the jury on January 30 after a three hour charge that ended with the warning that there is "no stain more deep or damning that a juror may bring upon his own character, than by being false to his oath and bringing in a false verdict." The next morning, Friday, January 31, Judge Davis announced that the jury was unable to reach a verdict and was unlikely to do so if given more time; he then dismissed the jury.

Confronted with a variety of other subjects, the cartoonist apparently considered the matter of Tweed's hung jury for more than a month. On March 19, 1873, Nast sailed for England for a nearly six-month change of pace and scenery, after the professional and personal rigors of the anti-Tweed Ring and anti-Greeley campaigns of the previous two years.

Three weeks after Nast sailed, *Harper's Weekly* printed on its April 12 cover his satirical response to the stalemated prosecution, "Blindman's-Buff. How long will this Game last?" (published April 2). The "blindness" (or impartiality) required for the pursuit of truth and justice in the courtroom is transformed here into an obstacle, in mimicry of the children's game blindman's-buff (which is also called "blindman's-bluff.") Justice herself reaches out in frustration for Tammany Ring and Erie Ring figures, who stealthily move away from her grasp. Pushed and about to be kneed from behind by an unidentified figure with "Verdict Of The Jury" on a paper in his pocket, Justice is certain to sprawl over the prone, twisted figure of David Dudley Field, a lawyer for both Tweed and Jay Gould of the Erie Railroad. Field conceals a book labeled "Tricks of Law."

The scene takes place in a theatrically lit corridor of the courthouse, by turns bright and shadowy. On the far left is Tom Fields, one of Tweed's cronies, whose conviction in October 1872 on two counts of bribery was overturned, allowing Fields to flee to Quebec, never to stand trial again. Next to him is Jay Gould, the wealthy and unscrupulous financier, who had been ousted as president of the Erie Railroad in March 1872, but had escaped prosecution and continued his lucrative business investments.

The Tammany four are grouped to the right of Justice: Richard Connolly behind her sword and scales; Oakey Hall peering around the corner, his face in the shade over her arm; Peter Sweeny on the corridor bench below, ducking away in alarm; and Boss Tweed on tiptoes, coyly trying to flatten his huge form out of reach against the wall, though illuminated as if by spotlight. The billboard at the rear indicates that once this frolic is over, "Bribery," "Corruption," and "Murder Trials" are the general order of business "Every Day In The Week."

The same issue reported that Tweed had resigned his seat in the state senate on March 27.

Nine months passed after the conclusion of Tweed's first trial until the Boss again found himself arraigned before Judge Noah Davis at a second, and decisive, trial commencing November 5, 1873. This time, the judge and prosecutors were braced for possible irregularities. Private investigators were engaged to keep an eye on prospective jurors, selected jurors, and court officers who might exercise a secret allegiance to Tweed. At the second trial, Judge Davis was conspicuously more rigid than in January, a mood intensified from day one when a motion by the defense accused the judge of bias against their client and asked that he not try the case. Davis was livid, and declared that the trial would go forward at once.

The arguments covered in January were briskly rehashed, with the two sides combined taking less than five days. Contrary to a clear advance warning—or feint—Andrew Garvey, the celebrated plasterer and Tammany contractor, was not called as a prime witness by the prosecution. He had vacillated under cross-examination in the first trial, so Tweed's lawyers were eager to see him take the stand again. When the defense objected to his absence, Judge Davis pointed out that they could call Garvey as a witness, to which Tweed counsel John Graham exclaimed that he "would as soon call Lucifer." The judge dryly retorted, "That is a matter of choice."

Following the abrupt close of the State's case against Tweed, the defense took only two days, called just three witnesses, and carefully refrained from putting the Boss himself on the stand. Following summations on November 18, Judge Davis, as in the first case, gave the jury a charge lasting three hours. At 3 a.m. the next morning, the judge announced that court would reconvene in seven hours.

A little before 10 a.m. on November 19, a calm Boss Tweed and his entourage made their way through hundreds of spectators into the crowded courtroom. The foreman of the jury requested Judge Davis to clarify instructions on one of the counts, after which they retired for another ten minutes. When the jury returned, the court clerk received an affirmative response from the foreman that they had reached a decision: William M. Tweed was found guilty on 204 of the 220 counts against him.

Before the verdict, Tweed and his counsel understood that the maximum penalty to which they were liable under the misdemeanor counts being tried was a single sentence of one year. After the verdict, prosecutor Lyman Tremain moved that Tweed—not yet tried for anything like major malfeasance—could be penalized separately for each misdemeanor count. "The time of mercy had passed," asserted Tremain. Tweed's counsel, John Graham, protested emotionally that the jury would never have found the defendant guilty had it believed that its decision could lead to a cumulative sentence of over 100 years.

At Tweed's sentencing on Saturday, November 22, Judge Davis remarked that the evidence against the former Tammany Boss was "overwhelming," and admonished him for violating the public trust: "Instead of protecting the public, you plundered it." Deciding against both the maximum-cumulative and one-year sentences, the judge "mercifully" imposed a prison term of 12 years, plus fines of $12,750. Tweed was jailed in the state prison on Blackwell's Island.

During the five days following the return of the verdict, Nast must have completed the cover page image commemorating what he surely hoped was the end of the long, legal road for Boss Tweed. The result was the cover of the December 13, 1873 issue of *Harper's Weekly* (available December 3): "Justice!" It features a grim-faced Justice, with her sword and scales, locking the cell door marked "W. M. Tweed." Behind her, a row of additional doors stand open for accomplices yet to be incarcerated, the first of which is labeled "NEXT." A shadowy fragment of the dome of the prisoner's head is barely visible through the tiny barred window of his new chamber.

Uncharacteristically, Nast's detached effort seems intended to evoke severity, finality, and austere dignity in the well-established manner of John Tenniel of *Punch* (London). There is no element of caricature to be found in it.

Boss Tweed's friend and long-time political associate, Sheriff Matthew Brennan, had arrested Tweed twice before—in October 1871 (see page 160) and December 1871—and now was supervising him in jail after his 1873 conviction and arrest. Obviously, he had given Tweed, who was the third-largest real estate owner in New York City, the opportunity to transfer some of his real estate to his family.

In this cartoon from the same December 13, 1873 issue of *Harper's Weekly*, Tweed thanks the sheriff for his humane treatment and says "I hope you will never know how it is yourself."

Sheriff Brennan soon found out. Henry "Prince Hal" Genet, a crooked Tammany member, was convicted of fraud. Before Genet went to jail, Brennan's lax oversight permitted Genet first to get roaring drunk and then to flee to Europe. As a consequence, Brennan served 30 days in jail for allowing Genet time to go home and "arrange his affairs."

THE SYMPATHETIC SHERIFF.

Ex-Boss. "I thank you for your humane treatment, and *I hope you will never know how it is yourself.*"

Samuel J. Tilden was an astute politician. A lifelong bachelor and a shrewd lawyer, he generally preferred to operate behind the scenes.

As long as Boss Tweed held incontrovertible power, Tilden apparently did not oppose him. Both were Democrats and long-time Tammany Hall members, and Tilden didn't rock the boat.

After the *New-York Times'* disclosures in July 1871, and the subsequent theft of vouchers from Richard Connolly's offices on September 10, Tilden finally stepped forward to play a role. Operating behind Andrew H. Green, his former law partner and fellow bachelor, and former mayor William Havemeyer, Tilden maneuvered Slippery Dick Connolly into taking a leave of absence, appointing Green as Acting Controller in his place, and finally indirectly to jail.

However, when Tilden took on Tweed head-to-head at the State Democratic Convention in Rochester in early October 1871, Tilden lost. Tweed's tactics and imported thugs controlled the convention. (See pages 156-157.)

After that Tilden took charge openly. He supervised the investigation of Tammany accounts, and spearheaded the prosecution of Oakey Hall, Tweed and other Ring members. For that he received deserved acclaim, and used it to win election to the state legislature in 1871 and the New York governorship in 1874.

However, Thomas Nast never became a Tilden fan because he strongly believed that Tilden was an opportunistic latecomer to the aftermath of the Ring's party.

Six days before Tilden's election as governor in 1874, Nast published "The Tammany Rat," a devastating satire on Tilden, on the cover of the *Harper's Weekly* issue of November 7, 1874 (available October 28). The cartoon is comprised of a chain of five interlocking circulars overlaying a central scene of destruction, all meant to illustrate Tilden's self-interested transformation from Tammanyite to opportunistic Tammany critic, as "The Great Reformer."

In the first ring, the rodent Tilden, while Democratic State Chairman, feeds from a sack under the Tammany Hall "Roof That Sheltered Him for Years." In the second, he is the first of several rats climbing to safety on a rock as the Tammany ship sinks in the background. The third has Tilden in human form narrowly escaping the crumbling Tammany Hall with his reputation intact, and heading for Broadway Bank to conduct his investigation of Tammany accounts. In the next vignette, he is a fox in a hooded priest's robe, preaching a Reform sermon to a credulous audience of geese and asses. In the final ring, he is a rat who is incongruously labeled a "rat-catcher." On an extended tail at the lower-right corner, the cartoonist predicts, incorrectly but with characteristic optimism, that the outcome of the election would mean the story of rat-Tilden was "Not To Be Continued In Our Next."

In the large, central image, the Democratic gubernatorial candidate, whose back is turned to the audience, clenches his fists as he delivers a superfluous kick to Tammany Hall, which has already collapsed into ruins.

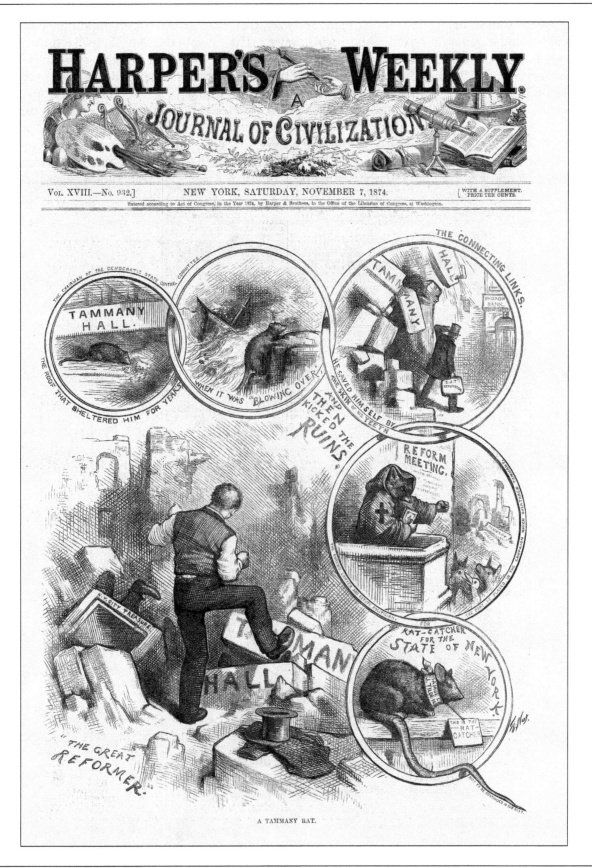

From the time of his inauguration in January 1875, Governor Tilden began building a careful case against the corrupt administration of the state canal system. The cover of the May 15, 1875 issue of *Harper's Weekly* contains Nast's "The Next Pardon in the Reform Farce (?)," showing a smiling Tilden handing a gubernatorial pardon to Boss Tweed on the pretext of the latter turning state's evidence against the Canal Ring. Behind his back, Tilden holds a paper labeled "Arrest for Canal Ring," and conceals from Tweed's view a scene of police officers storming a Canal Ring boat manned by crooks dressed as Italian banditti.

This satire rests on the report that the new governor had pardoned James Ingersoll so that he could turn state's evidence on Tweed, and on the understanding that Andrew Garvey had accepted an earlier offer of immunity from prosecution so that he could do the same. In fact, Tilden never did pardon Tweed.

Tweed's Appeal: Limited Success

After 19 months in Blackwell's Island prison for his **criminal conviction**, Tweed's appeal was successful. On June 15, 1875, the New York Court of Appeals (the state's highest court) unanimously declared that in sentencing William Tweed to 12 years for criminal acts, Judge Noah Davis had exceeded the statutory limit of one year. Consequently, the court ordered Tweed released from the penitentiary, having served more than the requisite time.

However, after gaining his freedom on June 22, the Boss was rearrested the next day on **civil charges** that he had misappropriated more than $6 million in public funds. Unable to raise the $3 million bail, he was sent to the Ludlow Street jail.

In the August 7, 1875 issue of *Harper's Weekly* (published July 28), Tweed's attorney, David Dudley Field, is featured in Nast's "Principals, Not Men" crying in the courtroom before Justice, under whose outreaching sword he pathetically beseeches mercy on behalf of his client. Tweed's $6,000,000 moneybag is clad in prison stripes. The "'Big' 6" also refers to Tweed's old volunteer fire company. Standing on the spiked side of the "Bar of (Obstruction) Law," the celebrated lawyer hugs the fugitive sack of loot protectively, and perhaps greedily. The book on the counsel's desk is entitled "Law or How to Avoid Justice." Tweed, largely obscured by his obese moneybag, peers out from behind it in a simulation of wide-eyed innocence. On the state seal in the upper-right the motto "Excelsior" ("Ever Upward") is combined with the dollar sign.

In the lower right, Nast incorporates the quote from Shakespeare's "King Lear" that prosecutor Charles O'Conor previously used when objecting to bail for Tweed on December 16, 1871. (See page 225.)

PRINCIPALS, NOT MEN—A LAWYER PLEADING FOR HIS "CLIENT."

Attacking the Court of Appeals

Thomas Nast was furious at the Court of Appeals for freeing Boss Tweed (for time served) after his **criminal conviction**. After warming up with "Princip-als Not Men," he published four more cartoons over the next two months which portrayed the potential results of Tweed's apparent victory.

In the issue of August 14, 1875, a sequel to "Princip-als, Not Men" predicts the furtive escape from justice that Tweed and his $6,000,000 moneybag will make with the help of attorney David Dudley Field. In the foreground, the "Legal Pointer" dog is put "Off the Scent," ensnared in bureaucratic "red tape," and fenced in by law tomes. On the other side of the latter, in the foreground, are recently published letters from Prosecutor Charles O'Conor and Judge Noah Davis criticizing the Court of Appeals for overturning Tweed's sentence.

OFF THE SCENT.

The Tables Turned

In the August 7 issue of *Harper's Weekly*, editor George William Curtis argued that the Court of Appeals did not merely discharge Tweed, but "left to [Tweed's] forbearance whether Judge Noah Davis shall forfeit his estate and take Tweed's place in his cell." Nast took the hint.

The cover of the September 11, 1875 *Harper's Weekly* featured Nast's "The Tables Turned. The Next Decision We May Expect," in which Tweed, wearing Justice's robe, scales, sword, and key, is about to close and lock the door of a cell in the "State Prison" on the figure of "Late Justice" herself. With her head cast despondently downward, "Late Justice" appears in prison stripes, with closely cropped hair, chained hands behind her back, and a weighty ball ("Law") and chain ("Red Tape") on her ankle. The Boss gleefully winks and places his finger aside his nose, as his counsel, David Dudley Field, looks on in the background with evident satisfaction and delight.

Tweed's great diamond gleams a mighty dollar sign, while another large diamond fastens the top of his robe on his right arm. Dollar signs embroider the bottom of Tweed's robe, just above "Late Justice's" shorn hair and the scissors used to cut it.

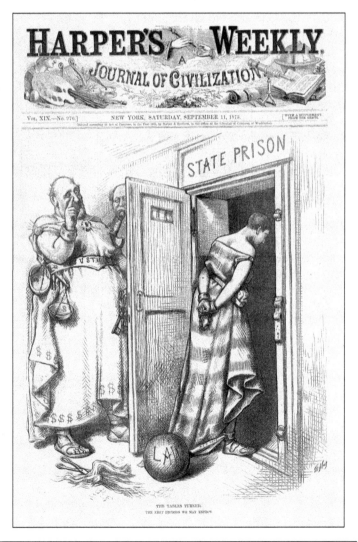

The Upright Bench

Another full-page satire in the September 11, 1875 issue of *Harper's Weekly* resulted in " 'The Upright Bench,' Which Is Above Criticism." Wearing prison stripes, Boss Tweed sits victoriously on top of a long, upturned bench (symbolizing the judiciary), as he waves aloft his hat in one hand and his $6,000,000 moneybag in the other.

In a visual display of Shakespeare's "King Lear" quote on disparate justice for the rich and poor, the judicial bench, marked "Politics," is divided at midpoint between the dollar sign above the line of criticism and the cent sign below it. Underneath the heavy wooden bench lies the crushed corpse of an impoverished petty thief, from whose grasp two stolen coins emerge.

Behind the wealthy and victorious Tweed is the entrance to the "Court of [Appeals]". Below him is a blindfolded, oscillating weather-vane rooster donned with the regalia of Justice: scales, which tilt toward the dollar sign, and a sword, which has slashed into the cent sign. On the partially drawn window shade, the state seal of a rising sun with the motto "Excelsior" (Ever-Upward) lends itself to a sarcastic reading of the entire cartoon.

A vacant jury box on the right awaits Tweed's third trial on the civil charge of misappropriating public funds, which would commence five months later in February 1876.

"THE UPRIGHT BENCH," WHICH IS ABOVE CRITICISM.

More Red Tape: Our Modern Mummy

"The Tables Turned," showing Justice being incarcerated, seems to have led Nast inexorably to his design of "Our Modern Mummy" for the cover of the October 16, 1875 *Harper's Weekly*. Loosely based on John Tenniel's illustrations of Tweedledee and Tweedledum for chapter four of Lewis Carroll's Through the Looking Glass (published in December 1872), Nast depicts Boss Tweed personifying both the Tammany Ring and Canal Ring conspiracies

The two figures suggest the continuity of state-supported crime in New York; the corrupt state canal system was being prosecuted when the cartoon was published.

Tammany Tweedledee jerks his thumb derisively at the figure of Justice, immobilized by "red tape"; she sits on the "Political Bench" atop a Supreme Court pedestal featuring an oversized dollar sign. He laughs at the notion that "She is going to punish us!" His identical twin, Canal Tweedledum, gleefully agrees, "That is the best joke yet."

In Nast's view, the partisan opposition of the Court of Appeals is responsible for the red tape which blindfolds and thoroughly binds the figure of Justice.

The cartoon was published on October 6, the same day that the New York Supreme Court—the lower court— denied the request of Tweed's counsel for a bill of particulars enumerating the crimes allegedly committed; a few days later, the Court also denied the request for a reduction in bail to $1.5 million. Two weeks later, an editorial in October 30 *Harper's Weekly* (in print October 20) expressed relief concerning the Supreme Court's rulings, noting, "It has seemed to very many people that Mr. Nast's striking cartoon of Justice helplessly bound in the Anaconda folds of red tape was but a simple picture of the truth, and that money and legal ingenuity combined could certainly outwit justice."

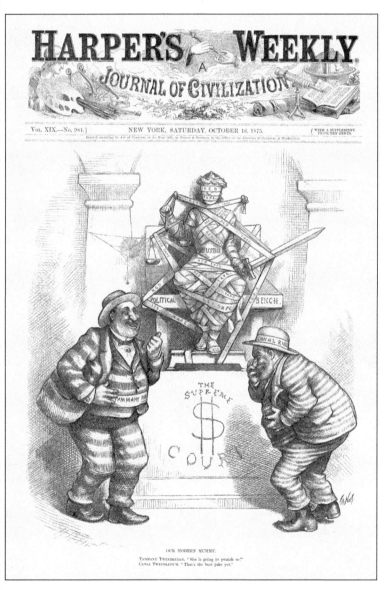

Prelude to Escape

During the autumn of 1875, Tweed's principal antagonist, Charles O'Conor, 71, was stricken with a serious (undisclosed) illness, which forced the formidable prosecutor to a lengthy confinement in the bedroom of his upper Manhattan home on Washington Heights. With O'Conor effectively out of the picture, Tweed's counsel pushed for the new case to come to trial.

On the other hand, "the friends of good government became alarmed," Matthew Breen later chronicled. "No great man's sick bed was ever watched with more anxiety. Newspaper reporters surrounded his residence… Every newspaper in the city had special bulletins posted several times a day…."

On October 8, 1875, the State of New York filed a second civil suit against Tweed, demanding an additional sum of about $934,000 for money funneled through Ingersoll, and another $1,000,000 in bail. On November 29, prosecutor Wheeler Peckham informed the defense that both lawsuits would be tried before the same "struck" jury, chosen by a rarely used, lottery-like process, which limited the defense to 12 challenges and thereby gave the prosecution a decided advantage. Peckham argued that this was necessary to "balance" the defendant's prominence and insure a fair and impartial jury. At Ludlow Street jail, Tweed's lawyers and the newspapers kept him abreast of the various developments.

Besides emphatic condemnation in George William Curtis's editorials, *Harper's Weekly* published an exposé in its November 13, 1875 issue (in print, November 3) by Albert G. Browne Jr., then an editor of the *Evening Post*, and formerly the official Reporter for the Massachusetts Supreme Court. Browne's article, subtitled "A Searching Criticism of the Decisions of the New York Court of Appeals in the City [i.e., Tweed] Ring and Canal Ring Suits," occupied almost six-and-one-half large pages of dense copy in a special supplement to *Harper's Weekly*. It accused the Court of Appeals of clear pro-Tammany bias over the five years since its creation in 1870, at the height of Tweed's legislative clout. Browne argued that as the Ring's last line of defense, the court functioned as a "permanent cabal" to do the conspirators' bidding. He concluded, "I believe … that the facts which I have marshalled show that such a court is not a safe depository of the supreme judicial power."

Tweed probably anticipated hostility from the New York Supreme Court, once under his control but now headed by his nemesis, Judge Noah Davis. What must have confounded and distressed him was opposition from the higher Court of Appeals. On November 16, 1875, the Court of Appeals announced a unanimous ruling that Tweed was not entitled to a "bill of particulars" of the charges against him; it also refused to lower his $3 million bail to a figure he might be able to raise.

Thus, the effect of the Appellate Court's surprise ruling in the criminal case in June 1875, which had freed Tweed, was reversed in its decision in the civil case that November, which kept him in prison. Although the cases involved different legal issues and standards, public pressure, including that from *Harper's Weekly*, may have played a role in the judicial turnabout.

At that point, the former Boss must have concluded that his legal options were finally exhausted.

By the end of November 1875, William M. Tweed, a proud man and by nature something of an irrepressible optimist, had good reason for wild swings of mood. For almost four years he had been under the threat of vigorous prosecution or actually imprisoned. He had seen the best defense that money could buy start to crumble against withering civic and public attack. His health was beginning to fail, and his financial resources were at last exhausted. Still, there seemed to be a chance that his situation might yet improve.

As Matthew Breen surmised, **Tweed may have feared that with criminal guilt no longer an issue, he would be facing a civil judgment for debt that might well keep him in jail for the rest of his life.** Facing that particular roll of the dice, Tweed apparently decided he could improve his chances by escaping from prison, remaining in the vicinity until the legal question was resolved, and then deciding what to do next.

At Ludlow Street jail, Tweed was granted privileges and liberties allowed to people imprisoned for debt but not to most other inmates, such as carriage rides and visits to his home and the homes of his adult children. On Saturday evening, December 4, 1875, he escaped while on such a sojourn and hid out in New Jersey.

The next morning, newspapers reported to their astonished readers that the Boss had escaped. Ludlow Warden William Dunham and Keeper Edward Hagen claimed to have taken Tweed to his home, where the three met the Boss's son, William Jr., in the parlor. Upon the pretext of greeting his wife, Tweed left the room and failed to return. A search of the house and surrounding area revealed no trace of the vanished former Tammany Boss.

The *Nation* of December 9 expressed skepticism about the jailers' story, implying that they colluded in Tweed's escape. However, according to one generally plausible account written and published 16 months later in *Harper's Weekly* (April 14, 1877), the former Boss's keepers, while clearly negligent, were not part of the plot.* Tweed had earlier paid a gang to plan and execute his escape, either while on one of his excursions away from the jail or through a fellow prisoner with connections.

Upon arriving at his home on December 4, he saw the sign indicating that "tonight was the night." Once inside, he wined and dined his jailers and his son. At the meal's conclusion, when one guard rose to wash his hands in the dining room's basin, the Boss excused himself to wash in another room, closing the door behind him. He then simply bid his wife adieu and walked out the front door to a waiting carriage.

---

* The anonymous author of the *Harper's Weekly* saga was finally identified as Carolan O'Brien Bryant, a press agent of the time, who claimed that his indirect source was Tweed himself. A detailed, and probably somewhat fanciful account of Tweed's 50 weeks away from New York, it makes interesting reading even today, and includes twelve illustrations, none of them by Nast. (See the Appendix on pages 290-307: "William M. Tweed. Romance of His Flight and Exile.")

After the vehicle made its way through Manhattan, Tweed was rowed across the Hudson River under dark of night to New Jersey, where another hack drove him to a farmhouse. There, he was shaved, given a wig and spectacles to wear, and assumed the identity of an ailing businessman—"John Secor"—seeking rest and relaxation. He stayed until early March 1876.

An alternative theory of the second night after Tweed's escape (Sunday, December 5) was published 38 years later (1913) by Greenwich resident Frederick A. Hubbard in "Other Days in Greenwich." The station agent who was on duty at the Cos Cob station that night (Cos Cob is the station after Greenwich) told Hubbard that the 9:15 train from New York City stopped 1,000 feet short of the station. He went out to investigate with a lantern, but was pushed from behind and the lantern extinguished.

The station agent had been reading about Tweed's escape in the newspaper. In the darkness, he could make out the bulky form of Tweed—whom he recognized from prior experience from 1870-1871 (see page 149)—get out of the baggage car and into a waiting carriage to go to Lydia McMullen's house. Later that night, he told Hubbard, Tweed was driven to Tarrytown, New York (where the Tappan Zee Bridge is now) and taken across the Hudson River to New Jersey in a chartered tugboat.

When asked 38 years later why he hadn't turned Tweed in for the $10,000 reward money, he told Hubbard that was not in his nature.

Tweed, who reportedly was the indirect source for Carolan O'Brien Bryant's account included here in the Appendix, makes no mention of Greenwich. If it was true, he protected himself and the McMullens to the last.

Years later, Thomas Nast indicated to his biographer, Albert Bigelow Paine, that Tweed's escape had been a "humiliation" to him. The admission was a highly revealing barometer of the intensity of the cartoonist's emotional involvement in the pursuit and prosecution of the Tweed Ring.

On the back page of its December 18, 1875 issue—published December 8, four days after the escape—Harper's Weekly printed Nast's "prophecy" from almost four years before (January 6, 1872), "Stone Walls Do Not a Prison Make," showing an oversized Tweed breaking out of jail with the aid of his jailers and friends. (See page 225.)

"STONE WALLS DO NOT A PRISON MAKE."—*Old Song.*
"No Prison is big enough to hold the Boss." In on one side, and out at
the other.

A week later, a parallel aura of shame combined with an Olympian detachment (again in the spirit of John Tenniel's work for the British publication Punch), is evident in Nast's severe judgment, "Good-By!", for the *Harper's Weekly* issue of December 25, 1875 (in print December 15). In a final gesture of ultimate disdain, the Grecian Lady Justice holds a distraught, disheveled New York at arm's length. As with his grim-faced "Justice" cartoon of two years earlier (see page 233), a disgusted Nast has no element of caricature in this picture, which occupies a double page for as much emphasis as he can give it.

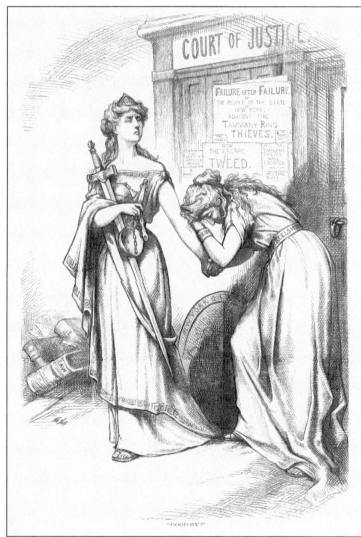

"GOOD-BY!"

The female personification of New York leans over to reveal a large placard denouncing the dismal record of the legal system: "**FAILURE** After **FAILURE**. The People of the State of New York Against the Tammany Ring **THIEVES**".

The door to the "Court of Justice" is padlocked, the law books are trashed, and a dark shadow is cast across the state shield and motto, Excelsior! ("Ever Upward"). At the lower left corner is a box marked "Ring Judges."

At the lower right hand corner is a box marked "$ Juries $."

Below the main placard: "Now the Escape of **TWEED**." To its left in a box, "The Court of Appeals Decision," and below that, "$ Sheriffs." To the right in a box: "All the Tammany Thieves Have Escaped" and in a lower box "Red Tape Suits."

Nast's first caricature of the vanished Boss was as the ghost of Hamlet's kingly father stepping off the rubble of Tammany Hall into the dark unknown: "In My Mind's Eye," in the *Harper's Weekly* issue of January 8, 1876 (published December 29, 1875).

The title is taken from a line of Hamlet's to Horatio in Shakespeare's "Hamlet" (Act 1, Scene II), and the caption is the ghost's mournful warning to his son (Act I, Scene V). "I could a tale unfold, whose lightest word Would harrow up thy soul; freeze thy young blood; Make thy two eyes, like stars, start from their spheres; Thy knotted and combined locks to part, And each particular hair to stand on end, like quills upon the fretful porcupine."

Looking terrified, though arrayed cavalierly in a suit of armor, Tweed carries a huge scroll of "Tammany Ring Regime Secrets."

Nast's illustration seems to have been modeled on John Gilbert's drawing of a similarly eerie moonlight scene, which appeared in Nast's 1860 edition of Shakespeare's plays. Gilbert's ghost of Hamlet's father also wears a plumed helmet, casts no shadow, and has his lower quarters fading into transparency.

"IN MY MIND'S EYE."

GHOST OF —— "I could a tale unfold, whose lightest word   Thy knotted and combined locks to part,
    Would harrow up thy soul; freeze thy young blood;   And each particular hair to stand on end,
    Make thy two eyes, like stars, start from their spheres;   Like quills upon the fretful porcupine."—SHAKSPEARE.

On February 7, 1876, the third trial of William M. Tweed commenced with a vacant chair marking the absence of the defendant, who had escaped nine weeks earlier. As the prosecution desired, the same "struck" jury was chosen for the "$6,000,000" trial and the "small" lawsuit. The judge was Theodore R. Westbrook, a Democrat who had served in Congress with Tweed two decades before and was thought by some to incline toward Tammany Hall. Despite rumors that the Boss would reappear to take the stand, the trial proceeded without him.

On Wednesday, March 1, testimony for the prosecution concluded, and David Dudley Field made the opening arguments for the defense. He moved to dismiss the charges against Tweed on the grounds that the Boss had stolen only a fraction of the missing $6,000,000 (about 25%), and so could not be held responsible for the entire sum. "Tweed's act did not cause the damage, whatever it was. The payments were made by Connolly to Garvey, Ingersoll, and others. If Tweed received a portion of the money, his liability is commensurate only with the amount received." Judge Westbrook denied the motion for dismissal, stating that it was established law that each conspirator was liable individually for all the money wrongfully taken.

The next day, Charles O'Conor made a surprise appearance in the courtroom, and began conducting the prosecution's case. During the remaining time, he adeptly objected to Field's various legal maneuvers and successfully kept the trial focused on Tweed's complicity rather than the propriety of the civil suit or secondary questions meant to derail the proceedings. O'Conor's skillful intervention proved to be a turning point in the trial.

Final arguments for both sides were made on Tuesday, March 7, and the next day Judge Westbrook gave the jury its charge, appearing, against previous predictions, to favor the prosecution. After deliberating for two and a half hours, the jury returned with a verdict against Tweed for principal and interest totaling $ 6,537,117. Field's motion for a new trial was denied.

A small Nast cartoon on the back page of the April 1, 1876 *Harper's Weekly* pictures Boss Tweed tearfully reacting to news that Secretary of War William Belknap was accused of taking bribes from contractors working at Indian trading posts. Published March 22, two weeks after the guilty verdict in Tweed's civil trial, the cartoon is set in a generic tropical location, in accordance with the common assumption that Tweed had already fled the country. Burdened with a parcel of "lawyers bills" in his hat, the former Boss, still in prison garb, reads adjacent headlines in the *New-York Times* announcing the jury's verdict in his case, as well as the accusations against Belknap. He pathetically weeps and blames public indignation over the secretary of war's malfeasance for influencing the jury's decision in his own case.

A CREATURE OF CIRCUMSTANCES.

"THE POOR OLD MAN." "If it had not been for that wicked Belknap and public indignation, the Verdict would have been 'NOT GUILTY!'"

Nast's "Tweed-Le-Dee and Tilden-Dum" appeared on the cover of the July 1, 1876 *Harper's Weekly*, in print June 21 and completed about nine days before that. It was precisely timed to reach readers one week before the Democratic National Convention in St. Louis. The cartoonist correctly anticipated that Governor Samuel J. Tilden would be the easy winner of the Democratic presidential nomination.

Nast challenged what he believed was the New York governor's exaggerated claim to being a government reformer, which the candidate exploited for the nomination. Reform was a major theme of the Democratic Party, emphasizing Tilden's defeat of the Tweed and Canal Rings in New York, as well as the need to cleanse the federal government of the corruption perpetrated during the Grant administration (1869-1877).

The cartoonist also discredited Tilden's denial of his connection with Tammany Hall. Throughout the campaign, Nast and *Harper's Weekly* linked Tilden with John Morrissey and Tammany Hall in a sustained effort at guilt by association. Although Morrissey was a key backer of Tilden, he had broken with John Kelly, the new leader of Tammany Hall, to form his own Democratic organization, Irving Hall. Furthermore, Kelly and Tammany Hall had opposed Tilden's nomination. One would never have known it by reading *Harper's Weekly*.

For this caricature of Tweed, Nast replicates one of the twin figures from "Our Modern Mummy" (see page 243), representing the Tammany and Canal Rings and loosely based on John Tenniel's "Tweedledee and Tweedledum" sketches for *Through the Looking Glass* by Lewis Carroll. In this illustration, the cartoonist's target is Tilden, the unseen "twin" of Tweed; together, they are just like Lewis Carroll's characters.

"Reform Tweed" is an escaped convict wearing a large "Tammany Police/Tammany Ring" belt, and collaring a pair of juvenile sneak thieves, one of whom drops three coins. Reinforcing the central image, the caption insinuates that in a Tilden presidency, as allegedly in his governorship, petty crooks will be arrested, while major culprits like Tweed will be rewarded with public office.

The raised billy club of "Reform Tweed" points to a poster reprinting an editorial from the October 7, 1875 issue of the *Nation*, which addressed the current widespread belief that voters must often choose between men of "pure motives" and those of "high ability." Voters demand that politicians simply stop public officials from looting the public till. If a politician sets out to do so, the public is not concerned whether he is "a statesman of the first rank" or what his stance on other issues is or has been. If the politician has self-interested reasons for pursuing reform, so be it—would that others would follow his example. Governor Tilden's rapid political success, the *Nation* asserts, is based on his having understood this situation. "He perceived sooner than his competitors that the time had come to stop preaching, and to begin making arrests and drawing up indictments."

Nast excised the editorial's opening passage, which praised Tilden's reform activities, and tacked on a profusion of descriptive placards on the wall to reconcile the *Nation* excerpt with points the cartoonist wished to make. **It was this cartoon that—three months later—enabled Spanish officials to identify and capture the escaped Boss.** (See page 255.)

TWEED-LE-DEE AND TILDEN-DUM.

REFORM TWEED. "If all the people want is to have somebody arrested, I'll have you plunderers convicted. You will be allowed to escape; nobody will be hurt; and then TILDEN will go to the White House, and I to Albany as Governor."

From his sanctuary across the river, Tweed had kept an attentive eye on newspaper reports of the case. The outcome would determine whether he returned to New York City or sought permanent exile abroad. Although he had become somewhat bored as the legal wrangling unfolded, he was thunderstruck by the appearance of his fearsome nemesis, Charles O'Conor. Tweed later explained that he felt the same as if had he been a murderer and the resurrected victim suddenly appeared in court to accuse him.

Sometime in March, Tweed—now using John Secor as an alias—moved his hideout from near Weehawken, N.J. (across the Hudson River from today's 39th to 47th streets in Manhattan) to Staten Island near the present Verrazano Bridge. In May, he sailed to Florida on a schooner, accompanied by the two companions who had been with him since his escape.

In Florida, he hooked up with a native guide in his late twenties, who John Secor (Tweed) introduced as his nephew, William Hunt. They camped out in the Everglades and ultimately sailed from St. Augustine to Key West, and then a relatively short distance to Santiago, Cuba. They had false passports, with Tweed's in the name of "John Secor," but no visas.

Arriving in Santiago on June 12, 1876, they were arrested by the Spanish military—Cuba was a Spanish possession—and held in custody. Word of the two Americans got back to the State Department in Washington, with Tweed's identity guessed. Republican officials from President Ulysses S. Grant and Secretary of State Hamilton Fish down wanted Tweed captured in order to provide political ammunition against current Democratic presidential candidate Samuel Tilden. Tweed's 1868 contribution of $5,000 to Tilden—when Tilden was Chairman of the New York State Democratic Party—was the link which Nast and others used as a cudgel.

By sweet-talking—possibly with money—American Consul Alfred Young in Santiago, Tweed was released from custody and sailed to Spain on July 27, almost literally "one step ahead of the sheriff." Consul Young was forced to resign soon afterwards as a result of Tweed's narrow escape.

Tweed's ship, the Carmen, took 42 days to arrive in Vigo, Spain on September 6, 1876. While it was in transit, the State Department, under the supervision of Minister to Spain Caleb Cushing, sent out wanted notices on Tweed to its consuls in Spanish port cities,. No photographs were available in Spain, but some of Nast's cartoons were distributed to serve the purpose.

The Vigo authorities identified Tweed from his July 1, 1876 image in "Tweed-le-dee and Tilden-dum." (See previous page.) Unable to read English and unfamiliar with the case, they assumed that the fugitive was guilty of kidnapping the two small urchins in the cartoon, and arrested him and his companion William Hunt.

Hunt was soon released and disappeared forever. Tweed spent three weeks in Spanish custody, after which he was returned to the United States aboard the Navy frigate *U.S.S. Franklin*, which departed Spain on September 27 and arrived in New York City on November 23. Chester Arthur, Collector of the Port of New York and future U.S. president (1881-1885), searched Tweed's baggage at customs.

Once back in custody, Tweed again went to the Ludlow Street jail, this time for good. He had lost more than 100 pounds on his two trans-Atlantic voyages, primarily from sea-sickness.

Nast and *Harper's Weekly* reveled in their joint role in actual law enforcement. After Tweed's capture in Vigo, "The Capture of Tweed—The picture That Made The Spanish Officials Take Him for a 'Child-Stealer' (published in *Harper's Weekly* for July 1, 1876)" appeared as a slightly smaller version of "Tweedle-Dee and Tilden-Dum" in the special supplement of October 7, 1876.

The small text printed below that cartoon—available on newsstands the day Tweed's ship left Spain—tells the story as *Harper's Weekly* knew it at that time, and is reprinted (in larger type) on the next two pages.

THE CAPTURE OF TWEED—THE PICTURE THAT MADE THE SPANISH OFFICIALS TAKE HIM FOR A "CHILD-STEALER."
[REPUBLISHED FROM "HARPER'S WEEKLY" FOR JULY 1, 1876.]

"We reproduce, for the amusement of our readers, Mr. NAST'S admirable cartoon which appeared in Harper's Weekly for July 1 of this year, a copy of which was placed by Mr. CUSHING in the hands of the Spanish authorities as a means of identifying the fugitive should he land at a port of Spain. It will be remembered that the first dispatches announced the arrest at the port of Vigo of one "Twid Antelme," on the charge of kidnaping American children—a mistake into which the local authorities were naturally led by Mr. NAST's cartoon.

"According to an account given in the New York *Herald*, TWEED, after his escape from the custody of Sheriff CONNER, was landed on a rock promontory about ten miles from Santiago de Cuba, by a boat which took him ashore from an American yacht. Here TWEED was discovered by a fisherman, much fatigued and exhausted, and conducted to the city of Santiago. The way was rocky and rough, and TWEED, owing to his weight, experienced much difficulty in walking. He was accompanied by a man called HUNT, who is supposed to have been a coachman for a long time in his service. The "Boss" was terribly sunburned, his face being as brown as a berry and very much blistered. The fisherman who guided the wandering pair received a gold "ounce" for his trouble, and led them not to a hotel, but to police headquarters. Had they been discovered on the coast by Spanish soldiers, instead of by the fisherman, they would probably have been shot on the spot on suspicion of being American filibusters on their way to "Cuba Libre."

"The police authorities, not satisfied with the fisherman's explanation, nor with TWEED's statement that he was an American citizen, sent him and his companion, HUNT, on board a Spanish man-of-war lying in the harbor, and there detained them as prisoners. TWEED, who was traveling under the name of "John Secor," succeeded in obtaining the release of himself and HUNT through the efforts of the United States consul at Santiago, who had no suspicion in regard to his identity, and took up his residence at a hotel, under police surveillance. He there lived very quietly. But meanwhile Consul-General HALL* entertained suspicions that there was something wrong about "Secor," in spite of the passport being en regle; and TWEED, feeling that he was watched, grew restless, and engaged passage for Spain on the bark *Carmen*, bound for Vigo and Barcelona. The night before his departure, Consul YOUNG telegraphed Consul-General HALL that "Secor" was WILLIAM M. TWEED. Mr. HALL, after a little unavoidable delay, obtained from Captain-General JOVELLAR** an order for his arrest; but the dispatch arrived at Santiago too late to be of service, the Carmen having sailed. The authorities at Santiago and Havana were at once made acquainted with the facts in the case, and the news was tele¬graphed to Madrid. These details were communicated to the *Herald* by a merchant of this city, whose name is not given, with whom "John Secor" corresponded while in Santiago.

* America's top diplomat in Cuba   ** Spain's top representative in Cuba

"TWEED's movements having been communicated to Mr. CUSHING, the American minister to Spain, he at once made arrangements with the Spanish government for the arrest of the fugitive on the arrival of the Carmen. Every precaution was taken to secure his person wherever he might land, and severe orders were given to the local authorities, especially to those of Vigo and the Galician coast. On the 6th of September, after a passage of forty-one days, the *Carmen* hove in sight off Vigo, and was immediately boarded by the Governor of Pontevedra, who at once recognized TWEED from the pictures in his possession. He was still traveling under the name of "Secor." Both he and HUNT were immediately secured, and transferred to the island of San Simon, in Vigo Bay, whence they were subsequently sent to Fort Castro de Vigo, where they were to remain until their departure for Havana, where, it is understood, they are to be delivered to the American authorities. There being no extradition treaty between the United States and Spain, the surrender of TWEED will be simply an act of comity on the part of the Spanish government. The *Madrid Epoca* of September 18, alluding to this fact, says it knows not what judicial course is to be taken by the Spanish authorities in the case. It adds that European governments would desire to see some definite legal arrangement made for dealing with such matters in the future.

"The Vigo correspondent of the London *Standard* writes, September 13, that TWEED appears to be in good health. He describes him as about sixty years of age, tall and stout, with a gray beard. The prisoners were conducted through the town on foot by carbineers to their quarters in Fort Castro."

Reprise

Nast always remained proud of his role in Tweed's capture. When illustrating a story in *The Illustrated American* magazine for September 6, 1890, he drew this picture of Tweed in Spanish custody in Vigo, Coincidentally, its publication date was 14 years to the day after the event took place. (See page 254.)

Still determined to exact revenge on the New York governor for his presumption in accepting the credit for toppling Tweed, as well as for aspiring to replace Ulysses S. Grant as president (Nast favored a third term for his hero), Nast continued his pictorial demolition of Tilden through the fall of 1876. Tilden, the Democratic presidential nominee, was currently engaged in a close race with the Republican nominee, Rutherford B. Hayes.

Nast did not like Hayes and did not depict him in his cartoons. Conversely, however, he helped Hayes by campaigning as strongly against Tilden as he had against three previous Democratic presidential candidates who ran against his all-time Republican heroes: Horace Greeley in 1872 and Horatio Seymour in 1868 vs. Ulysses S. Grant, and George B. McClellan in 1864 vs. Abraham Lincoln.

Continuing to tar Tilden with guilt by association with Tweed, Nast published three cover cartoons in September and one at the end of October just before the election. First, he heated the pot with "A Box Stew, or an Enviable Position" on the cover of *Harper's Weekly* issue of September 9.

Tilden is sitting on Tweed's unlocked box, tied with red tape, with Tweed inside looking wide-eyed in anticipation of getting out. Tilden is doing his best to keep Tweed contained before time runs out on the election; it is five minutes before midnight on the clock on the "Reform Fan that Blows Hot and Cold." Tilden's medallion has red tape instead of a blue ribbon with a "Hard and Soft Reform" inscription on it to describe the mixed feelings about Tweed that Nast ascribes to Tilden.

The wall has a picture of Tweed escaping under the Sheriff's nose, as well as a sign denoting Stanley's next expedition to find Tweed. (Journalist Henry M. Stanley, commissioned by the *New York Herald*, found missing explorer David Livingstone in the Congo in late 1871.) Another sign posts a "Reward to those that can find Tweed."

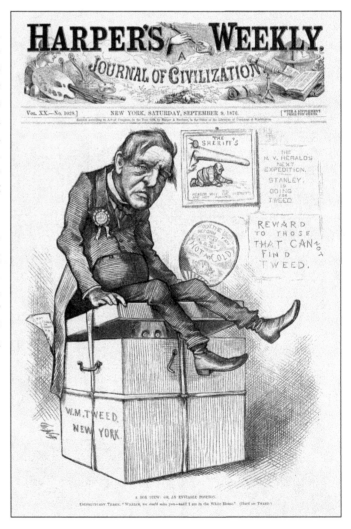

"Old Usufruct"

Nast returned to his "Tweed-le-Dee, Tilden-Dum" motif in "Any Thing for a Change," appearing on the cover of the September 16, 1876 *Harper's Weekly*, in print September 6. Coincidentally, that was the day on which fugitive Tweed's ship sailed into the Spanish port of Vigo.

Tweed rises like a Jack-in-the-box to offer his nemesis a prison suit. Surprised by the Boss's sudden appearance, Tilden employs a "reform" brush in an effort to dust "Tammany Mud" off his swallowtail evening coat (swallowtail was the nickname for members of the Tilden-Morrissey coalition, Irving Hall, which had broken with Tammany Hall).

The poster in the upper right reprints a headline from the August 27 *New-York Times* inquiring whether Tilden had lied concerning his income tax return (purportedly not paying tax on a legal fee of $20,000). In this cartoon, as well as the cover from the previous week, Nast seems to have based his Tilden caricature on a photograph because the image clearly shows the damage inflicted by a stroke Tilden suffered shortly after his gubernatorial inauguration.

The caption underneath the title reads: "Exile Tweed to Usufructuary Tilden. 'Let us usufruct on change. That's the best thing you can do about it.'"

The word "usufruct" is legalese for the right to "use and enjoy" property belonging to another person. It was a common railroad term, which Tilden knew well from his legal practice which focused on railroads.

Nast used it to stigmatize Tilden's reputation for sharp lawyerly practice, personal stinginess, and suspected tax evasion. Thanks largely to the cartoonist, candidate Tilden would be mercilessly tagged with the nickname "Old Usufruct," shorthand for a cheat, scrooge, or thief. Here, Tweed suggests they "usufruct or change."

A Hound on the Scent

For the cover of the September 30, 1876 *Harper's Weekly*, the cruel marks of paralysis in Tilden's face are even more apparent in "An 'Aggressive' 'Still Hunt.'" A "still hunt" means "stalking secretly" or "pursuing under cover."

The caption quotes Abram Hewitt, chairman of the National Democratic Party: "Governor Tilden has for years, like a hound on the scent, followed the members of the Ring patiently, secretly and diligently."

Such alleged aggressiveness and covert operations are countered by the cartoon's image. Tweed is the Tammany Tiger in the mouth of a Spanish cave, wearing the collar and tag of his old Americus Big 6 volunteer fire company. Tilden is a small, terrified mutt, with a "Usufruct" collar, who scampers an anxious retreat with his tail between his legs.

The Tilden dog is further hampered by a teapot, labeled "$5000 from W. M. Tweed," referring to a donation Tweed gave to Tilden in 1868 when the latter was chairman of the New York State Democratic Party. A teapot tied to an animal's tail (or to a coattail) is a symbol for a problem that is sure to trip up its wearer.

Tweed left Spain under arrest one week after "Still Hunt" was published on September 20.

Another Whale-Jonah Case

In the same October 9, 1876 issue as "The Capture of Tweed," Nast had another noteworthy cartoon reflecting "Jonah" Tweed's ride from Spain to New York in the belly of a whale. The whale, drawn with the head of a fish, has the features of Secretary of State Hamilton Fish—another ready-made Nast pun. Secretary Fish master-minded Tweed's capture and return, in order to be able to tie Tweed negatively to Samuel Tilden in the presidential election, which was only about a month away.

The words Nast put into Tweed's mouth: "Now *you* know how it is yourself" are the same (except for "now") that he put on Mayor Oakey Hall's signboard almost five years earlier. (See page 199.)

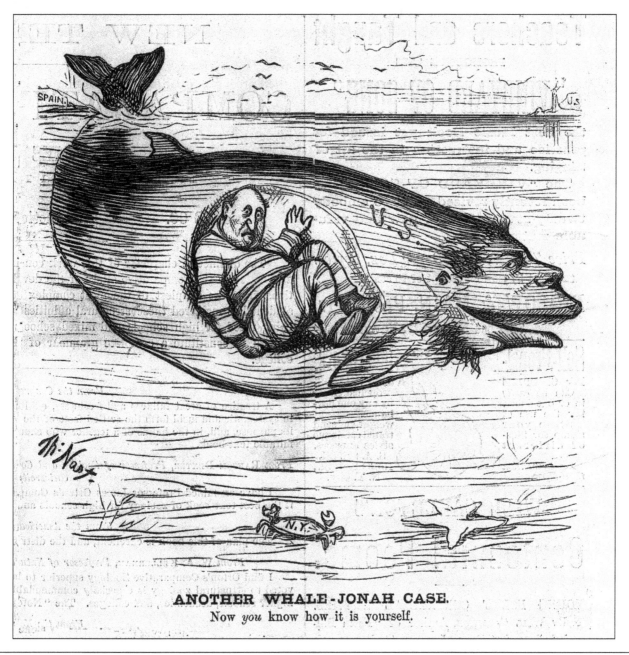

ANOTHER WHALE-JONAH CASE.
Now *you* know how it is yourself.

"Willie, We Have Missed You"

A fortnight later, the caricaturist visualizes the happy "reunion" of Tilden and Tweed as it might occur when the latter was forcibly returned from his brief trip to Spain. On the cover of the October 28, 1876 *Harper's Weekly* (in print October 18) is Nast's "Willie, We Have Missed You!" In another Tweedledee-Tildendum scene, the Boss, having arrived in a box, courtesy of "United States Express," embraces his old enemy, as each thumbs his nose in the direction of the reader. While Tweed, still dressed in prison stripes, hoists the sickly-thin body of his nemesis off the ground, the Boss seems to be placing another $5000 check in the presidential candidate's back pocket (unless he is supposed to be picking out the original check which Tweed gave to Tilden in 1868.)

Placards in the background balance Democratic national chairman Abram Hewitt's defense of Tilden's honesty (left) against Sheriff William E. Conner's improbable claim of Tweed's spotless record (right). Sheriff Conner was the official from whose jurisdiction the Boss had escaped, and to which he would be returned by federal authorities. Nast's third "Tweedledee and Tildendum" treatment may be loosely based on John Tenniel's final illustration of the twins from *Through the Looking Glass*, in which, partially facing one another, Alice helps prepare them for their great mock battle. "Let's fight until six, and then have dinner, said Tweedledum."

The sign just above the barrel on the left refers to Elbert A. Woodward's return to the United States from Canada. After his arrest in Chicago, he made a deal in New York to pay $150,000 in restitution, make a full confession, and testify against Tweed if required.

The Prospect in New York: "What Are You Going To Do About It?"

On the cover of the *Harper's Weekly* issue of November 11, 1876,—available November 1, six days before the election—Nast drew Samuel Tilden dumping a barrel of fraudulent votes into a ballot box. While the slogans on top link Tilden to current controversial issues—inflation, railroad scandals and the Confederacy—two reprints below the cartoon refer to vote fraud in the 1868 Presidential election.

On the left is "The Circular" of October 27, 1868, reportedly sent by Tilden, Chairman of the Democratic State Committee, with the intent of manipulating local vote counts. On the right is a "Letter to a Politician" from Horace Greeley, dated October 20, 1869, and referring both to naturalization fraud and repeat voting in the Presidential election of the prior year.

The "Circular" directly ties Tilden to Tweed in the vote manipulation process. In addition, Tilden's $5,000 contribution to Tweed is sticking out of his back pocket. For final emphasis, Nast repeats the 1871 refrain that he put in Tweed's mouth and used serially: "What Are You Going To Do About It?"

THE CIRCULAR
Rooms of the Democratic State Committee
October 27, 1868

My Dear Sir,—Please at once to communicate with some reliable person, in three or four principal towns and in each city of your county, and request him, (expenses duly arranged for at this end) to telegraph to WILLIAM M. TWEED, Tammany Hall, at the minute of closing the polls, not waiting for the count, such person's estimate of the vote. Let the telegraph be as follows: "This town will show a Democratic gain [or loss] over last year of—[number];" or this one, if sufficiently certain: "This town will give a Republican [or Demo-critic] majority of _____." There is of course an important object to be attained by a simultaneous transmission at the hour of closing the polls, but not longer waiting. Opportunity can be taken of the usual half- hour lull in telegraphic communication over lines before actual results begin to be declared, and before the Associated Press absorb the telegraph with returns and interfere with individual messages, and give orders to watch carefully the count. Very truly yours,
(Signed) Samuel J. Tilden, Chairman

LETTER TO A POLITICAN
. . . Now, Mr. TILDEN, I call on you to put a stop to this business. You have but to walk into the Sheriff's, the Mayor's, and the Supervisors' offices in the City Hall Park, and say there must be no more of it—say it so that there shall be no doubt that you mean it—and we shall have a tolerably fair election once more. Probably a good part of the Fifty Thousand supplied last Fall with bogus Naturalization Certificates will offer to register and to vote—some of them pretending not to know that they are no more citizens of the United States than the King of Dahomey is—but very few will vote repeatedly unless paid for it; and we shall not be cheated more than Ten Thousand if you simply tell the boss-workmen that there must be no more Illegal Voting instigated and paid for. Will you do it? Your reputation is at stake. The cowardly craft which "would not play false And yet would wrongly win," will not avail. If we Republicans are swindled again as we were swindled last Fall, you, and such as you, will be responsible to God and man for the out-rage. Prosecutors, magistrates, municipal authorities are all in the pool; we have nothing to hope for from the ministers of justice, and the villains have no fear of the terrors of the law. I appeal to you, and anxiously await the result. Yours, HORACE GREELEY New York, October 20, 1869

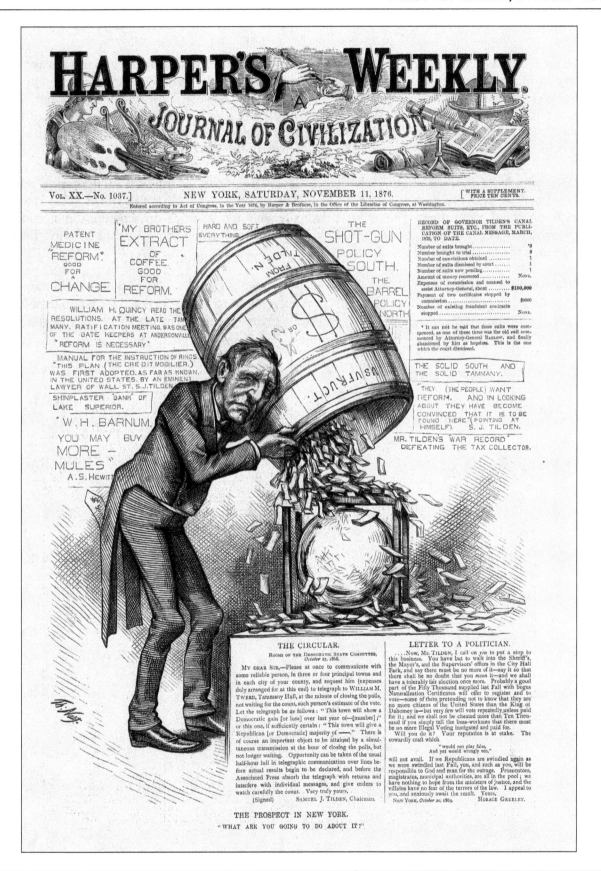

News to Tweed

After Bill Tweed was returned to New York and locked up in Ludlow Street jail, he was rumored to be negotiating a confession in exchange for his release. In fact, Tweed did write such a letter, dated December 6, 1876, the day this cartoon was published*. Conceivably, by implicating Samuel Tilden, it could hurt Tilden's chances for the presidency; currently, there was a deadlock in his contest with Hayes, even though the cartoon was published a month after the election took place, and it would be another eleven weeks before Hayes squeaked out a 185-184 victory in the Electoral College.

"News to Tweed" in the *Harper's Weekly* issue of December 16, shows Tweed peering out either from his jail cell, or possibly from his ship, at a purported letter from Abram S. Hewitt, chairman of the Democratic National committee. The letter is dated November 4—three days before the election—and warns the public against a "pretended confession of Tweed, already in type," as the steamer *Franklin* is returning him to New York from Vigo, Spain.

The caption: "Oh, Bill Tweed! thou art mighty yet." highlights Tweed's potential to damage Tilden. "To give State's Evidence is the Fall Fashion" probably refers to Peter Sweeny, James Ingersoll, Elbert Woodward and others who agreed previously to testify against Tweed. The empty boots may reflect a full confession with nothing left.

* See page 306 for the complete text.

ROOMS OF THE NATIONAL DEMOCRATIC COMMITTEE,
EVERETT HOUSE,
NEW YORK, *November* 4, 1876.

To the people of the United States:

I DEEM it my duty to caution the public against a pretended confession of WILLIAM M. TWEED seeking to implicate Governor TILDEN in the New York Ring frauds, which, I am informed, is already in type in advance of the arrival of the United States steamer *Franklin,* said to be purposely detained off the harbor of New York until the eve of the election, in order to give color to the fraud and prevent its contradiction. Possibly this notice may cause an abandonment of a device to which only politicians made desperate by the conviction of impending defeat would resort in order to mislead the ignorant and unwary. It is enough to say that the Ring was broken and TWEED and his confederates brought to justice by Governor TILDEN. This is one of his chief titles to the confidence of the American people.   ABRAM S. HEWITT,
Chairman National Democratic Committee.

TO GIVE
STATE'S EVIDENCE
IS THE
FALL FASHION.

NEWS TO TWEED.
Oh, BILL TWEED! thou art mighty yet.

Tweed is Double-Crossed

In a letter dated December 6, 1876, the imprisoned former Tammany Boss agreed to give the state attorney general, Charles Fairchild, a full confession based on the assumption that it was part of a deal for his release. Resisting an admission of moral culpability, Tweed began the letter by arguing that, because of "a mistaken sense of duty … to shield others," his previous intransigence and lengthy litigation "was truly more in the interest of others than in my own." Now, ailing and exhausted, Tweed conceded that he was "indeed overwhelmed" and believed that, "all further resistance being hopeless," he should "make [an] unqualified surrender." (See pages 306-307 for the complete text of Tweed's letter.)

He promised to turn over all his property, personal effects, and financial records to the state for examination, with the expectation, from Fairchild's public statements, that "the vindication of principle and the prospect of permanently purifying the public service are the objects you have in view, as being more desirable than the recovery of money." Tweed stated that he would not hire legal counsel for his own defense, but only for communicating and cooperating with the attorney general's office and the courts. Fulfilling his side of the bargain, Tweed testified at length on Ring operations.

Tweed ultimately was double-crossed, and Nast anticipated that by blaming his current villain, Democratic presidential nominee Samuel J. Tilden. Tilden was currently engaged in a close and bitter Electoral College dispute with Republican nominee Rutherford B. Hayes; a month after this cartoon appeared, Hayes won the presidency by one Electoral College vote.

"The Best of Friends Must Part," Nast's illustration for the cover of the February 10, 1877 *Harper's Weekly* (published on January 31) takes place under a moonlike timepiece prophetically showing "Tilden's Time" running out at 11 p.m. The Democratic nominee has broken his bond (the "Rotten Tammany Ring") with Tweed, and plans to make whatever politically expedient use he can of the confession that the Boss provided in expectation of his release from prison. The title of the cartoon derives from the lyrics of a traditional drinking song.

Tilden turns toward the road that he hopes will lead to the White House, which sits atop a precipice, marked with a large question mark. The path more certainly leads back to the New York governor's mansion, which he had vacated at the end of his term in early January 1877.

In Nast's most sympathetic caricature of Tweed, the former Boss watches Tilden's duplicitous actions in agonized disbelief. Tilden's pocket still contains his infamous (to Nast) $5000 campaign contribution to Tweed in 1868. In an interesting twist, Tilden hired both David Dudley Field, Tweed's former lawyer (mentioned in the caption), and Charles O'Conor, the former prosecutor of the Boss, as co-counsel to prepare and present the Democratic presidential nominee's case before the Electoral College Commission established to decide the election. The line under the title reads; "But their destination is not decided yet, by D. D. Field, Counsel of Fisk, Gould, Tweed, Tilden, & Co.

Foully Murdered

Harper's Weekly reported in its April 14, 1877 issue that Tweed's release from prison "has been provisionally agreed to, and will, as soon as due forms are complied with, be carried into effect." However, Fairchild, Tilden, and other officials, changed their minds (if they were ever so inclined) and refused to release the Boss.

The most bizarre and rancorous tailpiece to more than eight years of pictorial commentary on Tweed Ring exploits was Nast's sardonic "Foully Murdered" on the cover of the July 7, 1877 issue of *Harper's Weekly*. The cartoon is based on press reports that State Attorney General Fairchild had reneged on his promise, and declined to release Tweed from prison. Published on June 27, the artist had executed it in a burning fury some 10 days earlier, sacrificing exaggeration, and sometimes likeness, for undiluted emotion. The female personification of New York Justice lies dead—her throat slit—on a morgue bench. She is gagged as well as blind-folded, draped in sheets, and perhaps unrecognized or unclaimed as her exposed foot and big toe is untagged. Her professional tools—the sword "Excelsior" (the New York State motto, "Ever higher") and her scales for weighing good against bad—hang on the wall above, no longer in service. Boss Tweed gazes in astonishment from a corner of his cell window.

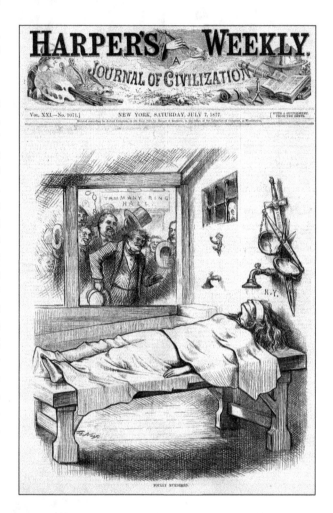

Outside the morgue window, a band of Tweed's former associates, who escaped penal sentences by various means, review the unlamented deceased in jubilation. They are (left-right): perhaps Elbert A. Woodward (the short man with a goatee), former clerk to the Board of Supervisors; standing in back, Andrew Garvey (also sporting a goatee), master plasterer and Tammany contractor and bagman; beside him, the spectacles of Oakey Hall have been thrown into the air in celebration; in front by the beam is a roughly drawn Tilden, who raises his hat to the slain Justice, and smiles wickedly; beside him is Tom Fields, former Tammany Republican cohort, who doffs his hat. The disheveled figure of Peter Sweeny dominates the scene in front as he waves goodbye to the corpse; with his face partially obscured on the right is George Barnard, the deposed Tammany judge who does not appear amused by the situation. The cheering figure in the back may have been intended to be former Comptroller Richard Connolly.

Tweed's predicament at the hands of the state attracted the sympathetic attention of the New York Board of Aldermen, where his political career had begun in late 1851. In September 1877, the aldermen initiated an investigation of why all the Tammany Ring principals except Tweed had been freed or allowed to settle with the state. On January 4, 1878, the Board of Aldermen approved, 13 to 7, a resolution calling for his release. With the publication of the aldermanic report, public sentiment began to swing more in line behind the prompt release of Tweed.

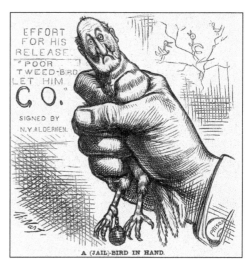

Nast reflected that public sentiment with his last cartoon of Tweed drawn while his former "Public Enemy Number One" was still alive.

"A (Jail)-Bird in Hand" appeared in the January 26, 1878 issue, published on January 16, twelve days after the Aldermen's resolution. The "poor Tweed-bird" looks almost philosophical in the grip of his jailor, perhaps reflecting Nast's own mixed feelings about Tweed's release.

A (JAIL)-BIRD IN HAND.

Probably because he had appeared to be acting against the interests of the new Tammany boss, John Kelly, in the matter of his predecessor, Fairchild was denied renomination as the Democratic candidate for state attorney general. The new state attorney general, August Schoonmaker Jr., also a Democrat, likewise refused to consider Tweed's request for clemency. However, after Boss Kelly urged Schoonmaker, in an open letter, to honor his predecessor's solemn pledge, Schoonmaker reversed his decision and agreed to release Tweed at the end of the current legislative session on May 15, 1878.

That date, though, came too late for the former Tammany boss. At noon on April 12, 1878, William Magear Tweed died in the Ludlow Street jail from heart disease complicated by diabetes and pneumonia.

Following an Episcopal funeral at the home of Tweed's daughter and son-in-law, at 63 East 77th Street, a modest cortege of eight carriages proceeded down Fifth Avenue and Broadway to Bowling Green, and then east to the Hamilton Avenue Ferry, which was taken to the Green-Wood Cemetery in Brooklyn. On a family plot overlooking New York Harbor, Boss Tweed was interred by his parents' graves. He was 55 years old.

Thomas Nast, who did so much to concentrate national attention and rage on the corrupt excesses of the Tweed ring, opted not to comment pictorially upon the old Boss's death.

In the wake of the Tweed Ring's overthrow, Thomas Nast received editorial tributes from all over the country. E. L. Godkin's comment on November 23, 1871, in the *Nation*, which he edited, is typical.

"To Mr. Nast it is hardly possible to award too much praise. He has carried political illustrations during the last six months to a pitch of excellence never before attained in this country, and has secured for them an influence on opinion such as they never came near having in any country. It is right to say that they brought the rascalities of the Ring home to hundreds of thousands who would never have looked at the figures and printed denunciations . . ."

Godkin's commentary was reprinted on the same day in the *Evening Post*, (which he also edited), but to which was added a more emphatic statement of Nast's pivotal role:

"The fact is that Mr. Nast has been the most important single missionary in the great work; and it is due to his telling work, more than to any other cause, that our municipal war for honesty has, from a local contest widened to a national struggle."

Only 31 at the time, Nast was at the zenith of his career. On January 28, 1872, he was entertained in a family sitting room of the White House by President Ulysses S. Grant and his wife Julia. Nast had arrived.

The *Times* gave Nast its highest praise on March 30, 1872.

"Mr. Nast has achieved a reputation which many men of twice his age might well envy, and which will probably outlast the reputations of most men who profess to form and direct public opinion . . . . "A man who can appeal powerfully to millions of people with a few strokes of the pencil, must be admitted to be a great power in the land. No writer can possibly possess a tenth part of the influence which Mr. Nast exercises."

During the following dozen years, Nast resurrected Boss Tweed as an evil spirit of powerful symbolic impact to use against whatever current politician the cartoonist opposed. His most prominent targets were three Presidential candidates:

1872   Democrat Horace Greeley, who had the audacity to run against President Ulysses S. Grant, Nast's all-time hero and personal friend. (See following pages 273-281.)

1876   Democrat Samuel J. Tilden, who Nast believed was hypocritical for jumping in late in the battle against Boss Tweed and the Ring, and then claiming excessive and undeserved credit for doing so. (See pages 236-237; 252-253; 258-271.)

1884   Republican James G. Blaine, who Nast and *Harper's Weekly* attacked for his prior alleged dishonesty in Congress, while supporting his winning opponent, Grover Cleveland. (See pages 282-283.)

The Connecting Link

During 1872, William M.—no longer "Boss"—Tweed was out of office and out of prison (on bail), but not totally out of Thomas Nast's cartoons. Tweed remained a shadowy figure of powerful symbolic impact for Nast to utilize for guilt by association against his selected political targets.

Nast replaced Tweed with Horace Greeley as his prime villain for 1872. As Nast had predicted a year earlier, Greeley was running for president against Nast's hero and current occupant of the White House, Ulysses S. Grant. (See page 43.) Greeley, the eccentric editor and owner of the *Tribune*, was easy to caricature with his unusual combination of clothing, vitriolic but changeable diatribes, and odd political bedfellows.

In early May 1872, the breakaway Liberal Republicans surprisingly nominated Greeley (who had been considered a possible candidate for vice president) for president, a choice seconded by the Democratic Party at their national convention in early July. In a series of cartoons, Nast addressed this bizarre combination of Northern liberals, led by a standard-bearer who had been an abolitionist and Union military enthusiast, with former Confederates and Civil War peace advocates in the Democratic Party.

The artist's back-page cartoon for the June 29, 1872 issue of *Harper's Weekly* (published June 19) provides a glimpse of Greeley as "The Connecting Link between 'Honest Republicans' and 'Honest Democrats.'" Three of the six figures joining Greeley were major players in the Tweed Ring scandal, including Tammany Republican Nathaniel Sands (on the far left), Mayor Oakey Hall and "Bill" Tweed. Liberal Republican Reuben Fenton, and Ben Wood, editor of the *Daily News* and former "Copperhead" (Peace Democrat) are identified by name. John Cochrane, a Republican politician who played a role in Greeley's campaign, is the plump man on Greeley's right.

THE CONNECTING LINK BETWEEN "HONEST REPUBLICANS" AND "HONEST DEMOCRATS."

"This is NOT an Organ"

A provocative full-page Nast cartoon of Horace Greeley as a dupe of the Republican Liberals appeared three weeks earlier in the June 8, 1872 issue. This was "The New Organ—(we beg the *Tribune's* pardon)—ization On Its 'New Departure': Any Thing To Get Votes." A subhead underneath quotes the *Tribune* from February 1871: "The brain, the heart, the soul, of the present Democratic Party is the rebel element in the South, with its Northern allies and sympathizers. It is rebel to the core to-day." The phrase "New Departure" was in wide use by "progressive" Democrats anxious to move beyond the sectional animosities of the Civil War and its "Lost Cause."

This was a powerful shot across the bow of the anti-Grant movement, intended to alienate regular Democrats who were preparing to adopt Greeley as their candidate during their national convention at Baltimore on July 9-10. It was also meant to underscore allegations that those Democrats were in control of this bizarre coalition. The attitude of the assembled Democrats in the cartoon ranges from indifference to boredom to hostility.

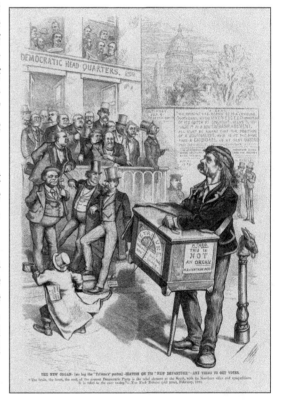

In giving up editorial control of his paper on May 15 for the duration of the campaign, Greeley had announced that the *Tribune* would cease to be a party organ. The prospect of an organ that was alleged not to be an organ was naturally irresistible fodder for Nast. The result was a caricature of acting editor Whitelaw Reid as the operator of the hurdy-gurdy—with a large placard on it stating "This is NOT an <u>Organ</u>"—trolling for votes in front of Democratic Headquarters, and using Greeley as his trained monkey.

The trio immediately in front of the monkey includes August Belmont, National Democratic Committee chair-man, and the 1868 Democratic presidential and vice-presidential nominees, Horatio Seymour and Frank Blair.

What is significant is the Tammany Hall assemblage which Nast has resurrected to support Greeley. They include (starting with third from the left) David Dudley Field, Judge George Barnard, Police Chief Hank Smith, Tom Fields, Peter Sweeny, Boss Tweed and Oakey Hall. Behind Tweed is Governor John Hoffman and, in partial shadow, Richard Connolly.

The man who looks like Teddy Roosevelt—between Tom Fields and Hoffman—is actually his uncle, Congressman Robert B. Roosevelt; the family resemblance is striking. While always a staunch Democrat, Roosevelt blasted the Tweed Ring at the Municipal Reform meeting held at Cooper Union on September 4, 1871. (See pages 56-59.) His inclusion with this group is somewhat unfair on Nast's part, even though Roosevelt was a Greeley supporter.

"Diogenes has found the *Honest* Man"

Throughout the presidential campaign of 1872, Nast incorporated visual and textual references to Greeley's letter accepting the Liberal Republican nomination, especially to the candidate's call for sectional reconciliation between Northerners and Southerners "eager to clasp hands across the bloody chasm which has too long divided them" (i.e., lingering sentiments from the Civil War). On July 11, 1872, Greeley's *Tribune* led its story on the Democratic nomination with an illustration of a white hand and a black hand firmly grasping one another. This must have been an encouraging signal to the cartoonist that he might now proceed to explore the graphic possibilities of "bloody chasms." A week later, the July 18 *Tribune* argued that Tammany, which was supporting Greeley's candidacy, had undergone a "complete revolution" since the fall of the Tweed Ring. Not surprisingly, Nast was unconvinced and suspicious.

In the August 3, 1872 issue of *Harper's Weekly*, Nast devotes four-fifths of a page to a view of Greeley shaking hands with Tweed, while patting him cordially on the arm. Reprising a theme Nast used to criticize Greeley's soft stance on Mayor Hall (see page 194), Greeley and Tweed appear as the Cynic philosopher Diogenes and the "*Honest* Man" he was seeking, but the cartoonist wonders which is which. Both carry papers labeled "What I Know About Honesty," but the sleeve of the former Tammany Boss is strategically covering the first three letters of what undoubtedly would read "Dishonesty."

The caption below the title is an excerpt from the *Tribune* describing Tammany Hall's exuberant reaction to Greeley's nomination by the Democratic Party: "As soon as the news that GREELEY and BROWN had been nominated was received, bunting was unfurled from every flag-staff on the City Hall. In the City Hall Park was displayed a large banner, bearing the inscription: 'TAMMANY RESPONDS TO THE NOMINATIONS OF THE NATIONAL CONVENTION AT BALTIMORE.' "

In the background, banners link the Tribune Building with Tammany Hall and City Hall.

DIOGENES HAS FOUND THE *HONEST MAN*—(WHICH IS *DIOGENES*, AND WHICH IS THE *HONEST MAN*?)

"As soon as the news that GREELEY and BROWN had been nominated was received, bunting was unfurled from every flag-staff on the *City Hall.* In the *City Hall Park* was displayed a large banner, bearing the inscription: 'TAMMANY RESPONDS TO THE NOMINATIONS OF THE NATIONAL CONVENTION AT BALTIMORE.' "—*New York Tribune, July 11, 1872.*

The Cat's Paw

One of Nast's principal plates for the August 10, 1872 issue of *Harper's Weekly* (in print July 31) shows Tweed as a large, cunning Tammany monkey controlling the paws of a feline Greeley to pull roasting chestnuts out of the "fire" on a hot iron stove. The term "cat's paw" refers to a person who is used by another for the latter's selfish gain, and is based on a 17th-century British fable of a monkey using a cat to pull chestnuts out of a fire.

The idea for the cartoon was suggested to Nast by one of the editorials in the July 13 *Harper's Weekly* in which George William Curtis pointed out to his Liberal Republican friends that they were being manipulated by the Democratic Party. Why do the Democrats want to defeat President Grant, the editor sarcastically wondered: "Is it that there may be great and generous reforms, or that they may achieve power? Did the monkey mean only to warm the cat's paws, or to pull out the chestnuts?"

THE CAT'S-PAW.—ANY THING TO GET CHESTNUTS.

Here, the chestnuts are political patronage positions in various departments of the federal government, such as "Treasury," "Post Office," and "Custom House," which renew Tweed's bygone dream of national conquest through a Hoffman presidency. On the backburner, the "Liberal War" against President Grant is a tempest in a teapot reaching the boiling point.

The Greeley cat is clearly uncomfortable. Its tail intertwines with that of Tweed's monkey over a spittoon associated with the crassness of Tammany Hall. The name attached to the end of the cat's tail is that of Greeley's inconsequential vice-presidential running mate, Gratz Brown. Nast usually reduced Brown to a tag on Greeley's coattail (or tail, as in this case).

Through the window, Columbia, representing the public, gazes with little expression at the scene she beholds.

The Tammany Tiger Loose (Reprise)

Three weeks later, Nast's "'What Are You Going To Do About It," If 'Old Honesty' Lets Him Loose Again?" appeared on the cover of the August 31, 1872 *Harper's Weekly*. The artist inverts the "Cat's Paw" idea by picturing Greeley whitewashing the ferocious Tammany Tiger through Whitelaw Reid's editorials in Greeley's *Tribune* (from which the candidate was on sabbatical). The scene is, of course, a close-up rendition of the coliseum setting in Nast's famous anti-Tweed Ring cartoon, "The Tammany Tiger Loose." (See page 163.) In place of Columbia in "The Cat's Paw" is Uncle Sam, who looks down in frustrated dejection. (See opposite page.)

The Tammany Tiger, who was "chained Nov. 7, 1871," wears an Americus (Tweed's social club) collar. His stripes, to which Greeley is applying "Reform White Wash," include "Corruption," "Illegal Voting" and "Wholesale Robbery." The paper in Greeley's pocket says "What I Know About REFORM," a not-so-subtle reference to Greeley's published book: "What I Know About Farming."

Something That Did Blow Over (Reprise)

For the October 5, 1872 issue of *Harper's Weekly*, Nast places "'Old Honesty' [i.e., Greeley] Among the Ruins of Tammany," which the artist first depicted after the Ring's election calamity in November 1871. Many of the same Tammany characters appear as in the earlier cartoon, "Something That Did Blow Over—November 7, 1871" (*Harper's Weekly*, November 25, 1871), although with a few notable changes. (See page 175.)

Mayor Hall has fallen from the precarious height atop a wobbling corner piece, in the previous satire, to being squashed under the split pillar of "Tammany Hall" at the front (right) of this cartoon. Boss Tweed is relocated from the center, where he was slumped on the rubble, aided with fan and alcohol bottle by two henchmen, to the far side (left) of this cartoon, where he rests glumly with his legs pinned under a fallen slab, pathetically hoping that "A Shell"—representing Augustus Schell, the interim Tammany boss— will shield him from further trouble. Peter Sweeny is behind Tweed. Not pictured in the earlier scene, John Hoffman, the outgoing governor, waves his hat forlornly in the center of this cartoon.

In the left foreground, Greeley stands upon the "Reform Platform," with his bucket of whitewash behind him, while in the right background, Congressmen James Brooks (in glasses) and Fernando Wood (with mustache) deliver campaign speeches for Greeley under a Tammany Hall banner. Newspaper editor Ben Wood (Fernando's brother) and Sheriff Matthew Brennan are cheering in the right foreground.

The paper in Greeley's pocket says "What I Know About Bailing," a derogatory reference to his having co-signed a $100,000 bail-bond which enabled Confederacy President Jefferson Davis to be released from prison in May 1867 after two years of confinement in Fortress Monroe, VA. Greeley was strongly and widely criticized for doing so. (See page 68.)

About six weeks after this cartoon appeared, Greeley would suffer his own ignominious defeat, losing the presidential race in a landslide, and then dying a few weeks after the election.

"OLD HONESTY" AMONG THE RUINS OF TAMMANY.

"Save Me From My Tobacco Partner"

Two weeks before the election, Nast portrayed Tweed on the November 2, 1872 cover of Harper's Weekly, available October 21, as a scary Indian chief with a raised tomahawk in his right hand and three tobacco leaves—"Greeley's $5,000.00 shares for which he never paid a cent"—in his left.   Tweed is a threatening—to a fleeing Greeley—cigar store Indian standing in front of Tweed, Greeley, Sands, & Co. Tobacco & Snuff Factory. In Greeley's pocket is a paper: "I hate tobacco but not tobacco shares. $5,000."

The title of the cartoon is "Save Me From My Tobacco Partner." "Old Honesty." "Do, Somebody, arrest him, or I shall never get to the White House!" Outside the other corner of the factory, a policeman is holding and reading a "Warrant of Arrest for All the Tammany Ring Thieves."

Nast assumes that Tweed, Greeley and renegade Republican Nathaniel Sands were partners in this commercial enterprise. It is conceivable that they only were all on the board of a non-profit Tobacco Association, but that is doubtful.

Other tobacco leaves hanging like scalps from Tweed's Americus Club belt say Tammany Republicans, Hank Smith, J. T. Hoffman and R. E. Fenton. Governor Hoffman, former governor and now Republican Senator Fenton, and former Tammany police chief Smith were all backing Greeley.

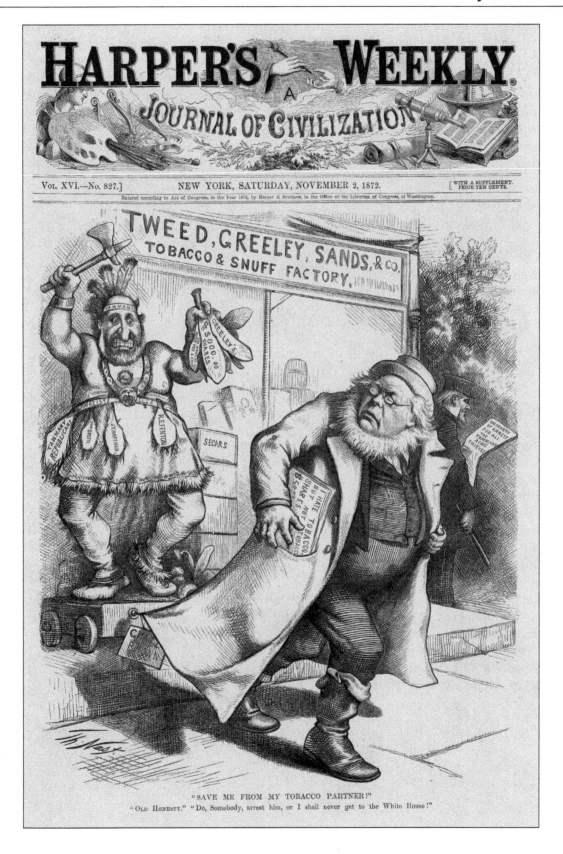

"SAVE ME FROM MY TOBACCO PARTNER!"

"OLD HONESTY." "Do, Somebody, arrest him, or I shall never get to the White House!"

1884: Nast vs. James G. Blaine (and the Ghost of Tweed)

282

In 1884, cartoonist Thomas Nast, editor George William Curtis, and *Harper's Weekly* broke their tradition of endorsing Republican candidates to support Grover Cleveland, the Democratic governor of New York, for president against his Republican rival, James G. Blaine from the state of Maine. The former U.S. Speaker of the House, Senator, and Secretary of State, was vilified by Nast, Curtis, and other liberals for his alleged involvement in railroad and other scandals, his opposition to civil service reform, and his rambunctiousness in foreign policy. Governor Cleveland, on the other hand, had won them over by backing civil service and other governmental reforms, as well as by opposing Tammany Hall. As the campaign heated up during the autumn of 1884, Nast incorporated the ghost of Boss Tweed into two anti-Blaine satires.

The first was "Grave Regrets," the cover of the September 27, 1884 *Harper's Weekly*, in which the Republican presidential candidate and the specter of the former Tammany boss console each other on the subject of their frustrated political careers.

Tweed's image appears in a cob-webbed cell-window, which seems to float in midair. His face is pallid but strangely luminous, while his prison-striped torso and arms fade into the dark shadow engulfing the scene. He laments the fact that he did not have Blaine's power as a political boss, which has resulted in the Republican presidential nomination on Blaine's third attempt.

Blaine glumly points out that he is backed by Robert Ingersoll, the skilled lawyer who defended the perpetrators of a post office scandal ("Star Route"), as well as by the *New York Tribune*, now run by Horace Greeley's successor, Whitelaw Reid.

GRAVE REGRETS.

THE SPIRIT OF TWEED. "If I hadn't been *too previous*, and had only belonged to the Republican party, and had been a big enough boss to get myself nominated, what a brilliant, intense American statesman I might have been!"

J. G. B. "And besides, I had the Star Route Defender, Bob INGERSOLL, christen me the *Plumed Knight*, and have the *New York Tribune* defend me *through thick and thin*."

1884: Nast vs. James G. Blaine (and the Ghost of Tweed)

283

In Nast's "Above Petty Personal Issues" pre-election cartoon for the November 1, 1884 *Harper's Weekly*," the ghost of Boss Tweed is now literally attached to Blaine as his shadow; Tweed once again regrets not having run for the presidency himself. The plumed hat worn by Blaine, and reflected in Tweed's hair, refers to Robert Ingersoll's comparison of Blaine to a "plumed knight" fighting for the good cause, an allusion that the cartoonist used to ridicule the Republican nominee.

Nast frequently pictured Blaine with a satchel to suggest that the politician was little more than a traveling salesman and, here, to more harshly equate his political career with prostitution. The label "20 Years" mocks the candidate's political memoir, *Twenty Years in Congress*. The figures peeking out from behind the door are Whitelaw Reid (left), the editor of the *New York Tribune*, and Congressman William Walter Phelps of New Jersey, Blaine's principal campaign advisors.

"ABOVE PETTY PERSONAL ISSUES."—New York Tribune.

Blaine. "The mere personality of a candidate for President is of small consequence."
Tweed. "I ought to have run for the Presidency."

However, Nast never again achieved the pinnacle of artistic and political success that he did in his 1871 and 1872 crusades against Tweed and Greeley, respectively. His 1876-7 campaign against Tilden made its mark, as did his 1884 campaign against Blaine, and he took great satisfaction when both of his villains lost.

During Nast's first 15 years at *Harper's Weekly*, he had the sponsorship and protection of Fletcher Harper, Sr., who supervised the publication. When Nast and editor George William Curtis disagreed on the appropriateness of a Nast cartoon, Fletcher felt there was enough room for two viewpoints and backed Nast. After Fletcher died in 1877, Nast lost his shield.

His unique gifts for caricature also faded. Like a home run hitter who smashed 60 in his two peak years, Nast fell back to perhaps 40 against Tilden and 20 against Blaine in their presidential campaigns.

OUR ARTIST'S OCCUPATION GONE.

TH: NAST. "It's all very funny to you; but what am I to do now?"

Nast was somewhat prescient with this cartoon in the *Harper's Weekly* issue of November 23, 1872, after Grant's victory over Greeley.

But Nast was more optimistic during the closing days of his campaign against Samuel Tilden in the *Harper's Weekly* issue of December 22, 1876, when the outcome of Tilden vs. Rutherford B. Hayes was still about ten weeks away from a final decision.

NO REST FOR THE WICKED—SENTENCED TO MORE HARD LABOR.

Finale ... After Harper's Weekly

Nast left *Harper's Weekly* voluntarily after 1886, upset by his occasional battles with Curtis, as well the rejection of some of his cartoons by the collective decision-making of the second generation of Harper management. In total, he contributed more than 2200 cartoons and illustrations to *Harper's Weekly* in the 25-year period from 1862-1886. Approximately 140 of them pictured Tweed.

On the personal side, Nast saw all his savings disappear in 1884—ironically because of his friendship with former President Grant. Grant's son, Ulysses, Jr., was a partner in the financial firm of Grant and Ward, which collapsed because of Ferdinand Ward's fraudulent activities. Both the former president and the cartoonist lost all of their capital, which had been invested in the firm.

In 1890, Nast did some cartoons for a New York publication called *The Illustrated American*, and reprised his Tweed Ring characters in a long serialized illustrated story by Edgar Fawcett called "A New York Family." He did find some new ways of showing them on playing cards, probably inspired by Boss Tweed's known habit of playing solitaire to fill his time while on the run and in jail. The perimeter caption for King of Diamonds Tweed (reflecting Tweed's huge diamond) reads: "What Are You Going To Do About It?"

TAMMANY'S FOUR KNAVES.

However, in the 1890's, the cartoonist was hard-pressed financially, and was desperate enough to accept the March 1902 offer of President Theodore Roosevelt, with whom he was acquainted, to become consul in Guayaquil, Ecuador at a salary of $10,000 a year. He knew the perils; before he left, he drew a prophetic cartoon of himself confronting the equatorial dangers of the sun and "Yellow Jack" (yellow fever) popping up like a jack-in-the-box as a skeleton-like death figure. Less than five months after arriving in Ecuador, he died of the dreaded disease on December 7, 1902 at the age of 62. His estate, including the home in Morristown, New Jersey, where he and his family had lived for 30 years, was valued at about $10,000.

Constantine De Grimm was a free-lance cartoonist who drew this caricature of Nast in 1892, when Nast was 52. Fifteen years later, it appeared on the cover of the Fiftieth Anniversary issue of *Harper's Weekly*, thereby highlighting Nast's premier importance to the publication. De Grimm had died in 1896, and this was the only occasion his work ever appeared in *Harper's Weekly*.

THOMAS NAST, THE ILLUSTRIOUS CARTOONIST OF "HARPER'S WEEKLY," WHOSE GENIUS OVERTHREW THE TWEED "RING," AND FOR YEARS WAGED A MEMORABLE FIGHT IN THE COUNTRY'S POLITICAL WARFARE

Tammany Hall did not stay powerless or corruption-free for long. John Kelly, Richard Croker, Charles Murphy and Jimmy Walker all served as notorious bosses over the next four decades.

Thomas Nast's larger contribution was less to the cause of good government in New York City than it was an enduring demonstration of the editorial cartoon as a vehicle for political and social change. For the first time in the history of a free press, a brilliant campaign of captivating and courageous cartoons, prominently displayed, had been harnessed to an editorial policy and strong reform effort. The public's imagination had been exercised, nourished, and given the understanding that it not only had a responsibility to care about an urban crisis, but also that its intervention could even make a decisive difference.

Nast supplied the emotion, continuity, breadth, color, and rage to bombard his Tweed Ring adversaries. If Samuel J. Tilden and Charles O'Conor finally turned the key that locked the cell door on Boss Tweed, it was Thomas Nast who generated and sustained public interest and wrath—nationally, as well as locally.

Nast probably thought of himself as a pictorial editor. Indeed, he was the first journalist who did not own his newspaper—or serve as managing editor—to play a major role in shaping public opinion.

While he may never have drawn or painted quite as well as some of his contemporaries, Nast had a particular genius in bringing wit, exaggeration, and irony directly to the support of his point. Some of Nast's 130-140 year-old symbols are still in everyday use. Best known are the Republican elephant which he invented; the Democratic donkey which he popularized; and the fat, jolly Santa Claus image which he created.

In 1916, an admiring cartoonist, Robert Carter of the *New York Evening Sun*, wrote to Nast's son, Cyril, "Your father used up almost all the ideas, and we [later] cartoonists are only rehashing them." That remains true today.

January 3, 1874

FINE-ASS COMMITTEE.

February 14, 1874

"ANOTHER SUCH VICTORY, AND I AM UNDONE."—Pyrrhus.

March 24, 1877

Appendix

290

William M. Tweed. Romance Of His Flight and Exile

WILLIAM M. TWEED.
ROMANCE OF HIS FLIGHT AND EXILE.
Harper's Weekly, April 14, 1877

The unfounded announcement of the death of Charles O'Conor, about the beginning of December, 1875, was read in Ludlow Street Jail by Tweed, with a feeling the reverse of what might be supposed, under circumstances which had given the Ring chief a notoriety on one side of the bar as great as the fame of O'Conor on the other. Until he realized the fact, Tweed could not imagine that the death of his great antagonist would prove so embarrassing to his interests. But, as he says, the anticipated event which excited so much sorrow in the community was more keenly felt by him than by any body else.

He was engaged at the time in negotiations for his release. Propositions for restitution and a settlement with the State by himself and his fellow delinquents were favorably entertained, one of the law partners of Edwards Pierrepont (then Attorney-General of the United States, and now minister to England) having the matter in hand. In the event of the decease of O'Conor, Tweed felt that there was no other person with whom he could hope to settle, and the toils in which he was left seemed so hopeless an entanglement that he fell into utter despair. He had battled for years already without result, except that he had squandered his ill-gotten riches upon lawyers and on courts, suffered imprisonment, with the prospect of a life term in Ludlow Street Jail in exchange for his previous place in the Penitentiary on Blackwell's Island. Worse than all else, he had sacrificed his property piece by piece, at ruinous prices, under the cloud of legal attachments, to raise the fees for carrying on his legal battles. This had reduced his means, so that, in view of disastrous shrinkage and foreclosures, he found himself brought face to face with actual bankruptcy. The approaching trial of the great six-million suit against him threatened a demand upon his cash resources for fees which he plainly saw he should fail to answer. His remaining possessions were not available to raise ready money, and credit, especially with the lawyers, was out of the question. His money gone, his courage broke down also, and he resolved on flight as the remedy both for his bankruptcy and his hopeless imprisonment. Could he obtain his liberty, he might save some fragments of his estate. From his prison bars he saw his fortune, like a raft broken in the rapids, scattered and helplessly drifting into irretrievable ruin. His costly and numerous counselors had deserted him in battalions, and with his shrinking purse came not only a change of his temper, but of his advisers and followers. In short, having lost the great judges and lawyers of the courts he had created and controlled, he found himself forced to fall back upon their clients, his fellow-prisoners of the jail.

Tweed's messmate in Ludlow Street Jail was Charley Lawrence, the silk smuggler, whose extradition led to the abrogation of the treaty with England. He had previously chummed with Tweed in the more agreeable sphere of the Americus Club, of which he was the official secretary, and, in fact, the chief steward and purveyor-general. This person being a client of Judge Pierrepont's office in the extradition matter, Tweed learned all the necessary details of the existing treaties and laws on the subject, from actual consultations in the jail in his presence, and having concluded upon flight, he resolved to reach Spain as the most expedient shelter, in view of the absence of any extradition treaty with that country.

William M. Tweed. Romance Of His Flight and Exile

291

Another of the inmates of Ludlow Street prison was a person of many professional aliases, who has since been more safely lodged in a penitentiary in Vermont. He is best known by the name of "Bliss," and was the engineer of the extraordinary Northampton Bank robbery. He was also "professionally" engaged in the famous Washington "safe burglary," which was the occasion of investigation under the late administration of General Grant. This person lodged on the upper floor, and had approached Tweed with the proposal to avail himself of the removal of the iron gratings of his window, which was on the ground-floor, and which would enable them both to escape, the whole matter to be managed from the outside by the associates of "Bliss." The proposition had at first been laughed at by Tweed. He had never previously entertained the idea of flight. He only replied, "What could I do with myself? Where could I hope to hide myself?" Concealment for Tweed was, as it seemed to him, an impossibility. But meeting his "professional" neighbor daily in the courtyard of the jail, where they took their exercise, the subject was more definitely discussed, and the outside friends of the "professional" being called in, Tweed was persuaded of the practicability of a plan which they presented, and for the execution of which he engaged to pay a stipulated amount of money. Flight, he had reasoned, must be his only relief. His conferences with his new advisers, peculiarly skilled in such matters, convinced him that this step, if entertained at all, must be taken with such absoluteness as to have no confidants or knowledge of his plans exist among his own friends. He must surrender himself exclusively to the control of those who undertook the job, leaving no entanglement or intelligence behind him by which he could be traced or overhauled. And, accordingly, no member of his family, nor his counsel, nor any friend or person whatever of his previous connections, knew of his proposed flight, or had any part in its execution; neither did they know of his whereabouts at any time, until it had become necessary for him to communicate with them, after his arrest in Cuba by the Spanish officials.

Tweed understood that he was to be taken in charge by a well-organized body of men, distributed throughout the country, having every facility, their connections and method being thoroughly tested and well established. He was furnished with a short key for telegraphic communication, and one for postal facility. The latter included a system of inclosures through five different envelopes, with addresses at removed points. He was to find occasion to visit his house in Fifth Avenue, corner of Forty-third Street, and deliver himself over, secretly and unattended, at his own door. The execution of the agreement included his landing in Spain, or under the Spanish flag, and on Spanish territory, safely and secretly. He was given the name of John Secor, by which he was to be known to his new connections, and his personal identity and his own name were to be concealed from all persons, without exception, from the moment he passed out of his own stoop. The exact minute of departure was fixed at eight o'clock in the evening, not more than one minute before to one minute after that hour exactly. The time of his flight was left undetermined. But he was to visit his house on certain days, and, when the whole train was ready, a sign was to be given by a certain secret mark upon the stoop, which he could see as he ascended the steps.

Accordingly, Tweed took occasion to obtain from the sheriff and his keepers the usual "privilege of the jail yard," to visit his family and transact some business. The sheriff being allowed by law to treat prisoners for debt to this privilege, as necessary for the purpose of enabling them to get bail and look after their suits, it becomes one of the perquisites of that officer, and also a principal responsibility and risk, for the exercise of which he gives his bonds. Tweed, being held on civil process, stood in a different light from his former attitude under a penal sentence. In leaving his jail he exercised a right in which he had only the sheriff to consult, being with him discretionary and a legitimate matter of fees or costs within the county limits. Several such visits having been made to his house at the usual hour, after dark, he secretly made some preparation of personal matters, and, putting his business affairs in as good order as possible, finally reached the 4th of December, 1875, which proved the occasion of his departure.

William M. Tweed. Romance Of His Flight and Exile

292

On the evening of that day he was driven in the customary hack, attended by two keepers, to his house. Ascending the stoop, he saw the sign.   It was about half past seven o'clock, and a dreary December evening.   The signal at once aroused him with a starting shock, and (as he describes the occurrence) his blood and his nerves were filled with an electrical excitement which thrilled every fibre of his frame. Controlling himself with some effort, he led his attendants to their wonted and welcome feast, which on this occasion was amply provided in the dining-room.

Mr. Tweed concealed his excitement by an affected display of appetite and a nervous and officious attention to his guests.   The clock on the mantel, which had been carefully regulated, seemed to him to be almost immovable, as the hands developed the slow minutes of the half hour preceding eight o'clock. The keepers ate, and he took care, also, that they drank. The meal engaged the profound attention of the men, and they put in their time effectively and promptly.   But Mr. Tweed says he thought he never had assisted at so anxious and dilatory a service of courses. He dreaded, on the one hand, to serve them so hurriedly as to have them rise and get in his way, and, on the other, he feared his detention with them beyond the close restriction of his moment of departure. This anxiety somewhat obscured the fluctuation of his resolution, which from time to time brought revulsions impelling him to give up the escape altogether.

But at just the right moment one of the keepers rose and went to the wash-basin in the room to wash his hands, and get ready for the luxurious and usual cigar after dinner. Tweed took the opportunity, rose also, and saying he would wash in the adjoining room, he passed into the hall, closing the door as he left the room. He quickly took the first hat and coat and slipped out the front-door. He was a fugitive! He saw the hack before the door without the driver, who also took advantage of the occasion in the kitchen. Not a person or a sound appeared to respond to his appointment.   It was not quite one minute past eight. The revulsion of his previous excitement seemed to have set in, and he began to experience peculiar sensations.

He had stolen forth from his home to place himself in the hands and guidance of a picketed gang of desperadoes! As he shrunk back under the shadow of the stoop, it seemed to him a long period of doubt and self-examination, until his attention was attracted by the noise of wheels, and he saw a common tradesman's wagon, such as is used by grocers and express drivers. He saw also a man's arm reach out from the cover, which was the sign that it was for him. As he descended the stoop he also saw a man passing slowly, which caused him to hesitate; but this person said, in a low tone, "All right; get in the wagon." So he scrambled into the covered wagon, which drove quickly around the block into Madison Avenue; but as they got there, a car having run off the track, some mounted police and passengers stood in the way, and the fugitive was stopped for two or three minutes. Before the car was righted and he had started again the suspense seemed to him an age. The presence of the police, the possibility of his detection and capture, the sense of flight, brought out a vivid realization of his situation. He had borne the indignities and the privations of his prisons and his punishment heretofore, but that seemed something voluntary. Like the Indian in captivity and torture, he did not heed it.

William M. Tweed. Romance Of His Flight and Exile

293

ESCAPE FROM THE SHERIFF'S HANDS TO THOSE OF THIEVES.

William M. Tweed. Romance Of His Flight and Exile

294

Mr. Tweed dates from this inception of his flight a complete change, which has since taken full possession of his character and his tone of mind. Many hours and days of like experience have since deepened his emotions, and all who have seen him since his return, and who knew him in his previous pride, have been struck with the revolution in his mental condition.

The wagon soon started again, and drove zigzag across the city toward the North River, which was soon reached, and beside a big truck on the pier they stopped. The driver said, "Get out on the river side."

Tweed got out, seeing that the truck covered him from observation as he alighted.

A man stood near the truck also, who indicated that Tweed was to descend into a rowboat, in which he quickly embarked and crossed to the Jersey side. The place of this departure may be indicated as in a comparatively direct line from Tweed's house at Forty-third Street, possibly not very far away from Weehawken Ferry. This is a lonely and unfrequented locality at night, and the opposite shores of Jersey present the first bluffs of the magnificent Palisades. The rocky shores of the river under the Palisades have been modified in their wildness of aspect by a road which reaches to Fort Lee, with occasional steep ascending roadways used by the quarrymen cutting out and carting the Belgian pavements.

THEIR FERRY FROM NEW YORK TO NEW JERSEY.

William M. Tweed. Romance Of His Flight and Exile

295

The row-boat landed Tweed at an unfrequented spot in this neighborhood, not far distant from the well-known place where Alexander Hamilton was killed in the duel with Aaron Burr.   There he was met by another vehicle in waiting for him on the shore road, when he was driven off into the region beyond the river and the Palisades, climbing and descending as occasion was, but in a direction and to a termination where he never had been before, and could not now ascertain or indicate. This lonely ride in the darkness was made in half or three-quarters of an hour, mainly at a rapid pace when not delayed by the unfavorable roadway. They passed into the peculiar region beyond the Palisades, where the aspect of the scenery may be found as wild and primitive as in the Adirondacks, and a refugee would be far more likely to escape observation. Skirted by picnic taverns and Sunday beer gardens, the population of this picturesque territory is chiefly German. Back from the river there are few travelled highways, and the few old farmhouses have a dilapidated and deserted appearance.

Reaching one of these decayed and unobtrusive homesteads, Tweed was received by another of his newfound friends, who greeted him quietly with assurances of kindness and safety. Being led into the house, his host tendered him the use of accommodations either on the ground floor or the one above. After examination, the second story was chosen.

In this refuge Tweed continued from his arrival, the 4th day of December, until about the first week in March.

After a fitful night's rest, the fugitive rose next morning to realize that he was an exile at his own threshold, as it were. From the neighboring bluffs or hills he could see his home in the city of New York, which he dared not visit, and where he was "born and raised. " When could he again return to it? His present resting place was intended to last until it was convenient for him to start for Spain, after a little further delay for preparations. But it was months before he set out, or could tear himself away from New York.

MR. TWEED CONTEMPLATES NEW YORK FROM THE PALISADES.

William M. Tweed. Romance Of His Flight and Exile

296

The first care in the morning was to put on his disguise and transform himself into his assumed personality, "Mr. John Secor," an invalid gentleman, seeking merely a little rest and fresh air, as well as relief from business pressure. So, his whiskers being shaven off, and his hair clipped short, he put on a wig. The removal of the whiskers gave his features, his jaws, and cheek-bones greater prominence, and with the wig and a pair of gold spectacles, he was quite transformed. The wig was of reddish-yellow hair, crinkled or curled in appearance, cut square, and quite well down on his neck.

The next anxiety of the day was to get the newspapers. It seems to have been a most exciting sensation to him when they were obtained. Nothing but Tweed. Column after column and whole pages on his flight, the search by the sheriff and detectives, the theories and conjectures of the reporters, the proclamation of reward officially, the communications and letters from every quarter. The uproar seemed unprecedented, and at once it had its effect upon him. It was occupation for his mind. He read each day, and had every paper he could get brought to him. The excitement of the search was peculiarly his. Many times, as some corner of the discussion seemed to point toward his hiding-place, he started up to go upon his voyage, then waited until the next day's batch of news, and was diverted from the idea. Reading the papers was his chief occupation. He seldom ventured out-of-doors in the daytime. A walk in the early morning, and an occasional late sundown ride in the covered country wagon through the unfrequented wooded lanes, filled up the routine of his time for several weeks. After that, he got an opportunity to watch the impaneling of the struck jury, and finally wound up with a naturally absorbing interest in the daily reports of the trial in the famous six-million suit against him, as elaborately presented in the New York papers.

It was during this opportunity of quiet and meditation, which his surrounding circumstances for the first time afforded him in many years, that the striking change began which has been observed in him since his return, and which the scattered indications in the brief diaries which he kept, clearly indicate. It is important to note this here, as a key to the concluding events of his extraordinary story.

DISGUISED, IN THE THIEVES' RENDEZVOUS.

William M. Tweed. Romance Of His Flight and Exile

297

The article published in *Harper's Weekly* on the Court of Appeals came out three days after the flight of Tweed. He never saw it until his return from Spain, but he read the discussions it had created, and saw the influence it exercised on the judiciary, which proved to be of the greatest importance to his destinies. O'Conor was not dead, but his condition was supposed to be such as to preclude any idea of his being ever able to resume his position in the courts again. The Ring men had nearly all fled, and there seemed to be nobody to carry on the unfortunate suits. The responsibility of a record which began to excite a good deal of odium against the judges could no longer be shifted from them, and no amount of political manoeuvring could head off the increasing scandal. Tweed had left no instructions about his cases, nor did his bondsmen or friends desire to move in them. But through the secret influence of the judges the matter was put on its legs, and Judge Westbrook, whose decisions had been reversed before, was made the medium of a change of policy, which had also been distinctly intimated in the denial of a minor motion in the case of Tom Fields, one of the Ring suits, by the Court of Appeals.

Judge Westbrook had written in the general term what is known as the cumulative judgment decision of the Supreme Court, supporting the sentence of cumulative penalties inflicted on Tweed, and which the decision of the Court of Appeals had reversed. He was identified with the decisions in the Ring suits from the first, having been sought by reason of his peculiar ability, and his acknowledged independence of the influences which had been so manifest elsewhere in the courts. When the case of the Assistant State Treasurer Phelps came before him, it was presumed that he would treat it in the usual way as a mere misdemeanor or a breach of trust. In fact, the delinquent Phelps, who had in his capacity as a public officer embezzled some forty or fifty thousand dollars, went to a high legal practitioner in Albany, and in a panic took advice as to his difficulties. The lawyer advised him of the trivial punishment and comparative immunity hitherto usual in such cases; and taking courage again, he returned to his official post, and increased the amount of his theft to upward of three hundred thousand dollars. But on his trial before Westbrook, the surprise was developed of sending him, under heavy sentence, as a felon to the penitentiary, and establishing such acts under the common law as punishable like any other robbery.

It is a curious coincidence, also, that during the administration of President Pierce, Westbrook was a member of Congress with Tweed, the latter having influentially exerted himself to procure the appointment of United States District Attorney for the man who has since so signally dissolved the "Tweed influence" on the bench. It should be remarked here, perhaps, that Judge Westbrook, having voted for the famous Kansas-Nebraska Bill, declined the appointment in question at the hands of Pierce, as it might seem like a payment for his vote—a delicacy not elsewhere manifested on that occasion by others. As a judge, his decisions and rulings have been marked by great clearness and simplicity, his gentleness of manner and delivery being entirely wanting in any effort at oratorical or dramatic effect.

In view of the severity of the attacks which have been made upon our State judiciary, this recognition, in a different key, would seem to be due to the judge who finally disposed of Tweed's case. Its importance in tracing the course of the latter is absolute. Tweed watched the proceedings as if he were a spectator and listener, where he sat in his retreat, viewing through his window the masts of the distant shipping and the house-tops, just dimly visible in the smoke of the horizon. Tweed knew well the temper of his judge, and in one regard it was the same to him whether he was on the ground to help, or out of sight and reach. Indeed, he conjectured that the inclination of the judge would be less severe, in view of the obvious absence of all appearance of influence from him (Tweed). He watched the defeat of the motion for a dismissal, and scanned with wonder the unprecedented and then novel proceedings for a "struck jury." Of course he could know nothing of the secret counsels held by the juniors at the sick-bed of O'Conor. The latter at Fort Washington, almost in a direct line across the river, and quite in sight of the hiding-place of the fugitive, had suddenly roused up from his long and extraordinary lethargy. He became convalescent, got out of bed, and rivaled Tweed himself in his growing interest in the trial.

William M. Tweed. Romance Of His Flight and Exile

298

Tweed had certainly made definite plans for his future in leaving his prison. But once at large, he lingered, intensely anxious that the result of the trial might admit of his return. He saw by the reports that the adroitness of David Dudley Field, in the absence of his old antagonist, Charles O'Conor, indicated an easy rout of the junior counsel, into whose hands the case for the people had dropped. The witnesses came on the stand from the public offices, from the city banks. Garvey and Ingersoll came. Mr. Tilden, the subsequent candidate for the Presidency, was put to the question. Tweed watched it all. He was certain, from appearances, that the prosecution of the suit was breaking down. The counsel, with their witnesses, and the proofs on the side of the people, seemed to him (as he describes it) like the stereotyped scene in a pantomime, where the great blower appears, and sends every body and every thing off the stage, or flying up in the air, at a puff. Such seemed the irresistible dexterity of the noted cross-examiner and codifier.

All these proceedings of the trial had been strung out, and had now reached the beginning of March. The suspense of Tweed had become intense. Upon the near event depended whether he should return to his native city or resume his flight and seek a permanent place of exile. He had occupied his present quiet retreat since the 5th of December, making three months. He continued under the control of the two men who had managed his escape and contracted for his safety. He did implicitly what they directed, and they held him in hand like trainers. He slept, he rose, he walked, he rode, ate, and drank only as they instructed him, and it may be remarked here, that this discipline and relation were maintained until he closed his engagement with them satisfactorily in Florida. His days back of the Palisades being spent in strict seclusion, all his mind naturally centered upon reading the daily reports of the trial. And as the great length of the proceedings naturally grew monotonous, even to him, he was suddenly startled one day, on receiving his papers, by seeing the announcement, in the customary sensation head-lines, that Charles O'Conor had re-appeared in his case before Judge Westbrook! Of all resurrections and ghosts, this seemed the most fearful to Tweed. As he describes it, had he committed murder, and had the body of his victim been suddenly brought before him to confront, he might have felt as he did when he read the strikingly dramatic scene in the court, when the white and emaciated form of the venerable pleader rose and resumed his cause before the judge.

All hope for Tweed at once seemed vanished. He had conjectured some brilliant technical stroke by his counsel which would quash the whole thing, as they did before the Court of Appeals. He had estimated the probabilities of "hanging" the jury on some disagreement. But the advent of O'Conor dissolved all. He did not wait for the end. He again gathered up his now scanty effects. If he (Tweed) did not make an end of this thing, O'Conor never would. Once more he was done.

The scene now changes. Tweed had finally surrendered himself to exile. He took up a temporary abode about half a mile from Fort Wadsworth, at the Narrows, in a fisherman's hut, with his two companions. This shanty had been used by some shad fishermen, but the obstruction which their poles made caused their removal by order of "G. W. B.," the famous guardian of New York Harbor. The shad-man's hut was therefore vacant, until the distinguished occupancy by this other great friend of New York city and its less liquid highways, "W. M. T." The cottage, like others of the kind, was of small dimensions, with a tier of bunks or berths, like the forecastle of a ship. Here the party staid for two weeks making preparations. How they escaped the Argus-eyes of the many joint and several Associated Press agents during this retreat on Staten Island is indeed a miracle—the very home of the agent of the Associated Press, Mr. Simonton, and the thickest haunt of the reporters, as well marine as ultramarine, special, regular, and regular special! Mr. Tweed not only lived at this shad-man's hut for two weeks, but even made a visit across the channel, and stopped a night in Brooklyn! This was fairly the beginning of a course of rough life and free adventure which lasted until his arrest in Santiago de Cuba.

William M. Tweed. Romance Of His Flight and Exile

299

The judgment for $6,000,000 and upward, which had now been entered up against him, sat as lightly, after all, upon his new resolution as the old badge of "Big Six" upon his breast in the early days of the old New York fire-laddies in the Bowery. He fully realized that the bail (not the judgment) was a barrier which had been most ingeniously devised to banish him forever from the old haunts. It was as firm and relentless a decree as ever Venice had enforced in her bitter and relentless edicts of the secret chambers of the Council of Ten. But he had, in fact, far more apprehension and concern now about the prospective ocean voyage and the detestable seasickness than about O'Conor, and the knapsack Westbrook had strapped upon his back. However, he dodged the main question of the seasickness by devising a coasting expedition by which, reaching Florida and thence crossing the Spanish Main, he might in easy stages land under the protection of the Spanish flag. His physique usually averaged some two hundred and eighty pounds, a most inconvenient bulk on a sea-voyage, and in sea-sickness a proportionate source of increased disturbances.

During his stay on Staten Island a light and fast-sailing little schooner was fitted out, and manned by himself and two companions, with a Negro boy. He started at last from the pier in front of the fort in a row-boat, in the night, and slipped away upon a pleasant breeze.

HE IS TAKEN FROM STATEN ISLAND TO THE SCHOONER.

In due course, and without any thing noticeable, they reached the lagoons on the coast of Florida. At one of the light-house stations they made a definite stoppage again, Tweed taking board with the keeper of the light as John Secor, an invalid gentleman seeking a restoration of health and the recreations of fishing and hunting. Here, too, he parted with his guides from New York, closing his contract with them at that place.

His new quarters stood out in the surf, upon a long and irregular strip of sandy sea-beach, outside of a bright and limpid lagoon between this beach and the mainland, the lagoon averaging about half a mile in width. Here, in this lonely shelter, he took a melancholy and meditative rest. He experienced for the first time in years a feeling of perfect peace and safety which began to fascinate him. His restless activity and the tumult from which he had escaped had prepared him for a strong appreciation of this forlorn abode. The keepers, a simple and contented family, knew nothing beyond this blank life of their duty and their scanty resources. Communication was easily had with the mainland, and the facilities of mails, and even the indispensable newspaper, were within easy reach.

William M. Tweed. Romance Of His Flight and Exile

300

His residence at this place marks a principal point in his adventures. Here, having parted with his "professional" friends, he was joined by the person who is known as Hunt in the reports of his subsequent arrest. This man, with a smattering of medical phrases and a practiced experience as hunter and guide, was one of a class of local characters, like the guides or trappers, the men of the mountains, the prairies, and the wild border-life of the West. In Florida the chief resource of profit for this class is to pilot the invalids and pleasure parties who seek that region for its climate during the winter months at the North. Here Mr. Tweed bade farewell to what the denizens call a "biled shirt"—an article which was replaced in this region by a woolen or hickory shirt, which may last the owner a couple of years (and frequently does without washing). The other articles of costume usually are a high pair of jack-boots, truncated pants tucked inside the boots, and a slouched or straw hat. The hunting knife, pistols, belts, blanket, and wallets are added, like pepper and salt, to suit the taste.

HOME ON FLORIDA KEY

SECOR AND HUNT CAMPING IN THE EVERGLADES.

The new guide soon led Tweed into his own haunts in the interior of Florida. With a camping blanket and necessary arms they set forth, and Tweed entered upon the fascinations of a life which seemingly offers no serious prospects of hardship in that climate. They kept out of the range of the regular tourists, and got well beyond the settled borders into the tropical wilderness. The everglades and forest life had the usual glitter and gorgeous aspects while the sense of novelty lasted. He speaks of many pleasures in his adventures during this expedition; but overtaken in due season by the torrid months, he was driven back, and took up his residence in the neighborhood of St. Augustine. It would be a commonplace matter to recite Tweed's local experience with the details of camp life, hunting, fishing, and seeking the usual expedients for killing time and the mosquitoes. It does not appear that Florida engaged his attention so much by its peculiar life, climate, and scenery, as it influenced him by the rest and self-review which it afforded him. Contemplating himself in the light of an Ishmaelite, and like the last of the Seminoles, Billy Bowlegs, driven out of civilized haunts into the everglades and the uninhabited wildernesses, he returned to the cooling breezes of the sea-shore near the suburbs of St. Augustine, and there deliberately planned a new sphere and a new life of usefulness, if not of repentance and reparation.

William M. Tweed. Romance Of His Flight and Exile

301

When he left this place in a fishing smack for Cuba, he had completed a definite set of plans to be carried out on his arrival in Spain.

Some forty miles' sail brought Tweed and his companion to the coast of Cuba, some ten miles outside the harbor of Santiago de Cuba. The fisherman who brought them from the American coast did not dare to confront the Spanish officials with a freight which he strongly suspected was contraband. It was a bright moonlight night as they made the point chosen for a landing.   Tweed had already become habituated to the by-ways frequented by his guides, and, even where he might have taken one of the regular steamers plying among the West India ports, he quite naturally continued his course as he had started, keeping himself away from the regular channels in which he might be inconveniently recognized.

There was no kind of habitation within sight, and the hour, notwithstanding the moonlight, precluded a search. Hunt wrapped himself in the blanket, and was soon asleep on the rock where they were left by the skipper. There was nothing unexpected or accidental in their situation. Camping out had been their custom for some months past. Avoiding the towns and settlements for the open country was also their habit. When the morning came, they looked around the shores of a bay that curved inland from where they were camping. On the opposite point a fisherman's cot was to be seen, and they observed a boy coming down to the beach. They beckoned to him with handkerchiefs, and he raised a lateen sail on the little craft and crossed to them, and bore them back to his father, who received them at the hut. After some breakfast prepared here, they arranged to be taken up to the city of Santiago de Cuba—which name the inhabitants shorten by using merely the last, "Cuba." Another rapid drift in the morning breeze with the lateen sails, and they landed upon the dock in the city. Here they were promptly confronted by the inevitable custom-house officers. A demand for their passports led to the production of what they had— an American passport without the Spanish visé at any regular landing-place. They were at once arrested. Their appearance was suspicious, and they were sent on board the Spanish man-of-war in the harbor, the *Cherucca*.

THE LANDING IN CUBA—SHELTERED FROM THE HEAVY DEW.

William M. Tweed. Romance Of His Flight and Exile

302

Tweed's arrival at Santiago is noted in his diary as the 12th of June, '76, about 2 P.M., and his release from on board the *Cherucca* at 1 P.M. on the 23d. The change and arrival of a new Captain-General at Havana had caused both suspicion and delay in their case. The Cuban patriots were manifesting much activity, and all American arrivals were strictly watched. Then a variety of rumors had started up about the two men arriving in this mysterious manner, which, although subjecting them to a strict surveillance, secured them, nevertheless, a distinguished and courteous entertainment by the officers of the Spanish man-of-war. The diary contains the names of these officers in detail, and indicates a familiar and kindly intercourse with the Captain of the Port, until Mr. Alfred N. Young, of Cincinnati, the American consul, procured their release on parole by becoming bond for them. They were accordingly able to take up their quarters at the principal hotel, kept in the name of Adeli Lascelles, where they occupied two comfortable rooms until their case should be passed upon at Havana.

A FILIBUSTERO ON THE "*CHERRUCA*."

The routine here was merely one of delay. Tweed notes his walks, his rides in the volante, the streets and public places, the churches and buildings, the hot days, and their Negro processions and carnivals. His social contact, through the American, French, and English consuls' residences, with the local society seems to have been free and cordial, with dinners, picnics, and excursions around the city. The 30th of June, Consul-General Hall telegraphs a reply to Mr. Young, the consul at Santiago: "The case of Secor and Hunt will be attended to as soon as papers arrive." A couple of captains of American merchant vessels, also delayed for custom-house infractions, made his companions at the hotel, and afforded him a sympathetic concert in maledictions against Spanish embargoes. On the 2d of July the telegraph announced the nominations at St. Louis of Tilden and Hendricks, of which ticket his anticipations were not altogether cheerful. His attention was recalled by the French consul to one of his previous schemes by an examination of some pictures of Rio Janeiro, where this gentleman had formerly acted as consul. Tweed remarks that he had originally contemplated making Brazil his place of refuge, but the arrival of the Emperor, Dom Pedro, in the United States made the idea unadvisable. The Centennial of America, the Fourth of July, he duly celebrated with the inevitable fire-works in the evening from the balcony of the Hôtel Lascelles, the demonstration being highly appreciated by a concourse of the "chattels," mainly in a state of nature, and absolute independence as to any apparel. On the 7th of July, having been detained a month, he concluded to settle down and make the best of it by employing a teacher of Spanish, and utilizing his time in acquiring a knowledge of the language. His teacher was a clerk in the customs, and a capable man, with whom he expresses his satisfaction, making fair progress in his daily lessons. On the 11th he notes the receipt of funds and the sale of his bills on the United States at ten per cent. premium. He began to grow "nervous and worried"

William M. Tweed. Romance Of His Flight and Exile

303

about his case at Havana, and waited with anxiety for every mail.   In view of the prospect of detention, he began to look about him for a house to rent, complaining, nevertheless, of the intolerable oppression of the climate, which began to tell on his health. The departure of his friend, the American consul, on a furlough to the United States, he mentions enviously, as also, the same day, he chronicles gloomily the execution of a person who is taken out and shot in the outskirts of the city. He saw the parade of the victim through the town, escorted by a guard of soldiers and a band of music. At the place of execution the man was put upon his knees, blindfolded, with his back to the soldiers, and shot. A little harder than three millions bail.

At last the Vice-Consul and the Consul-General, the Captain of the Port at Santiago and the Admiral of Marine at Havana, were brought into accord, and he was permitted to engage passage in the Spanish bark *Carmen* for Barcelona and Vigo. Having given security to report at Vigo to the Captain of the Port there, he went on board and sailed the 27th of July, paying $548 for himself and companion as the cost of the trip. Aroused on the morning of sailing by the bugle of the steam gun-boat *Tornado* (the captor of the *Virginius*), he saw with delight at last the slow departure of their bark down the harbor in the light breeze. Captain Julia and his officers are complimented in the diary for their courteous treatment. The daily record of the voyage has the usual monotony of any other log at sea. Skirting the Cuban coast in light winds and calms, he began a heavy experience of his long-deferred horror, seasickness, which stuck to his ample stomach until it had reduced his weight materially. His weight at home was more than 280 pounds, whereas on his return he had shrunk down to 160 pounds, and the sea had mainly done this work on him.

His notes upon the wind and progress of the ship present the usual daily chronicle until about the 5th of September, when they began to cross the track of the Mediterranean fleets, bound in and out from Gibraltar. Here the number of the vessels and the busy preparations on board the *Carmen* indicated the close of the protracted voyage. Its effect on him may be well illustrated by the remark in his journal: "I still keep on the cloth [summer] pants, a pair made for me in June, 1873, as the mark tells me. They are about ten inches too large around the waist, so I think I must have decreased some in size there since that time." Of his living he says: "No appetite. Bowl of soup for breakfast. Soup made of a few hard sailor biscuit boiled in hot water and seasoned with thyme, and then a quantity of oil poured into and boiled with it, making a cracker or biscuit soup; no other seasoning than the oil, which seems to be the prevailing mixture in all the cooking onboard." This diet, with a little sherry, he partook of merely in quantities to prevent the pangs of an empty stomach. Approaching Vigo, he expresses his longing for fresh meat at last, or a little fruit. He says: "I do try to eat what is provided, but I can not do it; my stomach instantly turns when I get a taste of garlic, and as that is the only flavoring they use in cooking, I am sure to get it in the first mouthful. I have not eaten more than two plates of soup and a few soda biscuits in two days, and I begin to feel the necessity for food."

William M. Tweed. Romance Of His Flight and Exile

304

On September 6, after a voyage of forty-two days, the *Carmen* arrived in the beautiful bay of Vigo. Boarded by the custom-house and health officers, the anchor was cast at quarantine, a small island in the centre of the bay, where the Lazaretto buildings stand, and to which they were transferred for the usual cleansing and fumigations. Tweed found himself formally arrested here; his diary, papers, and baggage were taken from him; and after seven days in the Lazaretto he was ordered to be taken to the castle or fortress as a prisoner of state. Tweed was taken from the little island of San Simon, where the Lazaretto stands, over to the city, and, in the custody of a guard of Spanish soldiers, he was marched up the hill toward the castle or fortress that crowns the city of Vigo. On his way along the steep road he had to stop and rest. Here he tried to communicate with the guard, but his defective Spanish enabled him to make out with difficulty that he must be held as a prisoner of state. In a maze as to what his fate must now be, he resumed his toil up the hill, and in due time reached his destiny in the castle. Ushered into an apartment, he found it to comprise a stone floor, stone walls, and a stone ceiling. There was nothing else except the door he had entered and a narrow window. They had the satisfaction, at least, of being shut in together and not separated. If they could not talk intelligibly to the guard, they could at least converse with and understand each other. But what was the use? They could not even satisfy themselves with conjectures as to the occasion of their position. Certainly the old difficulty about the passports could not have given rise to all this grim proceeding. It seemed very weary waiting until a servant-woman came, bringing two iron beds, with bedding, Spanish fashion, on her head. Indication was made by Tweed that he desired to see the officer of the guard or governor of the castle. But his efforts merely enabled him to have permission to get temporary wants satisfied from a hotel or tavern. Food, such as they desired to pay for, with beer or wine, and some matting for the floor, were provided; and they started in with some idea of patience and cheerfulness, waiting what might next turn up.

THE VOYAGE TO VIGO—SHIPS BEFORE THE MAST.

THE MAIL SECRETLY BROUGHT TO THE DUNGEON AT VIGO.

William M. Tweed. Romance Of His Flight and Exile

305

One morning when the woman who took charge of their room brought their food from the hotel, she attracted attention, by her gestures, to the slop-bucket she had just emptied. After she left with the sentinel, who always watched her when she came, Tweed examined the empty bucket, and found she had left him a note from his son. Having failed in every other attempt to communicate, he had succeeded in this. An answer was put in the bedclothes next morning, which the chamber-maid as duly found, and also delivered. In this manner Tweed came to learn something of the new phase of his case. He learned that he was held by the Spanish government, and supposed to be Secretary Belknap, a fugitive Minister of War of the United States. And this, at least, gave him the prospect of a release, his imprisonment being based on some mistake or Spanish blunder.

Another scene which grew out of the new postal arrangement was the finding of one of the epistles placed in the bedclothes by Soledad, the chamber-maid. One of these happened to fall into the hands of Hunt, who observed that the address to John Secor was superseded by what had until then been unknown to him, the real name of his companion, William M. Tweed. The result of this revelation proved temporarily unpleasant. Hunt exclaimed in astonishment, asking if his companion was actually the notorious Tweed. He broke out in indignation when he found such was the fact. He protested that he had never done any thing against the law to merit this association, and he stamped and swore and wanted the governor of the castle brought that he might vindicate himself and be set at liberty, or at least set apart from his notorious companion. He was not pacified, nor was there much comfortable feeling possible between them for the remainder of the fourteen days of their incarceration. By that time the *Franklin* had arrived, and they were taken duly on board, where explanation was more practicable. Hunt was clamorous on the way to the ship when he learned of the presence of the United States consular agent, protesting his American citizenship, his rights, and his entire ignorance of Tweed as such until the discovery in the castle.

Once on board the United States steam-frigate *Franklin,* Tweed found at last solid and intelligible ground to occupy. The commander said, as he received him from the Spanish soldiers and officers, that his instructions were to bring Tweed to New York; and to Tweed he also said what his mission was, and producing a photograph, said he was satisfied to receipt for him and bear him back accordingly, assuring him of his kindest feelings and of every courtesy and attention on the voyage back, placing at his disposal one of his best state-rooms, and extending to him the privileges of the officers' mess. As to Hunt, the commander had no knowledge, and would, if requested, extend to him the same privileges, or he was free to go ashore if he preferred.

William M. Tweed. Romance Of His Flight and Exile

306

SOLITAIRE ON THE U. S. FRIGATE *"FRANKLIN."*

Mr. Tweed's son had liberty to communicate freely with his father, which he availed of. As to Hunt, he speedily took himself out of sight of Tweed, and went off, returning, however, in restored good nature, with young Tweed, when he found there was no more danger of detention. As a token of reconciliation, and fraternity too, he left as a little keepsake the usual compliments of a certain class on parting with their friends in difficulty—a file, a whipsaw, and a jimmy chisel.

The rest of the story of Tweed up to his return to Ludlow Street Jail again has been widely published already. He was handed over to the sheriff on the 23d of November, 1876.

Secluding himself a little from lawyers and reporters, he has maintained, as to the public, an absolute silence since his return. The following letter to Charles O'Conor will show, however, that he had adopted an intelligent though an altered course toward the public:

"Ludlow Street Jail, December 6, 1876.

"Charles O'Conor, Esq.:

"Sir,—I take the liberty of addressing you this letter, in view of the fact that your position as the counsel designated by the State authorities in my matters has professed solely the public good, regardless of any factions or personal interest. Heretofore I have met my troubles with every resource at my disposal. Possibly in a mistaken sense of duty I have stood up too long to shield others as well as myself, bearing such losses and punishment as were meted out to my transgressions and my misfortunes. It was truly more in the interest of others than in my own that litigation and resistance were prolonged. Viewing the manner of my return to the wards of this prison, realizing the events in the city, in the State, and in the nation, which I am brought here to confront, it will not, I hope, seem to be a presumption or insincerity in me to say that I am indeed overwhelmed; that all further resistance being hopeless, I have none now to make, and only seek the shortest and most efficient manner in which I may make unqualified surrender.

William M. Tweed. Romance Of His Flight and Exile

307

"It is not my purpose to dispute, or appeal, or further resist the suits which you have against me in the name of the State and the people. I propose forthwith to place at your disposal a full surrender of all I have left of property or effects, and respond at once to such examination in this connection as may assure you and the public of the good faith of this assignment, as well as show the entire amount and disposition of all I have possessed, so far as you may wish it to be detailed.

"I am an old man, greatly broken in health, cast down in spirit, and can no longer bear my burden. To mitigate the prospect of a hopeless imprisonment which must speedily terminate my life, I should, it seems to me, make any sacrifice or effort. During the early stages of the suits and proceedings against me I was ready to make restitution and reparation as far as in my power. Entanglement with the interests and counsels of others delayed and defeated this. I regret that my means have now become so utterly inadequate. I would not make the futile offer if I had not some assurance, through your published statements, that the vindication of principle and the prospect of permanently purifying the public service are the objects you have in view, as being more desirable than the recovery of money. If in any manner you may see fit to use me in such connection, I shall be only too glad to respond. Trusting implicitly in your high reputation and character, I ask to make only a single reservation—not as regards myself, but wherever others may be concerned. Leaving my personal and property interests to be put to the fullest test of examination and publicity, I would hope to have any matters affecting other persons restricted to your private knowledge and discretion. Knowing as you do every material fact already, it would be unavailing for me further to resist or withhold any details you may demand. I only ask, in qualification of the utmost frankness, that your more reliable judgment shall take the responsibility of publication, and the use of such matters only as may be necessary for the ends you wish to advance.

"For the present I have no legal counsel. I shall not employ any, except to act in the spirit of this communication and conform to the usages of the courts. I send this by Foster Dewey, whom I have heretofore employed as secretary. He is directed to receive from you any instructions or suggestions, and answer in detail as to my circumstances,

"I remain, very truly, yours,

"William M. Tweed."

It is understood that Mr. O'Conor sent this letter to Attorney-General Fairchild with his favorable recommendation, and that Mr. O'Conor also signified his intention to terminate his more active connection with the Ring prosecutions, now practically ended. Acting upon this view, the Attorney-General has himself made several visits to Tweed, and has carried out the examinations of effects, and especially of information, which Tweed had to turn over. A large pile of checks, vouchers, and evidence is accordingly in the control of Attorney-General Fairchild. At the time this number of the *Weekly* goes to press his release has been provisionally agreed to, and will, as soon as due forms are complied with, be carried into effect.

As to what may become of Tweed, when he has surrendered all his property and turned over his papers, we are enabled to say that his flight was not altogether that of an aimless fugitive. He intended to enter upon important railroad work in Spain, which may still engage him if he sees his way to it upon his release. He was fifty-four years old on Tuesday, April 3.

William M. Tweed.—[From a Photograph by Brady.]
Harper's Weekly, January 21, 1871

Ackerman, Kenneth D. *Boss Tweed*. New York. Carroll & Graf, 2005.

Allen, Oliver E. *The Tiger: The Rise and Fall of Tammany Hall*. Reading, Massachusetts: Addison-Wesley Publishing Company, 1993.

Bernstein, Iver. *The New York City Draft Riots*. New York. Oxford University Press. 1990.

Bowen, Croswell. *The Elegant Oakey*. New York. Oxford University Press, 1956

Breen, Matthew P. *Thirty Years of New York Politics*. New York: Matthew Breen, 1899.

Brown, Joshua. *Beyond the Lines*. University of California Press, Berkeley. 2002.

Callow, Alexander B., Jr. *The Tweed Ring*. New York: Oxford University Press, 1966.

Davenport, John I. *The Election and Naturalization Frauds in New York City*. New York: Union League Club, 1894.

Genung, Abram S. *The Frauds of the New York City Government Exposed*. New York. By the Author. 1871.

Harper, J. Henry. *The House of Harper*. New York: Harper & Brothers, 1912

Hershkowitz, Leo. *Tweed's New York: Another Look*. New York: Anchor Press/Doubleday, 1977.

Hubbard, Fredrick A. *Other Days in Greenwich*. New York. J.F. Tapley Company, 1913.

Leonard, Thomas C. Chap. 4: "Visual Thinking: The Tammany Tiger Loose." *The Power of the Press: The Birth of American Political Reporting*. New York: Oxford University Press, 1986

Lynch, Denis T. *"Boss" Tweed*. New York: Blue Ribbon Books, 1927.

Paine, Albert Bigelow. *Thomas Nast: His Period and His Pictures*. New York: Harper and Brothers, 1904.

Rorabaugh, W. J. *Rising Democratic Spirits: Immigrants, Temperance, and Tammany Hall, 1854-1860*. Civil War History, June 1976. p. 138-157.

Rowell & Co., Geo. P. *American Newspaper Ratebook and Directory*. 1870. Nelson Chesman. New York.

Summers, Mark W. *The Press Gang*. Chapel Hill: U. of North Carolina Press, 1994.

Werner, Morris Robert. *Tammany Hall*. Garden City, New York: Doubleday, 1928.

Wingate, Charles. *North American Review*. New York, October 1876.

Printed in the USA
CPSIA information can be obtained
at www.ICGtesting.com
JSHW060043150824
68134JS00031B/2624